MATRIX
REIMPRINTING
USING EFT

MATRIX
REIMPRINTING
USING EFT

KARL DAWSON &
SASHA ALLENBY

HAY HOUSE

Carlsbad, California • New York City • London • Sydney
Johannesburg • Vancouver • Hong Kong • New Delhi

First published and distributed in the United Kingdom by:
Hay House UK Ltd, Astley House, 33 Notting Hill Gate, London W11 3JQ
Tel: +44 (0)20 3675 2450; Fax: +44 (0)20 3675 2451
www.hayhouse.co.uk

Published and distributed in the United States of America by:
Hay House, Inc., PO Box 5100, Carlsbad, CA 92018-5100. Tel.: (1) 760 431 7695 or
(800) 654 5126; Fax: (1) 760 431 6948 or (800) 650 5115. www.hayhouse.com

Published and distributed in Australia by:
Hay House Australia Ltd, 18/36 Ralph St, Alexandria NSW 2015.
Tel.: (61) 2 9669 4299; Fax: (61) 2 9669 4144. www.hayhouse.com.au

Published and distributed in the Republic of South Africa by:
Hay House SA (Pty), Ltd, PO Box 990, Witkoppen 2068. Tel./Fax: (27) 11 467 8904.
www.hayhouse.co.za

Published and distributed in India by:
Hay House Publishers India, Muskaan Complex, Plot No.3, B-2, Vasant Kunj,
New Delhi – 110 070. Tel.: (91) 11 4176 1620; Fax: (91) 11 4176 1630.
www.hayhouse.co.in

Distributed in Canada by:
Raincoast, 9050 Shaughnessy St, Vancouver, BC V6P 6E5. Tel.: (1) 604 323 7100;
Fax: (1) 604 323 2600

© Karl Dawson and Sasha Allenby, 2010

The moral rights of the authors have been asserted.

While Matrix Reimprinting and EFT have produced remarkable clinical results, they
must still be considered to be in the experimental stage and thus practitioners
and the public must take complete responsibility for their use of these techniques.
Further, Karl Dawson and Sasha Allenby are not licensed health professionals and
offer Matrix Reimprinting and EFT as personal performance coaches and holistic
therapists. This book is intended for information purposes only and is not intended to
substitute medical advice. The authors do not dispense medical advice or prescribe
the use of any technique as a form of treatment for physical or medical problems
without the advice of a physician, either directly or indirectly. Their intent is only
to offer information of a general nature to help you in your quest for spiritual and
emotional wellbeing. In the event that you use any of the information in this book for
yourself, which is your constitutional right, the authors assume no responsibility for
your actions. Please consult qualified health practitioners regarding your use of Matrix
Reimprinting and EFT.

A catalogue record for this book is available from the British Library.

ISBN 978-1-84850-249-9

Printed and bound in Great Britain by
TJ International, Padstow, Cornwall.

This book is dedicated to all the clients, trainees and practitioners
who have been part of Matrix Reimprinting
as it has grown and developed.

Contents

Foreword

The book you're now holding opens a doorway to a new reality. It is far more than a practical manual for a powerful new healing technique based upon Emotional Freedom Technique (EFT). It also offers a cutting-edge approach to understanding health and disease, drawing upon the work of leading scientists in quantum physics, the New Biology, epigenetics, trauma theory and new paradigm medicine. Matrix Reimprinting offers a whole new dimension in Energy Psychology which takes us far beyond classic EFT. Gary Craig, founder of EFT, often used to say that EFT was the 'ground floor of the new healing high-rise'. Matrix Reimprinting takes us several floors up that skyscraper, so we can gaze at the stars.

~~~

I still remember the incredible thrill, back in 2001, of watching asthma being healed in a minute on the introductory DVDs on EFT. I immediately trained in EFT and spent the next six months rethinking everything I 'knew' about emotions, consciousness and body-mind healing! As we know, these one-minute wonders only happen occasionally with EFT; more often, it takes time to ferret out the issues and specific events that underlie emotional or physical dis-ease. Nevertheless, EFT and Energy Psychology work at lightning speed in comparison with the 'talk therapies' that I trained in 30 years ago as a clinical psychologist – or even the shamanic healing techniques that I learned a decade or so later.

Since training in EFT, I've also trained in a plethora of other energy modalities, from TAT, Emo-Trance and Advanced PSYCH-K® to Matrix Energetics, Reconnection Healing and The Lifeline Technique. All of them have a lot to offer. Yet when I came across Matrix Reimprinting, I felt a huge surge of excitement. Here is an approach which integrates so much about the psycho-energetic nature of our reality, the trauma theory of disease and the latest research on the body-mind system – and which offers a tool for healing which is simple yet profound, elegant and imaginative. It is easy to practise on your own, or to give your clients as follow-up homework. It is creative and fun. And, crucially, it works!

I've always loved inner journeys and sub-personality work and have used Gestalt therapy, dream interpretation, voice dialogue, shamanic journeying and other-hand techniques at my workshops and with clients. As I learned more about trauma, dissociation and disease – from the work of Peter Levine, Robert Scaer, Bruce Lipton, Stephanie Mines, Ryke Geerd Hamer and others – I saw that these sub-personalities were often frozen, dissociated parts of the self which were holding traumatic memories, unresolved conflicts and negative beliefs and which needed healing and love. In shamanic terms, soul retrieval was required. Thanks to Matrix Reimprinting, I now believe that much of what I've done in the past has been mere 'talk therapy' with these frozen parts – which is slow and ineffective! But with Matrix Reimprinting, instead of merely talking to these parts (or 'ECHOs'), we can melt them in the timeless eternity of the subconscious – that is, in our energy field – so that they warm up, relax and move on. By freeing them from their feelings of isolation and powerlessness, we can enable them to make a *positive* contribution to our morphic field.

As Karl and Sasha make clear in this book, the real 'client' in Matrix Reimprinting is the ECHO. We are healing this frozen, traumatized part of the self that suddenly decided the world was dangerous, or that it was unloved, or that there was something wrong with it, or that it had to be good/perfect/special in order to be loved, or that set up a strategy for survival that might have been appropriate at the age of three or five but proved self-destructive and limiting at 30 or 45. Once you see the real client as the ECHO, an advantage is that the present-day client is no longer the one that needs help and so can take the higher vantage point of their Witness consciousness instead of identifying with the distressed or frozen part. This makes the risk of abreaction or re-traumatization minimal and helps clients to tap into wiser and more loving aspects of the Self. Since the ECHO is seen as carrying its own wisdom, it also makes the role of therapist relatively easy, since you simply need to guide your client in listening to their ECHO and following its lead.

By healing those parts of the self that have been 'frozen in time', mostly before the age of seven, we can free ourselves and our clients from stuck and limiting patterns which can block our prosperity, relationships, success and happiness and lead to anxiety, depression, phobias, addictions and other emotional problems. Since the New Biology shows that the mind controls our biology, and even our genes, healing our ECHOs can also prevent or even heal physical disease.

As I understand it, the vast majority of disease comes from resistance, or incoherent energy – that is, holding thoughts that are not aligned with our higher self. (The only exceptions are the very small number of people born with genetic disorders – and even those can potentially be helped with energy healing.) Physical symptoms can be seen as helpful mirrors of what has become 'frozen in time' in our psyche and needs to be brought into the light and warmth of consciousness. Poor diet and environmental toxins can affect our health, and viruses or bacteria can lead to symptoms, but only when the body is already weakened by emotional stress. As molecular biologist and former Stanford University biology lecturer Bruce Lipton points out, 95 per cent of illness comes from stress – *and 100 per cent of stress comes from faulty beliefs.* Matrix Reimprinting would suggest that every one of these 'faulty beliefs' can be traced back to frozen ECHOs in need of healing.

When I trained in Matrix Reimprinting with Karl, there was some discussion about whether our ECHOs needed to be reintegrated. In his liberating style, Karl said there weren't any rules – you just did whatever felt right to the client and the ECHO. In my view, our inner selves are rather like a family. In a healthy family, love and communication flow freely, yet there are clear boundaries and separate identities. Everyone contributes, everyone feels free, everyone thrives. In a dysfunctional family, by contrast, trauma leads to a breakdown in communication and the flow of love and emotion is blocked. Similarly, some of our inner selves might be repressed, controlled, criticized, excluded, ignored or scapegoated. Patterns then become frozen in time and are often passed down the generations – until someone challenges the pattern and breaks the 'chain of pain'. Matrix Reimprinting restores a healthy energy flow, so that dissociated selves can be welcomed home again. As in Hellinger's model of family constellations, love then flows freely. In this view, we simply need to reconnect with (rather than reintegrate) ECHOs, to bring them into our awareness and love and help them to move out of their frozen state. The ECHOs of our past can then become assets, rather than liabilities.

Anything can happen when you start meeting your ECHOs and seeing where they lead you! In one of my first Matrix Reimprinting sessions, my four-year-old ECHO urged me to talk to my father, who then took me to a moving scene from his own childhood. I found myself tapping on my father's eight-year-old ECHO and doing some intergenerational healing. In another session, I was led by my ECHO back to my own birth, and then into a past-life death on a battlefield that mirrored the same underlying theme. Another ECHO took me dancing along the yellow brick road in the Land of Oz, hand in hand with the good witch Glenda.

Since I began Matrix Reimprinting, I have revisited many traumatic memories from my past which I had already 'dealt with' using EFT. As a result, a personal issue that I had worked on for nearly 30 years has shifted profoundly in a matter of weeks. After working with my ECHOs, I also found myself handling a potentially traumatic situation with lightness, grace, acceptance and ease. And in a way which feels both subtle and profound, I feel more whole and present and alive.

EFT can remove the emotional charge from painful memories, yet it often leaves a void in its place. By contrast, Matrix Reimprinting heals the past memory and leaves a new memory in its place, so that conjuring up the old memory now brings up a joyful energetic imprint. We get whatever we send out into the field, according to the law of attraction, so holding these positive new images not only feels good but also means we are creating a whole new future. Since we are all ultimately One, this healing also sends ripples out into the cosmos. By healing our clients, we are healing ourselves. By healing ourselves, we are healing each other. By healing our past, we are healing our future – personally and collectively.

As you learn about ECHOs and Matrix Reimprinting, you stand on the threshold of a new adventure in healing emotional or physical disease and releasing our vast human potential. Enjoy this book – and above all, *use* this wonderful new tool. For yourself. For your clients. And for our world.

Gill Edwards,
September 2009
www.livingmagically.co.uk

Acknowledgements

Sasha and Karl would both like to thank:

Gill Edwards for kindly writing the foreword and giving feedback on the book.

Rebekah Roberts for typing the transcripts of the live sessions, plus all her love and support.

Sharon King for her contribution to Matrix Birth Reimprinting.

Ted Wilmont for friendship and feedback.

Colm Devlin at www.aametbuzz.com for all his support.

All the practitioners who contributed to this book by submitting case studies.

All the Matrix Reimprinting community.

Gayle Gang for the 'Tapping Points' artwork.

Hazel Trudeau for the Matrix Reimprinting poem.

Gary Craig and Roger Callahan for their phenomenal contribution to Energy Psychology in creating EFT and TFT – 'We stand on the shoulders of giants!'

Bruce Lipton, David Hamilton, Rupert Sheldrake, the Institute of HeartMath, Gregg Braden, Dawson Church and Dr Robert Scaer for the inspiration that their work provided.

Our fabulous editor, Lizzie Hutchins, who has made an amazing contribution to this title. Your clarity, precision and attention to detail are second to none and it has been an honour working with you.

All the fabulous people at Hay House – Michelle Pilley, Amy Kiberd, Marielle Kalamboussis, Monica Meehan, Diane Hill, Jo Burgess, Jo Lal and Joanna Lincoln – not only for publishing this book, but for all the hard work and brilliant advice that you have given us in the process.

Sasha would also like to thank:

My life partner, Rupert Wood, for being the backbone in everything that I do. I love you always.

Mum, Dad and Veronica, for all your love and support, particularly whilst I was finishing the book.

My brothers Ben and Daymo – I love you both dearly.

Brett Moran, Karl Dawson, Rebekah Roberts, Sasha Care, Fiona Shakeela Burns, Chris Gleed-Owen, Susie Shelmerdine and Sharon King for friendship and support.

Pete Yates and Anna Ingham at www.heartyoga.co.uk for helping me to wake up!

Harry Massey, Peter Fraser, Bruce Robertson, Andrea Evans, Sarah Skinner, Sarah Turner and everyone at NES for helping to further my understanding of the human body-fields.

Introduction

Karl's Matrix Reimprinting Story

I created Matrix Reimprinting in 2006, but the story of how I arrived at the technique starts many years earlier in 1987.

At 21 I had what can only be described as a profound spontaneous spiritual experience. For the two years that led up to this experience, I had an incessant need to spend time alone. As a social person who had always enjoyed the company of others, this was very new to me. Many life issues got in the way of finding time to be alone during this period, but eventually, in the summer of '87, I secured a holiday and found myself alone on a beach in Spain.

Eight or nine days into my 12-day holiday, my spiritual experience occurred. Although it is challenging to describe it in words, it was as though I suddenly felt a deep and profound connection with the universe. It seemed as if I could see deep into the spirit of the people I encountered and share universal truths with them that had previously been alien to me.

I'm not sure how my demeanour changed at the time, but it was clear that other people perceived me differently; even strangers would come to me and instantly open up regarding their issues and worries in life.

On my return from my holiday, the phenomenon continued. People who were not previously friends came round to my house to listen to me talk and share my insights. I attracted a group of 'followers', although this was not my intention.

Then, several months later, as quickly as this state had found me, it left me again. One day one of the 'followers' just looked at me and said, 'It's gone, hasn't it?' – and he was right. It was as obvious to others as it was to me.

For the next six years I travelled and worked all over the world, but underlying my desire to travel was one deep and pervading mission:

to get back to the beach, the place where I believed I would reacquire the talents and understandings I had lost.

While managing a bar in London in 1993 I met Adele, my now ex-wife, and we moved to America, where we had our first child, then to Hong Kong. Our second child followed. During this time I was still seeking the return of the spiritual experience and, as a result, was never fully present in the marriage, which eventually took its toll on our relationship.

Adele had a high-powered and successful career, so when we returned to England in 1996 it made sense for me to stay at home and raise our children. However, although this was the practical solution, I felt deeply unfulfilled in my role. My one solace was a novel I wrote but never published, which kept me in touch with the experience on the beach.

As my marriage worsened, I drank and smoked excessively and my sense of isolation increased. As a result, my confidence and self-value dropped to all-time lows. Inevitably, my health also spiralled downwards. My lower back, neck and shoulders caused me constant pain. I required glasses for the first time in my life. My digestion became severely compromised and I had allergies and sensitivities so severe that I was tested for bowel cancer. I started to become insulin-resistant and pre-diabetic. My energy levels declined and I experienced chronic fatigue, often taking the children to school and then going back to bed and sleeping during the daytime. Any task seemed to require a massive effort and I would dread simple things like a trip to the supermarket. As time passed I began to sink into a state of depression.

When I finally separated from my wife in early 2002, by which time I was in a terrible state both mentally and physically, I had several highly synchronous events which led me to visit a fasting retreat in Thailand. During this period I also came across EFT (Emotional Freedom Techniques).

Over the subsequent months things started to change for the better. My back improved greatly, my need for glasses went away, I had more energy and enthusiasm and my confidence increased. It didn't happen overnight, but slowly the good periods got longer and the bad periods got shorter. Eventually, over the next few years, I regained my zest for life.

Following my great results with EFT, I trained as a practitioner and spent several years working with clients before becoming an EFT trainer myself. Then, in early 2006, I passed the rigorous theoretical and practical exams to become an EFT Master, one of only 29 in the world.

As I naturally seemed to draw lots of clients and trainees who had autoimmune conditions and other serious diseases, I created the 'EFT for Serious Disease' training, which was popular with health professionals and laypeople alike. For a number of years this was my passion and my focus, along with training EFT practitioners worldwide.

Also in 2006, while running an EFT practitioner training in Australia, I had a serendipitous experience that dramatically altered the way that I worked. During an EFT session, one of the course attendees, who was dealing with a highly traumatic memory, stated, 'I can see the picture of my younger self so clearly, I could tap on her.' (If you are new to EFT, this statement will make more sense later.) I encouraged her to do so, with amazing results. And so Matrix Reimprinting was born.

Since then it has developed into a whole range of techniques. Unlike traditional EFT, it offers a range of protocols for different conditions, and the results I have seen with it have been phenomenal. Equally, those whom I have trained to use it have experienced remarkable outcomes with their clients or on themselves.

One of my many amazing results came when Sasha Allenby, the co-author of this book, resolved bipolar affective disorder when I worked with her for 20 minutes on one of the trainings. So it came as no surprise when she asked me, in 2008, if she could co-author this book with me. I am delighted to share this life-changing and empowering technique with you and I wish you peace and happiness as your journey with Matrix Reimprinting unfolds.

Sasha's Matrix Reimprinting Story

In 2005 I was completely disabled with myalgic encephalomyelitis (ME), a condition for which there is currently no known cure. Previously a very active performing-arts lecturer and personal development coach, I was initially devastated by the condition. But what appeared at first to be a drawback turned out to be a blessing in disguise. It started a journey of personal development that was so profound that I am now deeply grateful for the condition and all that it taught me.

Like many great journeys, mine started with a turning point. At the time, I was unable to bathe or dress myself. I lay in bed for 20 hours a day, continually playing negative messages over and over in my mind about how terrible my life had become and how hopeless my situation was. However, one day, in a flash of inspiration, I understood that although pain was inevitable, given my physiological condition, suffering was most definitely a choice. If I told myself over and over again that my situation was terrible and my life was over, I would disrupt my own healing – an understanding that I had learned from reading Louise Hay's work many years before, but only came to absorb as a personal truth in that instant. In that moment I made the decision to stop fighting my condition. I made a pledge to accept where I was and learn from it, and I labelled myself as someone who was 'in recovery' from ME, rather than 'suffering' from ME.

The journey that followed was as profound as my turning point. Everything that I needed to learn in order to recover fell into my path. It appeared that I was blessed. The question I often ask myself is, 'Would these things have come to me anyway, without a change of thinking?' I doubt they would have done, as it is my belief that the enormous shift in my consciousness attracted the right circumstances for my healing.

I dealt with the physical aspects of my condition using various techniques, with some good results. But psychologically I still had a number of issues. Most of these arose from invasive memories that had plagued me for years. I had tried various talk therapies and other healing modalities, including hypnotherapy, psychotherapy, counselling, meditation and acupuncture. I had also trained in yoga, shiatsu, Reiki and life coaching. Furthermore, I had extensive experience of changing destructive behaviour, as I had worked as a teacher of teenagers with behavioural problems. But, despite my search, I was no closer to ending the emotional pain that I lived in. All that changed when I encountered EFT.

I had a phenomenal first experience with it. I had crippling pains in my calves, which felt as though battery acid was dripping down my nervous system. I had been awarded Disabled Living Allowance due to these pains, and they had been present for about 15 months when I came across EFT. I learned the EFT tapping sequence from a book and applied it to the pains. After a few minutes I experienced a sensation that was like ice cracking up the back of my legs. Then there was a shooting pain that went from my legs, up my back and seemingly out of the top of my head. Simultaneously, I burst into tears, laughing and crying at the same time. This went on for several minutes and then I stopped cold. The pains that had crippled me so badly for so long had completely gone.

Following this amazing experience, I sought EFT practitioner training. I was particularly drawn to working with Karl Dawson, despite there being other trainers much closer to me geographically and travelling being such an issue for me in my physical state. I had no idea at the time of Karl's experience of working with ME, or the fact that he himself had overcome chronic fatigue-related health issues using EFT. It was as if the universe led me to him.

At the start of the first three-day practitioner training, I would say I was 40 per cent recovered from ME. By the end of the three days, I was about 70 per cent recovered. And to what did I owe this miraculous turnaround? It wasn't just because I had dealt with my physiological symptoms using EFT. In fact, I learned on the training that my physiological symptoms were only the very tip of the iceberg. It was simply because I had spent three days dealing with the trauma from my childhood and life experiences which had contributed to my wrong beliefs and distorted thinking about myself and the world. This was at the root of the physical illness that I was experiencing.

It is important to note that I am not suggesting that ME is all in the mind – quite the opposite. What I learned, and we will show in this book, is that all health conditions are in the mind *and* the body simultaneously, and what affects the psychology also alters the physiology. It is important to make this point, as there is still prejudice surrounding ME from the days when it was assumed to be a purely psychological condition. Here I am making a distinction between the old paradigm, which wrongly posited that ME was all in the mind, and the new paradigm, from the field of body-mind science, which shows how stress and trauma create disease. But first, more about my healing journey.

In addition to ME, throughout the whole of my adult life I had experienced bipolar affective disorder, which is commonly known as manic depression. Approximately every six weeks I would experience a profound feeling of depression, which I likened to being completely cut off from source. Intermittently I would also experience a drive that was so intensive I would be fixated on a single task to the detriment of balance in my life. I had had it for around 20 years before it was properly diagnosed; it had disrupted much of my working life, affected my relationships and impaired my zest for life.

When I attended the EFT training it was with the sole purpose of overcoming ME. I had no idea that it was even possible to resolve bipolar disorder, let alone that I would do so by the end of the three-day training. However, while working with another group member I got into severe difficulty. We were using EFT to resolve an abuse memory I had when suddenly I flipped into bipolar depression, which for me was the equivalent of being catapulted backwards at 1,000 miles per hour. In this state I was suddenly terrified of being in a room full of strangers. However, Karl spotted that I was in trouble and used Matrix Reimprinting on me (although this was at the very early stages of the technique and it didn't even have a name at that point). Not only did I quickly resolve the trauma, but I uncharacteristically flipped straight out of the depression. Up until this point in my life it had taken weeks to feel properly connected again after such an incident. The most incredible thing was that this was the last time I experienced bipolar depression. The memory that I had worked on had obviously been the main trigger for the condition.

Following the EFT practitioner training, I worked on my own extensively using EFT and Matrix Reimprinting. A few months later I was 90 per cent recovered from ME. And with a multi-disciplinary approach to my healing which included another Energy Psychology technique known as PSYCH-K®, dietary changes, supplementation and osteopathic intervention in the form of the Perrin Technique, I soon returned to 100 per cent health.

For the 18 months that followed my training I worked extensively with clients, mainly using EFT but more specifically Matrix Reimprinting. This was right at the start of the development of the technique – in fact, it didn't even have a title when I first used it with clients, I just picked it up from the work that Karl had done on me and, later, from demonstrations that he did about the technique. I was working as a full-time therapist and had approximately 40 clients on my books at any one time, mainly people with serious disease and adults who had been traumatized in childhood. It soon became apparent that I couldn't do a session with someone without using Matrix Reimprinting, and the progress I saw in people's lives while using this technique was astounding. Clients who had undergone years of psychotherapy and various other talk therapies would transform their lives in five to ten sessions (although those with serious disease usually needed to use the technique on a long-term basis to resolve their issues).

After the international release of my first book, *Joyful Recovery from Chronic Fatigue Syndrome/ME: Accelerated Healing with Emotional Freedom Techniques*, I felt drawn to write this book to get this information out to a wider audience. Despite my vast range of qualifications in a whole host of healing modalities, I can safely say that Matrix Reimprinting has grown to be my tool of choice for dealing with any physical or emotional issue. I look forward to sharing my enthusiasm for it with you.

EFT

As we've seen, Matrix Reimprinting originated from EFT. If you are not familiar with it, it's a self-help tool that is used to resolve or improve any physical or emotional issue, destructive thought pattern or form of behaviour. It was created by Gary Craig, who adapted it from Thought Field Therapy (TFT). EFT is a simplified version of its predecessor. It involves tapping on points along the body's meridian system – the system used in acupuncture. While tapping on the points, you bring to mind physical symptoms or negative memories. This helps to release life stresses or physical issues from the body's energy system and allows it to return to emotional and physical health.

Because you tap on the body and think of the issues at the same time, EFT is a technique that involves the mind and body simultaneously. It has generated impressive results with chronic fatigue syndrome/ ME, rheumatoid arthritis, MS, IBS, diabetes, asthma, cancer, Crohn's disease, colitis, vitiligo, alopecia, hypothyroidism, anxiety, panic attacks, stress, depression and post-traumatic stress disorder, among a whole host of other physical and emotional conditions.

In EFT it is recognized that to heal any condition we have to heal the mind and the body simultaneously, and that most of the myriad of diseases that are part of our society have their origins in life stresses and traumas. These traumas can easily be resolved with EFT, and the results ultimately affect the physical body.

Matrix Reimprinting uses the same acupuncture points as EFT, and they are tapped in the same way, but the protocols are very different. A basic grasp of conventional EFT is therefore useful in order to use the Matrix Reimprinting techniques, but if you have no experience of EFT, you can still learn Matrix Reimprinting from this book, as we will give you a grounding in EFT before we introduce the Matrix Reimprinting techniques.

Introducing Matrix Reimprinting

Matrix Reimprinting is based on a number of key principles. The first is the quantum physics theory that we are all connected by a unified energy field, known as the Matrix. Our more challenging life experiences are held as pictures in the Matrix in the form of Energetic Consciousness Holograms, or ECHOs. With Matrix Reimprinting we can interact with these ECHOs to transform these past pictures and replace them with supportive ones. This changes our health, happiness and wellbeing in the present.

Our ECHOs also hold us in negative states of belief which are destructive to our physiology. We can use Matrix Reimprinting to resolve these negative beliefs and return to health.

As well as the Matrix Reimprinting protocols, throughout the book there are also a number of Matrix Reimprinting sessions with Karl and Sasha, and case studies from a host of other practitioners who have been using this technique with incredible results.

So, whether you are a complete newcomer to EFT and Matrix Reimprinting or a seasoned practitioner, this book contains a wealth of resources that you can use to transform your own life, the lives of your clients, family and friends, and the unified energy field itself. We welcome you to the start of the ultimate journey of personal and global transformation.

PART I

The Matrix, the Body and the Mind

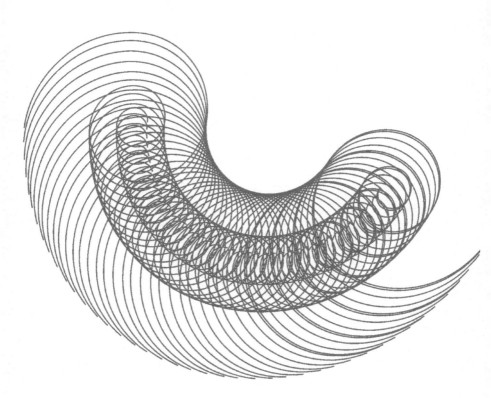

CHAPTER 1

The Matrix

Matrix Reimprinting is based upon the understanding that we are all connected by a unified energy field, generally referred to as the 'field' or the 'Matrix'. This understanding was first brought to light in the 1940s by the father of quantum theory, Max Planck. In the twenty-first century, it has been popularized by films such as *The Secret, What the Bleep Do We Know?!* and, more recently, *The Living Matrix*, and books such as *The Divine Matrix* by Gregg Braden and *The Field* by Lynne McTaggart.

A very basic understanding of this Matrix is needed in order for you to use the Matrix Reimprinting techniques. If you are not scientifically minded, rest assured that you do not need to be a quantum physicist to do so – in fact, you can perform Matrix Reimprinting simply with the knowledge that we are all connected by a unified energy field. Some of the best Matrix Reimprinting practitioners that we have trained have perhaps watched one or two of the films mentioned above and really resonate with the understanding that we are connected by the Matrix, but would be challenged to describe even the basic science behind it.

So our aim here is to give just a very brief and simple explanation of the science that supports Matrix Reimprinting. If you want to learn about it in greater detail, we suggest you explore the books and DVDs listed above. But all you will need to grasp in order to practise Matrix Reimprinting are the following principles:

1. *We are all made up of energy that vibrates so fast we appear as solid matter.*

2. *We are linked by a web that connects us all, known as the Matrix.*

3. *We send our thoughts out into the Matrix and those thoughts are attracted back to us as life experiences.*

4. *We can change how we experience life by changing the pictures in the Matrix.*

Let's look at those principles in more detail:

1. We Are All Made Up of Energy

Before the emergence of quantum physics, all matter was believed to be solid. It was understood that some types of matter were more solid than others – metal more than people, concrete more than animals – but generally, matter was perceived as an unchanging mass. However, what quantum physics has taught us, in a nutshell, is that the world is not solid. It is actually composed of electromagnetic energy, which in turn is composed of various atomic and subatomic particles. Our solid world is in fact an illusion – underlying it is a vibrational reality.

It is the fact that the particles that we are comprised of vibrate so fast that makes us appear solid. An analogy we like to use is the electrical fan: when it stops, you can see the gaps in between the blades, but when it spins, it appears to be one solid object. Similarly, as the atoms that make up our physiology vibrate, we appear to be a single entity, but really we are energy in motion.

2. We Are Linked by a Web

Part of the previous scientific paradigm included the presupposition that up to 90 per cent of our cosmos was comprised of empty space. In *The Divine Matrix*, Gregg Braden points out the flaw in this logic: 'If it's really vacant, then there's a big question that must be answered: How can the waves of energy that transmit everything from our cell-phone calls to the reflected bright light bringing this page's words to your eyes travel from one place to another? Just as water carries ripples away from the place where a stone is tossed into a pond, something must exist that conveys the vibrations of life from one point to another.'[1]

Quantum physics has taught us that what once was believed to be empty space contains the great net that connects everything in our universe: the Matrix.

3. We Send our Thoughts Out ... and They Are Attracted Back

Our understanding of this unified energy field has also brought with it the knowledge that we are creators of our own realities, because what we focus on sends ripples into the Matrix that reflect back to us in our experiences. The film and book *The Secret* by Rhonda Byrne and works by Esther and Jerry Hicks such as *Ask and It Is Given* have awakened countless people to the understanding that we get what we focus upon in life. Many of us have now learned that the universe responds to consciousness and our thoughts become our reality. Our beliefs, fears, hopes and dreams are all reflected back to us by the Matrix in the world that surrounds us.

This 'Law of Attraction' is vibrational. We attract experiences of a vibrational frequency that is similar to our own. Whatever we are putting out comes back to us in a life experience that matches our own signal.

To some people, the idea that we 'create our own reality' in this way has seemed offensive. This is because it may be seen as putting blame on those who have created a reality which is less than desirable. However, as we will explore later, much of what we attract is related to our earlier life experiences and we can change our point of attraction by directly working with these experiences using Matrix Reimprinting. So we are not to blame for the reality we have created, but rather empowered to do something about this reality with this knowledge and understanding.

4. We Can Change How We Experience Life by Changing the Pictures in the Matrix

In relation to this, we would like to offer a unique view on why the Law of Attraction hasn't appeared to work for some people. All the life experiences that we have had create pictures in our Matrix. If they are positive and supportive, they help us to attract more of what we want. But if they are negative and destructive, we attract more of the same. Simply wishing for different experiences when we have these destructive pictures in our field will not change our point of attraction. But when we start to work with Matrix Reimprinting, we actually change the pictures in our fields, and thus the direction of our lives, by attracting different experiences.

When Karl first heard of the Law of Attraction, he imagined a big hand, pretty much like the one on the National Lottery campaign in the UK, coming down from the sky and picking people out to have better life experiences! Now he understands about the pictures in the field, he realizes how inaccurate this was. Instead we attract experiences that are similar to our pictures and people with pictures that are similar to our pictures. And until we change our pictures, we will continue to attract more of the same.

Before we explain how we change the pictures in our fields with Matrix Reimprinting, let's take a look at other fields that exist as part of our reality and how these also affect our behaviour and our point of attraction.

Local Fields

As well as the unified energy field that connects all beings, there are also local fields around our own body which shape not only our physical form but also our behaviour, our customs and our habits. These fields are different from the Matrix, because they are local to us. But at the same time they are sub-fields that are part of the Matrix. Let us look at how they affect our everyday reality.

Fields – Patterns of the Past

In her early twenties Sasha regularly used amphetamines and hallucinogens to block her emotions around her childhood and life traumas. Her habit spanned eight years, beginning when she was 19 and ending when she was 27. For a particular period in her early twenties she had a pattern with the street drug known as speed. She would take it every Friday night, stay awake most of the night and wake abruptly early on Saturday morning. Her partner at the time would stay in bed and sleep all day Saturday, and she would lie next to him, unable to motivate herself, and obsess about things that she had said or done. In effect, she would torture herself psychologically for several hours at a time. She continued this pattern for a number of years. However, although by the time she was 25 she no longer used speed, she would still wake up early every Saturday. What's more, she continued to be plagued by the same pattern of obsessing over her actions at this time, and Saturday would always be a painful and disturbing day for her, accompanied by anxiety and self-doubt. This pattern continued well into her thirties, until she eventually managed to break it with Matrix Reimprinting and EFT.

For a number of years, Sasha also worked with teenagers with severe behavioural problems. She taught therapeutic drama as a means of encouraging them to reflect on their actions and address their destructive behaviour and often criminal activity. With street crime, she enabled them to act out the role of both victim and perpetrator, so that they would experience all the issues involved. In lessons they made great progress and Sasha was delighted. It felt as though she was changing the world! However, most victories were short-lived.

During the course of his ten-year marriage, Karl had an increasing amount of trouble with his lower back. He had a prolapsed disc and a trapped nerve. As the unhappiness in his marriage increased, so did his symptoms. Due to the constant pain, he even told his son, Daniel, that he would no longer be able to play sport with him. When his marriage ended and he began to work on many of his issues, his back problems subsided. However, every Christmas, when he spent the whole day with his ex-wife and children and was back in the old patterns, as the day progressed the back pain would return. It would take him a few days afterwards to feel 'normal' again. Years later, while he was working with a holistic healthcare practitioner who was using a diagnostic tool known as META-Medicine® (which we will discuss in Chapter 3), he was told that the problem was related to self-devaluation. He was originally outraged at the suggestion, but then it started to make a lot of sense to him. He *had* felt devalued in his family situation. He had been a house-husband and his wife had been a very strong and domineering character. And returning to the old house at Christmas-time would retrigger how his marriage had made him feel.

So what does all this behaviour have in common? The answer is 'fields'. All our behaviour, either self-supporting or self-destructive, has its own field, which in turn influences us to react in a given way.

The concept of fields is not a new one, and there are already a number of known fields, such as the Earth's gravitational field and magnetic field. In addition, biologist Rupert Sheldrake's work suggests that all living cells, tissues, organs and organisms have their own fields, which he calls 'morphic fields'. These fields shape each individual species. We owe a huge debt to Sheldrake, as his work has inspired a number of the Matrix Reimprinting techniques.

Morphic fields are habitual and the more they are repeated, the stronger they become. They are influenced by what has gone before, through a process called 'morphic resonance'. Each individual cell, organ or species takes a specific form because of its morphic resonance with similar cells, organs or species from the past.

Behavioural Fields

As well as shaping form, fields also shape sociological patterns, customs, behaviour and habits of the mind. They impose rhythmic patterns on the nervous system which affect the sensory and motor regions of the brain, impacting behaviour.[2]

Every species, including humans, has some sort of inherent instinctive behaviour. We learn this through morphic resonance with the members of our species who have gone before us. Learned behaviour is different, and becomes established through resonance with ourselves. Our morphic fields become habituated when we repeat certain patterns and behaviour.

Learned behaviour and the fields that accompany it are in fact an important part of our socialization process. There would be no structure in our life without these fields. Every form of behaviour, from the simple act of brushing our teeth to the more complex one of communicating with members of the opposite sex, has its own field, which has been created by our life experiences and is reinforced by self-resonance.

Many of these behavioural fields may be supportive and nurturing. If, for example, your life is structured and organized then you have probably formed positive behavioural fields around functioning. If your life lacks structure then your behavioural fields may be more chaotic. And if you have very obsessive qualities about being ordered or are even expressing a condition such as obsessive compulsive disorder, your behavioural fields around being organized have become too strong.

Changing Behavioural Fields

So how do we change our behaviour? We have all heard the saying 'You can't teach an old dog new tricks.' In the light of our understanding of behavioural fields, what this is actually referring to is the challenging nature of changing a behavioural field.

Let's look at a common scenario. There's something you want to change about yourself and you believe this time you really can do it. You may tell everyone you are going to do it. You set a date. For most people it's a Monday or the first of the month. The first of January is obviously the most popular choice, because that's when everyone else changes, so it has to be the best time, right?

On your start date you put all your energetic resources into changing. You have a good first day. You feel confident and may even talk about your success. This goes on for a few days or even weeks. As time passes you start to feel really sure of yourself. You might even think you have conquered your 'bad habit'. If it's eating chocolate, for example, you might think it's OK to have just a little bit now and then. If it's exercising regularly, you might deviate from your schedule slightly. It's OK to skip it once or twice, isn't it? Or it may be that someone has upset you, so you justify slipping back into old ways just for a while, to get over it. It's a temporary blip anyway. You'll be back on track tomorrow. But chances are that you won't be back on track. Because, *bang*, you'll be straight back into the old pattern and back to square one. Sound familiar?

So let's take a look at this universal pattern. What's really happening here?

The more you repeat something, the stronger its field becomes. So if you have a long-standing way of behaving, its resonance has great strength, and thus a great influence over you. When you decide with your conscious mind that you want to make a change, put a lot of energy into this decision and actively make the change, you start to tune into a new field, an opposing field if you like. Consider this in relation to Sheldrake's remark: 'A field brings about material effects while the system is tuned into it. But if the tuning is changed then other fields come into play: the original field disappears.'[3] By tuning into this new field you feel completely different. The new field has its own resonance and you may feel confident, sure and able because of this resonance.

However, if you decide, too soon, that you have 'cracked it' and you believe, too early, that this new field is totally stable, you may slip back into your old ways with all the confidence that you have from the resonance of the new field. And the trouble is that as soon as you do slip back, you tune back into the old field – that old field that resonates so strongly with you. According to Sheldrake, 'the most specific morphic resonance acting on a given organism will be that from its *own* past states, because it is more similar to itself in the immediate past, than to any other organism'.[4] So you are instantly familiar with the old field. It's like an old friend, but the sort that you keep going back to despite knowing how destructive the relationship is for you.

If you've been caught in this cycle for a number of years and have been wondering things like 'Why aren't I strong enough?' or 'What's wrong with me?' then take a moment to sit back and let yourself off the hook. Because it is very challenging to change behaviour with willpower alone, because willpower comes from the conscious mind, and the conscious mind does not override the subconscious mind, or the fields. In fact, we believe that the subconscious mind and the fields may be one and the same (we will discuss this further in the following chapter). And if you have used other interventions that haven't worked for you, even Energy Psychology interventions that have seemed to work for everyone else, this explains why. By resolving the old trauma you may have stopped yourself from tuning into the old field, but you may not have tuned into a new field. And as a result the new behaviour has not stabilized.

So, what's the solution? With Matrix Reimprinting we will introduce you to a unique Field-Clearing Technique which will help you to tune into and stabilize new fields. But this is only one part of the process. We will also show you how you can go back to whatever may have triggered your destructive or habitual behaviour in the first place and clear any energy from the past that is holding you in that old pattern. Furthermore, we will explain how to create new pictures in your field, so you can begin to align yourself with the new habit or behaviour. We will basically show you how to create a new image of yourself and then stabilize this with a new and supportive field.

Following Through

Once you have new pictures in your field, you will start attracting new experiences into your life. We often lightheartedly refer to the Kevin Costner film *Field of Dreams*, which has the recurring phrase: 'If you build it, they will come!' If you create new fields, the right people will come into your life and it will begin to change. But it is also important to follow through these opportunities. There is a popular story in the personal development industry that runs as follows:

A fisherman's boat capsizes in the middle of the ocean and he ends up holding on to it. He tells himself, 'God will save me.'

Another fishing boat comes along and tries to pull him out of the water. He declines, saying, 'God will save me.'

A dolphin offers him a ride back to shore. He replies, 'Thank you, but no. God will save me.'

Along comes a whale, who also offers a ride. He replies, 'God will save me.'

Eventually he drowns.

> *When he arrives in heaven he asks God why he didn't save him. God replies, 'I sent a fishing boat, a dolphin and a whale. Why didn't you save yourself?'*

So, once you change your pictures in your field, your point of attraction will start to change, but you will still need to take action for your life to truly transform.

We will explore further how to transform your life experiences in Part III of this book. But first let's explore the relationship between memory and our local fields, and how this relates to Matrix Reimprinting.

Memory

There is much to suggest that memory is not stored in the brain, as previously thought, but in local fields. This notion will form the basis of much of the work that we will do later with Matrix Reimprinting, so an understanding of this will help with your comprehension of the Matrix Reimprinting techniques.

Orthodox medical theory has for some time assumed that memory and habits are stored as 'material traces' in the brain. However, countless experiments have been performed to try and prove this, and none has been successful.[5] Also, according to neuroscientist Francis Crick, there is a practical issue with the idea that memory is stored in the brain. Human memory often lasts decades, yet it is believed that, with the exception of DNA, nearly all the molecules in our body turn over within days, weeks or, at most, months. Memory cannot, therefore, be stored in the brain, as the brain also experiences molecular turnover.[6]

It would seem that humans and animals inherit a collective memory from all previous beings of their kind and in turn contribute to that memory.[7] In addition we all have our own individual memories, which are also thought to be held in morphic fields. We tune into them through self-resonance, when patterns of activity in the nervous system are similar to patterns of activity in the past.[8]

Through Karl's extensive work as an EFT Master, working specifically to clear the energetic disruption around his clients' past memories, he had begun to suspect that memory was held in the field, and then he came across the work of cell biologist Bruce Lipton. In his DVD presentation *As Above, So Below: An Introduction to Fractal Evolution*, Dr Lipton discusses how we have self receptors on each of our cells, which tune into the self in the Matrix.

Learning

It also appears that learning is transmitted through morphic resonance. Although we do not condone animal experiments, the most comprehensive study on learning and morphic resonance deserves a mention here. The study involved rats in a water maze. The first generation of rats made an average of 165 errors before they were able to successfully complete the maze. Subsequent generations made fewer and fewer errors. By the thirteenth generation they made an average of only 20 errors. The remarkable thing is that when the experiment was repeated elsewhere, the first new generation of rats made an average of only 25 errors, with some of them getting it right first time. It seemed that the new rats had picked up where the old rats had left off and had downloaded the information needed to complete the maze through the collective unconscious via morphic resonance.[9]

Countless examples of morphic resonance are also seen in nature. One interesting example of learning in this way is seen in the interactions between horseshoe crabs and shore birds. For 250 million years, each May in Delaware Bay on the east coast of America, horseshoe crabs have laid their eggs on the beach, out of the reach of fish predators. However, some one million shore birds come to feast on the eggs, some of them journeying 10,000 miles. The crabs, having walked the Earth with the dinosaurs when birds didn't exist, have not altered their programming to account for the birds. However, the birds have learned, through morphic resonance, to return to the beach at the same time each year to eat crab eggs.[10]

Emotional Fields

In our experience of working closely with the emotional health of others for a number of years, it would also seem that each emotional state has its own field. A number of leading voices in personal development have highlighted this idea, but from a slightly different perspective. Most notably, Esther and Jerry Hicks, in their phenomenal work with the collective consciousness known as Abraham, have discussed the vibration of different emotional states. A component of their teachings includes raising your vibrational state in order to better align yourself with Source Energy. They list the emotions on a scale:

1. *Joy, knowledge, empowerment, freedom, love, appreciation*
2. *Passion*
3. *Enthusiasm, eagerness, happiness*
4. *Positive expectation, belief*
5. *Optimism*
6. *Hopefulness*
7. *Contentment*
8. *Boredom*
9. *Pessimism*
10. *Frustration, irritation, impatience*
11. *Being overwhelmed*
12. *Disappointment*
13. *Doubt*
14. *Worry*
15. *Blame*
16. *Discouragement*
17. *Anger*
18. *Revenge*
19. *Hatred, rage*
20. *Jealousy*
21. *Insecurity, guilt, unworthiness*
22. *Fear, grief, depression, despair, powerlessness*[11]

They suggest that when you are in one of the lower vibrational states that you should reach for a state which is slightly higher than the one you are experiencing and continue to climb the emotional ladder in this way. And it would seem that what they are describing is a change in emotional fields.

You may recognize your own emotional fields as you re-experience emotions. Remember, morphic resonance is habitual, so the more you repeat an emotion, the more resonance it will have. This is why it can be easy to fall back into destructive emotional patterns. However, techniques such as Matrix Reimprinting, EFT and TFT directly influence and transform emotional fields and later in this book you will learn how to transform your own destructive emotional fields into supportive and positive ones.

Fields of Disease

After discovering Sheldrake's research on morphic fields and morphic resonance, Karl naturally began to apply these theories to his understanding of disease. What occurred to him was that each disease had its own particular morphic resonance. This field is created first by downloading the collective unconscious of those who have experienced it in the past and then by the individual adding their own interpretations and expectations of that disease and repeating the behaviour patterns associated with it. One possibility is that those who overcome incurable conditions manage, through a variety of interventions, to alter the morphic resonance associated with the condition, and thus are healed.

When Sasha overcame chronic fatigue syndrome/ME, a condition for which there is currently no known cure, she believes that the variety of therapeutic and self-help tools that she employed helped her to transform the morphic resonance of the illness. At the start of the condition she was heavily influenced by the collective unconscious of others who had the illness. A huge amount of negativity surrounded the condition, and misunderstanding had led to misdiagnosis and the discriminative treatment of a large number of those who had gone before her. Having experienced some of this prejudice herself, as it took her the best part of a year to get a diagnosis and her symptoms were dismissed on a number of occasions by medical professionals, Sasha found it was easy to tune into the collective field of ME and take on board the popular beliefs about the illness, including the notion that recovery can take years, even decades, and very few people make a full recovery at all. However, a shift in consciousness came about by applying a host of techniques, along with a variety of supplements and a change in diet, and Sasha believes that this helped her to transform the morphic resonance of the illness.

Scanning the Human Body-Field

When Karl and Sasha first started working with the concept of fields, they were doing so without any tangible evidence that these fields existed. However, they have since encountered a tool which scans the fields of the human body and displays its findings on a computer screen. The program, which decodes the human body-field with startling accuracy, was created from the work of Peter Fraser and assimilated into a technological computer program by Harry Massey. In *Decoding the Human Body-Field*, Fraser extends our understanding of the fields of the body. These are understood to be integrated with the body, not separate from or outside it. Fraser also identifies morphic fields which shape the body and the organs. There are different fields for the connective tissues within the body, which also house the meridians and carry the emotions. And these fields are integrated by the heart field, to maintain health and wellbeing.

If these fields become disrupted, illness and disease can occur. The system created by Fraser and Massey, known as Nutri-Energetic Systems®, or NES, can pinpoint emotional disruption, nutritional imbalance, toxicity, disruption of the flow of information in and around individual organs, and many other issues which are showing up in the body-field.

Although NES have their own systems for treating these disruptions, their technology can also be used in conjunction with other healing modalities to identify possible causative factors for illness and disease. The technology provides a breakthrough in our understanding of the fields of the human body, because it allows us to visibly see the disruption in a person's body-field and therefore accurately create resolution.

Although being able to scan the human body-field is not necessary for us to effectively carry out Matrix Reimprinting, what this technology has shown us, even in the earliest stages of experimenting with it, is that there is a correlation between the disruption shown on the NES analysis of the body-field and the related life traumas that a person has experienced. Later on we will show how to treat life traumas with Matrix Reimprinting and clear disruption from your body-field.

CHAPTER 2

Body–Mind: Connecting Thoughts, Beliefs and Biology

In the 1970s and '80s there was a surge in the understanding that the mind affects the body. During this period, the self-help movement evolved, and pioneers such as Louise Hay highlighted how affirmations and thoughts could affect health and wellbeing. However, at this time there was little science to back up the links between mind and body.

The main issue was that those who understood the body–mind connection were challenging the popular Western scientific model, which leaned heavily on the Darwinian approach to science. In this model, the body was viewed not only as a machine, which could break down, but also as a device to carry the head around! So disease was fought purely with medication, there was little room for the suggestion that thoughts and beliefs could affect health, and any suggestion that they did was frequently dismissed as a New Age theory.

Sasha's earliest memory of this model being challenged was a documentary that she saw in the very early '80s which showed how cancer patients could affect their ability to heal by believing that they could recover. Although not even ten years old at the time, she remembers clearly the paradigm shift that this presented to her. Labelled a 'sickly child', she had been raised to believe that the only answers to her health lay with the doctor, yet here were men and women who were affecting this killer condition with their minds.

Although it was decades before Sasha learned to affect her own body with her mind, the memory of that paradigm shift has always stuck with her.

So when did it all change? What was the turning point? Well, funnily enough, one of the key contributors to the scientific evidence of the mind affecting the body was the pharmaceutical industry – the very industry that had a vested interest in the sole reliance on pharmaceutical drugs. Ironically, they helped verify the body–mind connection by constantly proving the placebo effect.

The Placebo Effect

The placebo is seen as a nuisance in the pharmaceutical industry – it 'gets in the way of research'. Whenever a new drug is trialled, the pharmaceutical companies have to also trial an inert substance, a placebo, to check on the effects of the drug. What is fascinating is that in many cases the inert substance works almost as well as the drug. It would seem that a person's *perception* of what a drug is going to do for them has a positive effect on their healing.

Fascination with the placebo effect caused pharmaceutical scientist David Hamilton to leave his prestigious position in the industry and devote his time to researching and writing about the body–mind connection. His books on the subject include *It's the Thought That Counts: Why Mind over Matter Really Works* and *How Your Mind Can Heal Your Body*, and both these books pool together countless research experiments which highlight the nature of the placebo effect.

In one study, for example, pregnant women were given a drug that they were told would stop their vomiting and nausea. They were then asked to swallow a device that measured the stomach contractions associated with nausea. The drug that they were given did stop the nausea contractions as suggested. However, the women had actually been given syrup of ipecac, a drug that should have made them even sicker. The power of suggestion had not only overridden the nausea but also the effect of the drug.[1]

These and countless other studies show how our thoughts, feelings and beliefs about the effects that a drug will have on us form part of our healing response. So, if we can heal ourselves with the power of belief in an inert substance, then we can also heal ourselves with the power of thought itself. However, as well as having a positive influence on our body, our mind can have a very powerful negative influence too. We may be able to create health with the placebo effect, but we can also negate it with the nocebo effect.

The Nocebo Effect

The nocebo effect is the power that negative thoughts can have on our health. This notion has been prevalent in the medical industry and it has been shown on a number of occasions that when a doctor gives a wrong diagnosis the patient can actually die of the condition in response.

People's beliefs about the effect that medicine can have on them have also caused death on occasion. A number of examples of this are cited in *Healing Breakthroughs: How your Attitudes and Beliefs Can Affect Your Health* by Dr Larry Dossey. In one instance, a patient who was allergic to penicillin was given a placebo but told, just after he'd swallowed it, that it was actually penicillin. He went into anaphylactic shock and died immediately.[2] This case is a clear example of the power of the nocebo effect.

Dr Dossey also highlights the case of a middle-aged woman who had a narrowing of the tricuspid valve on one side of her heart. She had previously experienced low-grade chronic congestive heart failure, but medical intervention had been successful. While she was having a check-up at the hospital, a prominent heart specialist was taking a group of trainees on a routine examination tour. He entered the room and announced to the trainees, 'This woman has TS,' before leaving abruptly without any further communication with her.

Moments later, she began to hyperventilate, her pulse went up to 150 beats per minute, she was drenched with perspiration and her lungs were filling with fluid. The attending doctors were baffled and asked her what was wrong. Her reply was that the specialist had said that she had TS, which she believed to mean 'terminal situation'. One of the doctors explained that TS meant 'tricuspid stenosis', which was the description of the condition of her heart valve. However, the woman could not be reassured, her lungs continued to fill with fluid and she lost consciousness. Later that day she died from intractable heart failure.[3]

So our mind, trained from an early age to believe in the authority of the medical profession, can cause a cascade of chemical reactions which lead to disease and even sudden death. Effectively, we can be programmed into ill health. But it is not only the medical profession which can create this nocebo effect – we can create it for ourselves.

In the same book Dr Dossey describes what he calls 'Black Monday Syndrome'. You may be surprised to learn that more fatal heart attacks occur on Monday at 9 a.m. than at any other time of the week. According to Dr Dossey, 'the best predictor for a first heart attack is not any of the major risk factors (high blood pressure, high cholesterol, smoking, and diabetes mellitus), but rather job dissatisfaction'.[4] It appears that our thoughts and feelings about the loathing, dread or challenge of our work can create a heart attack. How can this be so? According to leading psychopharmacologist Candace Pert, we create a chain of chemical reactions in the body which are triggered by our thoughts and emotions.

The Interaction between Body and Mind

There are chemical links between our physical cell structures and our emotional experiences. Candace Pert has made a lifelong study of these links and what she has discovered is that there are receptors for emotions on every cell of the body, not just in the brain, as previously thought.

Prior to Dr Pert's research it was believed that when our emotions made us blush or feel bliss, for example, the body was responding to a signal from the brain. Dr Pert's research has revealed that these responses are actually being produced not just in the brain but throughout the whole body.

The key to our emotional responses is found in tiny messenger molecules known as neuropeptides. Every cell in the body has thousands of tiny receptor molecules on its surface, much like sense organs. Their role is to pick up signals from the space that surrounds them. When a signal is received by the receptors, it is transferred to deep within the cell. This directs the cell to divide and grow, spend or conserve energy, repair, fight infection, and so on.

The signals communicate cell to cell through hormones, neurotransmitters and peptides, which are collectively known as ligands. These ligands provide 'an infrastructure for the conversation going on throughout the bodymind'.[5] They are responsible for 98 per cent of the data transferred in the brain and body. Dr Pert's work has led her to refer to peptides and receptors as 'molecules of emotion'. She says that 'the emotions are the link between the physical body and nonphysical states of consciousness and the receptors on every cell are where this happens'.[6]

She also highlights that the peptides and receptors don't produce the emotion in a cause-and-effect relationship. Instead, her research suggests that the molecules actually *are* the emotions. The feelings that we have are in actuality the 'vibrational dance that goes on when peptides bind to their receptors'.[7] Beneath our feelings a phenomenal amount of emotional information is being exchanged on a subconscious level. This has led Dr Pert to assert, 'Your body is your subconscious mind.'[8]

In Matrix Reimprinting, we hold the belief that the subconscious mind also extends into our local fields and into the Matrix. It is our belief that the cells tune into the self in the local fields and our physiological responses change accordingly.

Returning to the subconscious mind and its effects on the body, there are a number of proven ways in which we can affect our body on a day-to-day basis with the power of our mind. These include visualization and affirmation.

Visualization

The power of the subconscious mind can be seen in the fact that people are able to visualize themselves back to health. This is a very obvious example of the links between the mind and the body.

In *How Your Mind Can Heal Your Body*, David Hamilton has collected together a plethora of research outlining how visualization can lead to healing. The book contains a whole host of personal stories from laypeople who have healed everything from cancer to autoimmune conditions to fibromyalgia with the power of visualization. Sasha's own healing story is also featured in the book, as visualization was one of the techniques she used.

Affirmation

Popularized by Louise Hay, affirmation is another example of the effect of the mind on the body. Repeating a positive statement, an 'affirmation', can have a healing effect. In the popular movie *The Secret*, we are told of a lady who healed from breast cancer by repeating the words 'Thank you for my healing' over and over again until the tumour no longer existed.

Your words and thoughts actually strengthen synaptic connections in your brain and alter your neural patterns. This in turn affects your whole body-mind, your point of attraction and thus your reality.

Neural Plasticity

Why do visualization and affirmations work? It is now understood that it is due to what is known as 'neural plasticity'. In his outstanding book *How Your Mind Can Heal Your Body*, David Hamilton explains that every thought causes microscopic changes in your brain's structure: 'In a sense, thoughts leave physical traces in the brain in much the same way as we leave footsteps in the sand.'[9]

When you think, your brain cells, known as neurons, reach out and make connections with one another: neural connections. Both your physical experiences and your thoughts create new connections, and the more you repeat a thought or experience, the denser the neural connections become. So by visualizing, David Hamilton points out, you 'actually change the microscopic structure of the brain'.[10] Affirmations work the same way.[11] With both affirmation and visualization it is literally a case of mind creating matter. Our thoughts alter the physical structure of our brain.

The Role of the Heart

The old scientific paradigm assumed that our emotional responses came from the brain alone. We now know that this is not the case. Research from the Institute of HeartMath indicates that emotions involve the heart and the body as well as the brain.[12] It has revealed that the heart actually has its own independent nervous system. This is a complex system which is referred to as 'the brain in the heart'. It 'receives and relays information back to the brain in the head, creating a two-way communication between heart and brain'.[13] 'Surprisingly, the heart sends *more* signals to the brain than the brain sends to the heart!'[14]

In fact the heart generates the body's most powerful electromagnetic field. It is 60 times greater than that of the brain and permeates every cell in the body. The magnetic component is approximately 5,000 times stronger than the brain's magnetic field and can be detected several feet away from the body with sensitive magnetometers.[15]

So the brain and the heart communicate with one another and also with the body and the world around us. The signals they send have an effect on how we act and feel. 'Jagged and irregular heart rhythms send a message to the brain that indicates we are upset. On the other hand, smooth harmonious heart rhythms send a signal to the brain that tells it everything is OK and working in harmony.'[16]

The heart rhythms are affected by our emotions. Anger, hatred, frustration, fear, worry and upset create irregular heart rhythms. On the other hand, love, compassion, confidence, appreciation and security create regular heart rhythms.[17] When we understand this we begin to realize how important it is to resolve our emotional triggers with techniques such as Matrix Reimprinting.

The heart's rhythm has a powerful influence on processes throughout the whole body. At the Institute of HeartMath scientists have demonstrated that brain rhythms naturally synchronize to the heart's rhythm and that the blood pressure and respiratory rhythms entrain to the heart's system during sustained feelings of love and appreciation.[18] They also propose that the heart's field acts as a carrier wave for information that provides a global synchronizing signal for the entire body.[19]

Fascinating evidence of the complexity of the heart can be seen in the stories of those who receive transplanted hearts. They often take on the characteristics of their donor, while knowing nothing about them. Paul Pearsall, in *The Heart's Code*, relates how an eight-year-old girl was given the heart of a murdered ten-year-old girl. She saw such vivid images of the murder – including the place, the time, the weapon used and the clothes that the murderer wore – that the police were able to catch and convict him.[20]

The heart also sends out information into the Matrix, as its fields are measurable ten feet from the body. With this new and exciting research about the power of the heart, there is now confirmation that the heart, mind and body are linked.

EPIGENETICS

There are a number of different fields of research which further highlight the power of the body–mind connection. The most notable is epigenetics, meaning 'the control of genes from outside the cell'.

Genes

For some time orthodox science and medicine have held the opinion that the genes are in charge of our health. Under this paradigm health is seen as a matter of luck, reserved for those with 'good genes', and sickness as a short straw for the unlucky ones with 'bad genes'. This belief system has prevailed for some time; however, a revolution in biology, which has been termed 'the New Biology', has now shown that the cells of our body are affected by our thoughts and beliefs, and this in turn affects our health and wellbeing on every level.

This evolution in science enables us to transform ourselves from victims to masters of our health, but it has not yet reached our healthcare systems or the general populace, and beliefs about genetic determinism still prevail. In his book *The Biology of Belief*, Bruce Lipton points out that the world is filled with people who are living in fear that their genes are about to turn on them at any moment.[21] And, as we will see, this fear itself creates a self-fulfilling prophecy, because our thoughts about our health ultimately have an effect on how healthy we are.

There is also a further problem with placing so much control over the genes, as highlighted by Dawson Church in *The Genie in Your Genes*: '...it locates the ultimate power over our health and wellbeing in the untouchable realm of molecular structure, rather than in our own consciousness.'[22] The moment we believe that our genes alone are in charge, we surrender our personal power over our health and become victims of chance. And again, this disempowerment only serves to negate our healthy state.

It is important to note that the New Biology does not discount the role of genes altogether and there are a number of conditions that are undoubtedly the result of a single-gene disorder. But it now appears that only a very small percentage of diseases fall into this category. According to Dr Lipton, 'Single-gene disorders affect less than two per cent of the population; the vast majority of people come into this world with genes that should enable them to live a happy, healthy life.'[23] This is in startling contrast to our old beliefs that genes caused all disease.

So it would seem that genes are not the main problem. In fact, some of our biggest killers in the Western world, including diabetes, cancer and heart disease, are no longer considered to be the result of a genetic disorder alone. Instead, it appears that they are the result of a complex interaction between multiple genes and environmental factors. In *The Biology of Belief*, Dr Lipton highlights that: 'Scientists have linked lots of genes to lots of different traits, but scientists have rarely found that *one* gene causes a trait or disease.'[24] This new understanding has caused a radical shift in our perception of health.

Environmental Signals

So how do we get sick, if the genes aren't in charge? It has now been shown that genes are in fact controlled by environmental signals. They are activated by both our inner and outer environments.

Our inner environment includes our emotions, our biochemistry, our mental processes, our sense of the spiritual, and so on. Our outer environment includes the food we eat, the toxins we are subjected to, our social rituals, sexual cues, etc.[25] Our genes are switched on and off in response to signals from these environments. All our biochemical, mental and physical processes, along with our cellular activity, are also controlled by signals from our inner and outer environments. These are what keep us alive. But what happens when they go awry?

According to Dr Lipton, there are three things that interfere with the signalling processes of the body: trauma, when an accident causes a disruption in the brain signal; toxins, which interfere with the body's signalling chemistry; and the mind – if our mind sends inappropriate signals, our systems become imbalanced and diseased.

You may be asking yourself why your mind might send the wrong signals to your body. The answer is down to perception. Each of your cells has many thousands of tiny receptors which enable it to read its environment. They are similar to switches and respond to a huge number of environmental signals, adjusting your biology accordingly. When your perceptions are accurate, this is a positive means of survival. But if you are programmed with misperceptions and read your environment inaccurately, you engage your responses inappropriately. So you can inappropriately activate your genes and thus cause disease and dysfunction. In Dr Lipton's words: 'Perception "controls" biology, but ... these perceptions can be true or false. Therefore, we would be more accurate to refer to these controlling perceptions as *beliefs. Beliefs* control biology.'[26]

So how we see the world, and our thoughts and feelings about it, affect our gene expression. In *The Genie in Your Genes*, Dawson Church highlights how this complex interaction between mind and body takes place: 'As we think our thoughts or feel our feelings, our bodies respond with a complex array of shifts. Each thought or feeling unleashes a particular cascade of biochemicals in our organs. Each experience triggers genetic changes in our cells.'[27]

So it is no longer a case of mind over matter, but more a case of mind *creates* matter. Our thoughts, beliefs and mental patterns impact on our biology on every level. There is now the scientific evidence to prove what self-help teachers such as Louise Hay have known instinctively all along – negative and undermining thoughts are destructive not only to our self-esteem but also to our physiological wellbeing.

Sasha was astounded when she entered psychotherapy while she was overcoming ME and was asked to make note of her internal chatter. Having studied yoga and worked as a life coach for some years, she considered herself a positive, upbeat and lively individual. But positivity was actually an act for her in those days, something she projected onto the world rather than felt deep within herself. When she really, truly tuned into her self-talk and carefully observed it throughout the day, she found she was running herself down approximately every ten seconds! Her inner monologue, although not damning, was constantly self-judging. That yoga session was OK, but she could have been more focused. That meal she cooked was OK, but needed less salt. That phone call was OK, but she could have been more honest. In fact, she even had a section in her journal entitled: 'One thing I could have done better today'! Despite all her years working to help others change their behaviour and raise their self-esteem, somewhere along the line, she realized, she had totally missed the point. It appeared to be true in her case that we all teach what we need to learn the most. And this was precisely why she was ill (along with the myriad of life traumas that she was holding in her energy system, which we shall come to later). So one of the main things she needed to do was shift her thought patterns to ones of self-love and self-nurturing, rather than self-criticism. We will show you how to do this with Matrix Reimprinting later in this book.

Thoughts, Beliefs and the Subconscious Mind

Why are so many of us allowing our thoughts and beliefs to ruin our health in this way? Surely if we realize what's going on, we can just change our thoughts and beliefs and heal our diseases?

The answer is that we can, but it's not as straightforward as just deciding to think differently. In fact, if you have ever tried to change your mental patterns by willpower alone, you will know that this is the case.

We all have the ability to decide to do something consciously, and until recently great emphasis was placed on our conscious mind, but research has now shown that 95–99 per cent of our behaviour is actually controlled by the *subconscious* mind. Moreover, the subconscious mind processes 20 million environmental stimuli per second while the conscious mind interprets just 40. And while the conscious mind can handle a few tasks at a time, the subconscious mind can handle thousands.

If you're not convinced, think about all the things that you carry out on autopilot during the day, from getting up to having your breakfast, brushing your teeth and going to work. We are on autopilot for much of the time, and this autopilot is the subconscious mind. In *The Biology of Belief*, Dr Lipton highlights that: 'The subconscious mind, one of the most powerful information processors we know, specifically observes both the surrounding world and the body's internal awareness, reads the environmental cues and immediately engages previously acquired (learned) behaviours – all without the help, supervision or even awareness of the conscious mind.'[28]

Our beliefs about life, the world, our place in it, our abilities, our health and our prospects are also held in our subconscious mind. These beliefs have come from our life experiences and our learning. Some of them may be nurturing, self-supporting and encouraging. But others are likely to be self-deprecating, undermining and self-critical. Positive or negative, they all have an effect on our biology.

The First Six Years

Of particular significance are beliefs formed in the first six years of life. This is because of our brainwave activity in those years. Between birth and two years old, babies are mostly in a state of *Delta* brainwave activity, and between the ages of two and six, children are predominantly in a state of *Theta* brainwave activity. *Delta* and *Theta* are the brainwave states that hypnotherapists drop their clients into in order to make them more suggestible. This explains why children are like sponges, absorbing the beliefs, attitudes and behaviour of the adults around them. From the perspective of fields, they learn from the information that is transmitted at a vibrational level through the morphic fields surrounding them.

This undoubtedly has positive elements, such as the formation of boundaries. Boundaries are necessary for survival. Without them, a child does not know the difference between safety and danger. But as adults, we keep running the same programs that we received in childhood and this can be to our detriment.[29]

Shame is one of the most common tools used to form boundaries, for example – children learn early on that a disapproving glance or a harsh word from their parents means that they have crossed a boundary. This causes a problem when parents, filtering the child's behaviour through their own perceptions, are too critical or severe. From a spiritual perspective we always acknowledge in our work with others that their parents were doing their best and are likely to have learned to be overly judgemental or self-critical from their own parents. But this behaviour leads to negative self-beliefs, and later in life, if left unresolved, these can lead to sickness and disease.

Fortunately, over the last few decades a plethora of Energy Psychology techniques have emerged which have enabled the transformation of beliefs. TFT and EFT are two of these techniques and we will discuss them later on. Matrix Reimprinting has advanced these techniques and works effectively to resolve beliefs formed in the first six years and even in utero. Later you will learn how to transform your negative self-beliefs to improve your health and wellbeing on every level.

CHAPTER 3

Stress, Trauma and Disease

In recent decades stress has been dubbed one of the biggest killers of our times. It is a notion that is bandied about in the West by almost everyone. Notice how many times you refer to it in the day or hear others doing the same. Yet it is frequently misunderstood, miscalculated and underestimated. When we take it back to its bare bones, it can be simply defined as negative perceptions and thoughts about our situation creating disease in our body. In this chapter we will explore the science behind this.

Psychoneuroimmunology (PNI)

One of the scientific fields which links stress and disease is the field of psychoneuroimmunology, or PNI, which is a term coined by Robert Ader in the 1970s. PNI shows the connection between the brain and the immune system and how they communicate with each other using various chemical messengers. It has shown us that stress and anxiety can influence the function of the immune system and thus create sickness and disease.

Growth and Protection

One of the keys to understanding why stress creates disease can be found by studying the interaction between our two main categories of survival, which are growth and protection. When we reach adulthood, our growth processes do not halt, as we replace the billions of cells that wear out in our body every day. In addition we have our protective mechanisms. These not only help us to ward off threats from pathogens but also to read signals in our environment which might suggest a threat to our safety and respond accordingly.

Bruce Lipton indicates that the mechanisms that respond to growth and the mechanisms that respond to protection cannot function optimally in our body at the same time. Anything that endangers us or is a threat to our survival naturally takes priority over the repair of cells, tissues and organs. We are biochemically programmed to protect ourselves first and repair ourselves later. This makes perfect sense for survival, but what if, through a myriad of false beliefs or misperceptions, we subconsciously see threatening signals from the environment that aren't there? What if, as a result of our stressful and traumatic life experiences, we engage our survival mechanisms continually and inappropriately, and our body is not able to repair itself sufficiently? When we grasp this notion we can start to understand how our misperceptions can leave us in a stressed state and thus open to a disease state.

Furthermore, when cells perceive a threat, they close down and stop detoxifying. This means they do not take in protein properly. So long-term 'fight-or-flight' reactions compromise our health on a cellular level.

This was a revelation to Sasha when she was recovering from CFS/ME. When she came across this information, she suddenly understood that because of the constant stress she had placed herself under, through her distorted perceptions, negative beliefs and life traumas, she was continually in a state of stress and protection rather than growth or healing. No wonder she was sick, and no wonder her body wasn't healing. It was only by changing her perceptions, adopting positive beliefs and releasing the energetic disruption around her life traumas that she was able to enter a state of growth and heal her condition.

The Effects of Stress

So what exactly are the effects of stress? As a populace we generally understand that stress creates adrenaline, but most people only have a vague notion of how this links to disease and remain unaware that stress itself is a matter of perception.

In *The Genie in Your Genes*, Dawson Church illustrates the different perspectives that can lead to stress: 'Your system may be flooded with adrenaline because a mugger is running towards you with a knife. It may also be flooded with adrenaline because of a stressful change at work. And it may be flooded with adrenaline in the absence of any concrete stimulus other than the thoughts you're having about the week ahead – a week that hasn't happened yet, and may never happen.'[1] The way you view the world ultimately triggers the stress responses in your body.

Think about all the different attitudes people have about being late, for example. There are those who have to be at any meeting half an hour early, no matter what, otherwise serious panic sets in. Sasha used to be one of these people! Then you've got your three-minuters. They are usually OK if they get there just before something starts, but are ruffled if they don't. Others have to be bang on time and will sit in their cars or even stand outside in the cold in order to arrive on the dot. Then you've got your latecomers. These guys can roughly be divided into three categories: those who make a big scene about being late, exteriorizing their stress and embarrassment; those who sneak in, red-faced, interiorizing their embarrassment; and that rare breed who saunter in at whatever time they get there, minus any form of personal suffering. They are late. So what? Who cares? Sasha's partner is one of these. And interestingly, she used to think that she had to make him more like her – more bothered about what people thought if he was late. Of course, that was why she was sick and he was well, but it took her a while to learn that important lesson!

In this example, our life experiences around being late, our fears around other people judging us, our fears about not being good enough, and the stress this causes, are all a matter of perception. So what are the stress responses that this perception can generate? Let's take a look at what happens in the body when we get stressed.

The HPA Axis

The body responds physiologically to stress through a system known as the hypothalamus-pituitary-adrenal (HPA) axis. This helps regulate body temperature, digestion, mood, sexuality and energy expenditure, as well as the immune system. It's also a major part of the system that controls our reaction to stress, trauma and injury. It is the brain's pathway for hormonal control. While the immune system protects us from internal pathogens, the HPA axis protects us from external threats. Once it is triggered, the immune system is suppressed, so consistent triggering of the HPA axis is harmful to immunity and therefore health.

When there are no threats, the HPA axis is inactive. But when the hypothalamus in the brain perceives a threat, it engages the HPA axis by sending a signal to the pituitary gland. Think of the pituitary gland as a kind of master gland. It organizes our 50 trillion cells to deal with an impending threat. It also sends a message to the adrenal glands, thus stimulating our fight-or-flight response.[2] Stress hormones are then released into our blood and the blood vessels of our digestive tracts are constricted, forcing blood into our arms or legs and launching our body into action. With the blood out of our digestive systems, we can no longer digest, absorb or excrete, which explains why digestive issues accompany long-term stress.

Our Western lifestyles, and more accurately our perceptions of our stressors, mean that adrenaline is continuously released into our bodies through the HPA axis. Some of us become adrenaline junkies, as the release of adrenaline provides a temporary high. The high is always followed by a crash, though, and because of that we continually seek the high again through repeating conflicting and dramatic situations, or through stimulants such as coffee, and thus the cycle deepens until we reach burnout.

Cortisol

As well as adrenaline, your body has another stress hormone: cortisol. When adrenaline starts to come down in the body, cortisol rises. The more often you activate your adrenaline, the higher the levels of cortisol will become in your body. And cortisol is damaging to your very being. While your body is making it, it isn't making dehydroepiandrosterone, or DHEA, which is responsible for many of the health-promoting and protective functions in the body. Low DHEA levels have been linked to numerous diseases, while high cortisol levels have been shown to increase fat, reduce memory and learning ability and are linked with bone loss and reduced muscle mass.[3]

Anger and the Immune System

Extreme stress emotions such as anger also compromise the immune system. In one study, participants were asked to focus on two different emotions – anger and care. While they did, their secretory IgA (immunoglobulin A) levels were measured. Immunoglobulin A is the first line of defence of the immune system. The study found that simply recalling an angry experience caused a six-hour suppression of the immune system. On the other hand, feelings of care or compassion boosted IgA levels.[4]

Stress Summary

It is therefore fair to summarize that stress is completely detrimental to the body. It puts us in a state of protection, meaning that we can't renew or detoxify our cells, it activates our fight-or-flight response, and it increases adrenaline and cortisol in the body.

Next we will explore trauma, the most extreme form of stress, and its damaging effects on our physiology.

TRAUMA

Trauma, though less widely discussed than stress, is something all of us are likely to encounter at some point in our life.

The 'big T' traumas can be defined as sexual assault, violent personal assault, being taken hostage, military combat, terrorist attack, torture, environmental disasters, severe motor-vehicle accidents and major illnesses – basically anything life-threatening. In children it can also be defined as inappropriate sexual experiences without violence.[5] These traumas may not be something we come across every day, particularly in the West. But there are also the 'small t' traumas, those events, particularly in the early years, that shatter our sense of security. Such events can be particularly traumatic if they happen unexpectedly, if we are not prepared for them, if we are powerless to prevent them, if they happen repeatedly, or if someone is intentionally cruel to us. The sudden death of someone close, a car accident, a fall, a sports injury, surgery (particularly in the early years), the break-up of an important relationship or the discovery of a life-threatening illness can also all be classed as 'small t' traumas.

As we have already established, 'small t' traumas are particularly damaging if they are experienced in the first six years of life, due to the fact that we are in a hypnogogic, non-conscious state during this period. An unstable or unsafe environment, a serious illness, medical procedures, separation from parents, physical, emotional, verbal or sexual abuse, domestic violence, bullying and neglect are also sources of trauma at this time.

Boundaries in Children

There are a number of reasons why trauma is so damaging to young children and one of the main ones relates to boundaries. Boundaries, as we have seen, are necessary for a child to develop, but while they are forming, children are at their most vulnerable to traumatic stress.[6] Traumatic stress occurs when children's boundaries are ruptured or impinged upon, causing them to lose their sense of being safe from the world around them. This usually leaves similar problems in adulthood.[7]

In the book *The Body Bears the Burden*, leading trauma specialist Dr Robert Scaer outlines how, when the safety boundaries have been ruptured, the severity of other traumatic events that follow in life can be a matter of perception. Any new implied threat will be likely to be interpreted as more traumatic than it is in reality.[8] This is part of our survival mechanism, because our subconscious mind is protecting us from something it does not want us to re-experience. The problem here is that if we continue to misinterpret minor situations as traumatic, the effect on the body-mind is extremely detrimental.

Subsequent Threat

When there is a life threat, the body responds through a series of pathways in the brain. This is described in detail by Dr Scaer in *The Body Bears the Burden*[9] and we have distilled the basics here.

If our senses perceive a threat, a message is sent to the thalamus. This is a cluster of cells in the middle of the brain which forms a relay station for messages between the brain and the body. The thalamus then sends the information to various areas of the brain, one of which is the amygdala, a group of nerve cells which processes memory and emotional reactions, and the amygdala attaches an emotional meaning to the information.

The information is then sent to the hippocampus, which is the centre for processing conscious memory. The hippocampus forms a conscious structure for the threat-based information. After this, the information is sent to the orbitofrontal cortex, which evaluates the threat for severity and either heightens or tones down our survival behaviour. If the information is deemed by the orbitofrontal cortex to be a threat, it activates the hypothalamus, which in turn triggers the HPA axis. As we discussed earlier, this results in the increase of adrenaline and cortisol.

The problem is that if we have experienced trauma, our evaluation of a new threat will be distorted and we will continually trigger the HPA axis. Subsequently our health will decline because, as with stress, the cortisol levels will become elevated and the DHEA levels lower.

The Freeze Response

One of the most fascinating aspects of how the body responds to trauma is the freeze response. This is the least understood component of the fight/flight/freeze response. We talk about the fight-or-flight response quite frequently, and our language is filled with references to it, but the freeze response is mentioned rarely and understood less. In fact it is often inaccurately seen as a sign of weakness. Time and again when we have worked with people with EFT and Matrix Reimprinting and they have described a traumatic time during which they went into the freeze response, they have done so with a sense of shame: 'I didn't fight back', 'I should have run away', 'I didn't move, I just let it happen.' Yet the freeze response is a biological state which is designed to aid our survival.

We are grateful to Dr Robert Scaer, whose research on the freeze response has helped to further our work with Matrix Reimprinting and trauma. His work has involved observing animals in the wild and noting their behaviour during trauma. If you watch an animal being pursued by a predator on TV you will see that it will often collapse and become limp even before being seized by the predator. This is usually a last resort for animals when flight or fight has failed. And when it freezes in this way, the animal releases a flood of endorphins, so that if it is attacked, its pain will be minimized. Furthermore, in a surprising number of cases the attacking animal loses interest when its prey stops moving, which is another biological reason why the freeze response is triggered.[10]

What happens after the freeze response, if the animal does survive, is of greatest interest to us here. In virtually all cases, it will begin to tremble. This can range from a shudder to a dramatic seizure. According to Dr Scaer, analysis of a slow-motion video of this trembling shows that it resembles the last act of the animal before it froze, usually the act of running. So the animal discharges the freeze response by shaking, deep breathing and perspiring. After doing so it will get up, shake itself off and apparently be none the worse for its ordeal. By doing this it seems that it has released all unconscious memory of the attack.[11]

For animals such as the gazelle, which has numerous predators, the freeze response can take place several times a day on a minor scale. The animal may freeze when it sees its predator and then, in the absence of threat, release a slight muscular shudder before returning to its previous activity.[12]

We are different: we don't discharge the freeze response. In fact, if we shake after a traumatic event we are often encouraged to calm down. Because of this, we store the trauma instead. (Though it is worth noting here that some tribal human cultures do discharge the freeze response.) Interestingly, zoo animals and domesticated animals do not discharge the freeze response either. And we often see traumatized zoo animals and strange behaviour in domesticated animals which is not common to wild ones of the same species.

EFT Master Carol Look originated the idea that we could go back to an event where we did not discharge the freeze response and discharge it using EFT. We will discuss how we have furthered this idea with Matrix Reimprinting later. First of all, let us look at what else happens to us when we experience severe trauma.

ENERGETIC CONSCIOUSNESS HOLOGRAMS (ECHOS)

In traditional psychotherapy it has long been understood that when we experience severe trauma, a part of us splits off to protect us from it, dulling or blocking our memory of it. At the same time another part of us relives it over and over again, below the threshold of awareness, so it is as if the trauma has never really ended for us. It has always been believed that the part reliving the trauma is located somewhere in the brain. However, in the same way that memory traces have never been actually proved to be in the brain, these stored traumas have never been located there either.

What Karl has discovered through his extensive work with trauma over the years is that these traumas are actually held in our local fields. His theory is that when we experience a trauma, the part of us that splits off actually forms a separate energetic reality outside our body-mind. He has named these dissociated energetic parts 'Energetic Consciousness Holograms', or 'ECHOs' for short. They hold the energy of the trauma for us as a strategy for protecting us.

The concept of parts is not a new one. In traditional counselling and psychotherapy, parts are often described as 'inner children'. It has long been accepted that we are affected by these parts of ourselves and that our traumatic and stressful life experiences are repeated due to our relationship with our dissociated parts. However, it has always been assumed that we store these parts on the inside, hence the name 'inner child'. Karl's suggestion that they are stored in our fields is therefore a radical new one. Furthermore, he suggests that when we tune into the energy of the original memory, we tune into the ECHO in the field, and this brings the original energy of the memory back into our body.

If we have experienced lots of traumas (either 'big T' or 'small t'), we will therefore also have lots of ECHOs. These ECHOs are like parts of us frozen in time. They have their own personalities based on how we were at the time of the traumatic event. When we tune into their energy in the field, we take on their personality and energy. You may have experienced this yourself when in response to something stressful you find yourself becoming a three-year-old, a five-year-old, a seven-year-old and so on. In some cases there is even a physical transformation of facial expression and body language. If you have observed this in others, you may have noticed that it is as if a child is suddenly in front of you. If you have experienced it yourself, it is as if you have suddenly become a childlike version of yourself.

How do we end up tuning into the energy of the ECHO? It is triggered by something that reminds us of that earlier traumatic event. It may be a tone of voice, a look, a word, a sound, a smell, a taste, a colour, and so on. This triggers an alert in the subconscious mind which tunes us back into the original ECHO. Suddenly we are flooded with the energy of the memory, although we may not be conscious of it. On the other hand, it may be completely overwhelming. In very severe cases we see conditions such as dissociative identity disorder (DID, previously known as multiple personality disorder), where a person has a number of different personas. Given that DID occurs when a person has experienced extreme trauma, we believe that this condition comes about when the ECHOs are so powerful that they cause the individual to switch identity. In DID, each personality has its own physical characteristics, even to the extent that one personality can be diabetic and another not. It stands to reason, then, that a person with DID is tuning into different ECHOs in the field. If the different personalities were stored inside the body, it would not account for the physiological changes that they experience. Although DID is an extreme example of tuning into ECHOs in the field, we all do it to some extent if we have unresolved trauma.

Our ECHOs hold on to the trauma to protect us from it, but they can only do so for so long, as it takes a lot of energy for them to hold it at bay. This is one of the reasons why a lot of trauma, left unresolved, leads to disease. And you may notice that as people get older, if they have unresolved trauma they become more and more affected by it.

With Matrix Reimprinting you can work directly with ECHOs to help them release the energy of a traumatic event. Not only does this change your relationship to the event, it also changes your point of attraction. Remember the Law of Attraction: what you focus on is what you attract? If you have lots of traumatized ECHOs in your field, you will keep attracting more of the same, however hard you try to be positive. So, when you release the energy around the ECHOs, you will start attracting something different as well.

Trauma and Disease

The effects of trauma on the emotions can be devastating. People often go through various stages of shock, denial or disbelief. There is often an accompanying sense of shame or guilt. Concentration can be affected, and anxiety symptoms and fear are common. Some people even disassociate and feel as if they have actually left their bodies.

There can be physical symptoms, too, often unexplained aches and pains or other ailments. Victims of unresolved trauma often visit the doctor frequently with physical symptoms that flair up dramatically and disappear just as quickly. Sasha did so until she resolved her life traumas with Matrix Reimprinting and EFT. She had colds and flu approximately every six weeks, violent skin rashes, lumps that would come and go very quickly, and her health would change like the wind. She was often treated with doubt by the medical professionals and felt sure that hypochondria was suspected. Since discovering Matrix Reimprinting and EFT, however, she has gone through several years with only minor health issues.

Insomnia or nightmares very frequently accompany trauma, both of which throw the body into a state of protection. Fatigue is also common, not only due to a lack of sleep but also because of the frequent triggering of the HPA axis and the rise in cortisol. This leads to edginess and agitation, a frequent racing heartbeat and being easily startled. It is little wonder that those in this highly triggered state often have severe health issues. It is also a relief to understand that once the energy around the unresolved traumas has been cleared with Matrix Reimprinting, healthier states can be restored.

META-Medicine®

In her book *Heal Your Body*, Louise Hay explains how our attitudes to life and the language we use can cause specific ailments. This incredible book came from her intuition, after she had healed herself of cancer, and from her understanding of the human condition through her vast work with others. Interestingly, there is a field of scientific research which has now proved what she sensed intuitively. This came out of German New Medicine® and is known as META-Medicine®. It is not a therapy, but a diagnostic tool which links different life stresses and traumas to specific diseases and ailments.

In 2004, Segerstrom and Miller, psychologists from Kentucky University, established that nearly all diseases are caused by stress. But what has not been established in the Western medical model is which stressful events cause which diseases. According to META-Medicine®, when a person goes through a stressful event, one that is unexpected, dramatic and isolating, and they have no strategy for dealing with the situation, their whole body changes to give them the best chance of solving the stressful problem. The changes are seen behaviourally, socially and environmentally. And, as each organ has a specific role in the body, when there is a later dysfunction in an organ, we can determine through META-Medicine® the type of stressful event that caused it to alter its function in the first place. Then an overreaction to the unique stressful event can easily be identified.

Interestingly, alterations in the brain structure are also seen. In META-Medicine® each particular area of the brain has a link to an organ. You may have seen something similar in reflexology, where a map on the foot has a link to each organ. In META-Medicine® it is recognized that when a person goes through a given stress, the organ best designed to solve that particular conflict changes its function to support the person through that issue. While it is doing so, emotional-information energy becomes trapped both in the organ and the corresponding area of the brain. What is fascinating is that to a META-Medicine® coach the trapped emotional-informational energy is visible in the brain via a CT scan as a ring both on the affected organ and the corresponding part of the brain. A META-Medicine® CT scan reader can therefore tell a person which of their organs is under stress or is healing.

Having this very precise diagnostic tool, we can quickly determine which traumas have triggered which diseases and then resolve them with Matrix Reimprinting. In fact Richard Flook, the head of META-Medicine® in the UK and author of *Why Am I Sick?*, is fond of saying that META-Medicine® and Matrix Reimprinting are a 'match made in heaven', as META-Medicine® helps to get to the root cause of a trauma and Matrix Reimprinting is the best way of resolving that trauma. (*For more on META-Medicine®, see Resources.*)

How Early Trauma Can Trigger the Disease Cycle

After a number of years of teaching 'EFT for Serious Disease', Karl was able to distil the disease process down into a cycle which many of our trainees and their clients have been able to relate to. Of course, there are always some variations to this cycle and it is not closed, fixed or definitive. As when anything is simplified into a model, there is a certain amount of generalizing. However, this cycle seems to fit most of the disease processes that we have encountered.

We believe that the disease process starts with any negative core beliefs that are developed in the first six years of life. We have already discussed how the first six years are crucial. Any stressful life experiences at this time, anything that we are told about the world and our place in it, any pressures, any traumas, anything that damages our self-esteem or self-worth, if left unresolved, will later affect our health and wellbeing. We have also learned how ECHOs hold an energetic blanket around our early traumas, protecting us from them, and how over time their ability to do so diminishes. This is why as we get older the disease process takes hold.

A lot of children are told at this early age that they are naughty, shy, stupid, undeserving, selfish, untidy and lazy. This forms a tendency to negative self-talk, and stress starts to become a predominant life feature. Many children form the belief that they are just not good enough, not pretty enough, not bright enough, not fast enough, not special enough.

And then of course there are the poor diet and lifestyle choices that are increasingly challenging to avoid in the fast-paced Western world that we live in. Poor eating patterns may start in childhood or develop later in life, but they put a huge strain on our system.

Any negative beliefs that we learned in the early years are then reinforced by upbringing and life pressures. The chances are that the very people who helped us create those beliefs continue to reinforce them on a regular basis. There is no blame here, by the way, as the people who are enforcing those beliefs have usually had similar experiences in their own lives and are behaving the way they are because of their own imprinting and behavioural fields.

As we get older still, we may also choose to abuse substances or self-medicate in order to cope with the stress that we are experiencing due to the traumas that we are holding in our fields. And so the cycle deepens.

Even if we have been lucky enough to avoid ill-health in childhood, as we age many of us who are caught in this cycle of disease develop a tendency to frequent infections, colds and flu. Culturally we are encouraged to tackle these with antibiotics and medication. This leads to an increase in body acidity and compromising of the gut flora, and conditions such as candida can then take hold. When candida becomes prevalent in the body, the gut flora loses its full ability to absorb nutrients and there is a toxic build-up and a subsequent further debilitation of the immune system. For many people this leads to allergies and food intolerances.

The body then goes into constant stress, typified by an increase in HPA stimulation, adrenal burnout and rising cortisol levels in the body.

What follows is lowered physical and mental ability to deal with life and a worsening of symptoms.

However, if this picture has left you with an impending sense of doom, do not despair, because the solutions are within your reach. With Matrix Reimprinting you can resolve your traumas and transform your self-limiting beliefs to heal your life.

PART II

Introducing Energy Psychology

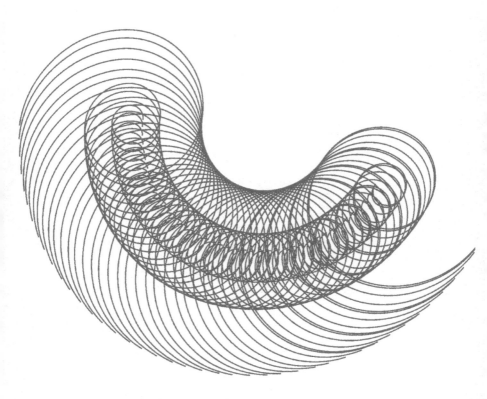

PART II
INTRODUCING ENERGY Psychology

CHAPTER 4
TFT and EFT

There are now a number of therapeutic techniques that come under the umbrella heading of Energy Psychology. Here we will focus specifically on TFT and EFT, as these are the techniques that led Karl to create Matrix Reimprinting. You will need a basic grasp of EFT in order to use the Matrix Reimprinting techniques.

Please note, if you are already an EFT or TFT practitioner then you may choose to skip this chapter.

A Brief History – from TFT to EFT

In the 1980s Roger Callahan, an American hypnotherapist and psychotherapist, began developing a technique known as Thought Field Therapy (TFT). This began almost by accident when he resolved a client's phobia by following an intuition.

Callahan had been studying the ancient meridian system of China – the system used in acupuncture. He was working with a client on her water phobia when she complained of feeling sick to her stomach. Callahan thought of the meridian system and how there was a point for the stomach under the eye, so, as an intuitive experiment, began tapping under her eye. After a few moments she exclaimed that her phobia had gone and jumped up to test her fear next to a pool outside. She was instantly free of it.

Callahan realized he had hit on something extraordinary. He started to research phobias and emotional problems and their links with the meridian system. And so TFT was born. He created a series of algorithms, like recipes, which involved tapping on various meridian end-points around the body, depending on which condition was being treated.

Callahan had a number of students. One of them, Gary Craig, had graduated from Stanford University as an engineer, but his passion for personal development had led him to pursue a career as a personal performance coach. He was fascinated by Callahan's work and he began to experiment with it himself. His question was: could he make it simpler and more accessible?

Craig spent some time experimenting with the various algorithms. He tried collapsing them down into one basic one and felt the results were pretty much the same. The advantage of this was that people could learn it themselves and it could also be used for the conditions and issues for which no algorithm had been created. And so Gary Craig began to deliver what he termed Emotional Freedom Technique (EFT) to the world.

At the time of writing this book, over one million people worldwide have downloaded the EFT manual from his website and EFT has been used in health services, schools and clinics worldwide. It is widely practised by internationally recognized doctors such as Deepak Chopra, Norm Shealy and Eric Robbins. Joseph Mercola, whose website is one of the most popular sites in the natural health industry, uses it. Molecular biologist Bruce Lipton also recommends it. It is rising in popularity due to the fact that it is fast and easy to use and it often works where nothing else will.

Some of the most notable studies in EFT have been conducted by both Gary Craig and Dawson Church on war veterans with post-traumatic stress disorder (PTSD). They showed significant improvements in just six sessions.

More about How EFT Works

What we are going to present to you here is a simplified version of EFT as we teach it and understand it. We are simplifying the process, as you will only need the basics of EFT to perform Matrix Reimprinting. The EFT that we present here is independent of Gary Craig and if you want to explore conventional EFT further, see the Resources section in the back of the book.

EFT is based on the Traditional Chinese Medicine system and involves tapping on acupuncture points with your fingers. While you do so, you bring to mind and verbalize, in a specific manner, physical symptoms or negative memories. This helps you to release life stresses or physical issues from your body's energy system and return to emotional and physical health.

So how does it work? When you are in good health, energy flows freely through the meridians in your body. This has been recognized for thousands of years and techniques such as *tai chi*, *shiatsu*, *qi gong* and so on are designed to keep the energy flowing. Trauma and stress, in their many forms, create blocks in the energy system. If the energy is not moving properly, it does not reach and sustain vital organs, and disease is imminent.

How Emotions Affect the Body

We have already seen how inappropriate emotional responses can adversely affect health. These responses come from triggers in your subconscious relating to your life experiences. So when something happens in your life and you react a certain way, you are doing so because of these triggers, or rather, because you are reminded of something that has gone before. This is why we all act differently in given situations, as we have all had different life experiences which have created different triggers for us.

Interestingly, when we remember a traumatic event, our subconscious cannot tell the difference between whether it is happening now or in the past. The same chemical responses are triggered in either case. On a small scale, this happens frequently. If you bring to mind an embarrassing memory, do you cringe or go red? This is your mind affecting your body, and also an indication that your body is experiencing the embarrassment as though it is happening now.

What You Can Change with EFT

With EFT, you can bring to mind and release negative emotional issues, physical issues, thought patterns and/or behaviour. It won't take away your natural responses to life issues, but it will take away unhealthy responses. For example, if someone close to you has passed away, it won't take away the natural grieving response. But it will remove unhealthy responses, such as holding on to the pain because you don't want to let go of the person.

What EFT Is Not

EFT is not a placebo. It works whether you believe in it or not. We are aware that from a Western medical model it may seem far-fetched that tapping on meridian points while repeating phrases can transform emotional and physical health. However, there is now a lot of evidence to back it up (see the Resources section).

There are a number of other things that EFT is not. Just to clarify, it is not a distraction therapy. Distraction techniques involve taking someone's mind off the problem. With EFT we actually focus on the problem.

It is also not Exposure Therapy. Exposure Therapy forces a person to confront their fears, while EFT relaxes and neutralizes the problem.

It is also not symptom substitution. Symptom substitution is where you fix one problem and another takes its place. With EFT we are resolving problems rather than substituting them.

Furthermore, EFT is not a talk therapy. Talk therapies involve working with the conscious mind, whilst EFT works with both the conscious and subconscious mind. You may find that issues that you thought you had resolved with talk therapies still hold some emotional intensity for you when you start tapping. This is because although you may have resolved them in your conscious mind, they may not have been resolved in your subconscious.

Success Rates

In the hands of a qualified and experienced practitioner, EFT can result in up to a 95 per cent success rate. Complete beginners usually achieve around about a 50 per cent success rate. So, experiment with these techniques and see if they work for you, and consult a qualified practitioner if you are not achieving the results you require.

THE BASIC EFT PROTOCOL

Step 1: Select the Problem

The problem you select may be either physical or emotional. You can also work on habits of thought or patterns of behaviour. The reason why we focus on the problem in EFT is that the problem is where the energetic disruption in the body lies. So resolving the problem will release the energetic disruption.

It is vital that you are specific in identifying the issue to get effective results. So if you are feeling fear, for example, break it down into its various parts – a pounding heart, nausea in the stomach, a sinking feeling in the chest, and so on. Then deal with the parts one at a time with the EFT protocol, taking the most challenging one first.

Step 2: Rate the Problem out of Ten

Give the symptom or issue that you are dealing with a number out of ten for its intensity in the present moment, zero being 'not a problem' and ten 'as intense as it gets'. This is known as the SUDS level (subjective unit of discomfort).

Ensure that you rate the problem in the present. For example, if you have nausea in your stomach, how bad is it right now? On this scale, ten would be the worst it could possibly be and one would be barely noticeable. Giving the problem a rating helps you to see the progress that you have made during each round of EFT.

Step 3: Carry Out the Set-up

The set-up is a way of overcoming any resistance to change. In EFT the resistance to change is known as 'psychological reversal' and the set-up helps us to overcome our unconscious tendencies to hold on to issues or problems.

Tap on the karate chop point on the side of the hand (see *the figure opposite*). This is the fleshy part on the side of the hand in line with the little finger. Use the tip of the index and middle fingers of the opposite hand. At the same time, say the set-up phrase out loud, which is:

'Even though I have this [specific symptom or issue], I deeply love and accept myself.'

For example:

'Even though I have this churning stomach, I deeply love and accept myself.'

'Even though I have this racing heart, I deeply love and accept myself.'

Repeat the set-up phrase three times while continuing to tap on the karate chop point. This should diffuse the energy around any resistance to change.

The set-up is not always essential in EFT, as there is not always psychological reversal. As a newcomer, it is advisable to include it. As you become more experienced, you can experiment with leaving it out and see if you still get the same results.

Please note you can alter the wording of the set-up phrase slightly to find wording that is preferable to you. Some people use 'totally love and accept myself', others prefer 'deeply and profoundly love and accept myself' and some say 'I'm working towards loving and accepting myself' or 'I'm alright' or 'I'm OK.' It is a matter of personal choice, so use what feels right to you.

Step 4: The EFT Sequence: Tapping with a Reminder Phrase

Reminder Phrase

Determine your reminder phrase. This will help you to stay tuned into the problem. It is a shortened version of your set-up phrase.

So if your set-up phrase was 'Even though I have this racing heart, I deeply love and accept myself', your reminder phrase would be 'This racing heart.'

Tapping

Tapping on the EFT points will restore the flow of energy in your body's meridian system. See the diagram below for where to tap. Tap on each of the points in turn with the end of your index and middle finger (apart from when you tap on the top of the head, when you can use all four fingers of one hand). As you tap on each point, repeat your reminder phrase.

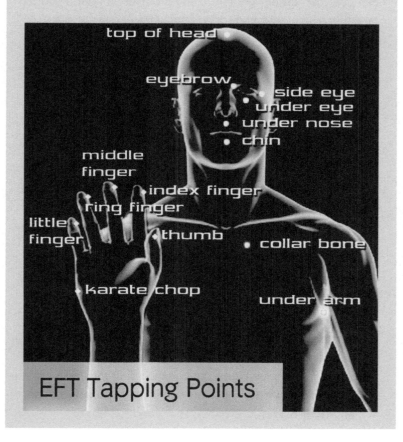

Each person has their own preference concerning the pressure used for tapping, but ensure that you tap firmly enough to make contact with the points but not so hard that you cause physical discomfort. Both Karl and Sasha prefer to tap very gently, as it is more therapeutic.

Tap down the body, starting from the top of the head and finishing on the karate chop point. Tap around seven times on each point, though it's OK if you tap more or fewer times. Also, it is fine if you accidentally miss points out in the process.

With the exception of the points under the nose or on the chin, the EFT tapping points are on both sides of the body. You can use your left or right hand, and it doesn't matter if you tap on either side of your body or on both sides at once. It is also OK to change sides.

Tap down the body, in the following sequence, repeating your reminder phrase as you tap on each point:

- First tap the top of the head on the crown with the flat of your fingers.
- Then tap the inside edge of the eyebrow, just up and across from the nose.
- Next tap the side of the eye, on the bone around the outside corner of the eye.
- Then tap the bone under the eye, about an inch below the pupil.
- Next tap under the nose, in the small hollow above the lip.
- Then tap under the bottom lip, midway between the point of the chin and the bottom of the lower lip.
- Next tap on the collarbone point. Find your collarbone and locate the 'U' shape at the top of your breastbone, where a gentleman's tie knot would sit. At the bottom of the 'U' shape, move your fingers out one inch until you find a slight dent on either side. These are your collarbone points (also known as K-27).

- Then tap under the arm about four inches below the armpit. This point is approximately in line with the nipple for men and the bra strap for women.
- Optional points are found by tapping the front of your wrist with the flat of your fingers.
- Further points are also found on the fingers. With your palm facing you, tap the nearside corner of the thumbnail and each fingernail.
- Finish by tapping on the karate chop point.

This completes the EFT tapping sequence.

Step 5: Reassess the Intensity of the Problem

At the end of this round, check the SUDS level (score out of ten) to see if the intensity of your symptoms has changed. It should either have disappeared altogether or gone down. If you still have some of the problem remaining, or the intensity has gone up, continue with subsequent rounds of tapping.

Step 6: Subsequent Rounds

Continue with subsequent rounds until the problem is a zero and has subsided. If you are working on the same symptom, you will not need to carry out the set-up phrase for each round. But if the symptoms begin moving round the body and you start working on something new (for example, if you switch from a racing heart to a churning stomach), you will need a new set-up phrase.

Step 7: Challenge the Results

Once you have got the problem down to a zero and there are no more physical symptoms, try hard to imagine the original emotion or pain, so that you can clarify that the process has worked for you. Close your eyes and think of the problem really vividly. If there is no intensity, you know that that particular part of the symptom or issue is resolved. If you do get some more intensity, then there is more work to do.

Step 8: Persist

If the problem remains after the results have been challenged, persist until it is a zero in intensity.

Refining the EFT Protocol

To refine your use of the basic EFT protocol and ensure that results are improved upon:

Refine the Set-up

You need to say the set-up out loud with feeling and emphasis to help you tune into the problem. Also, in order to get effective results with EFT, the set-up needs to be specific. If it's too global, you won't tune into the problem. For example:

Global: 'Even though men reject me...'
Specific: 'Even though Glen dumped me on Valentine's Day...'

Global: 'Even though I am an anxious person...'
Specific: 'Even though I have this racing heart...'

Chase the Pain

Often in EFT when you start tapping on a particular symptom or issue, it will begin to move around the body. It might change in intensity. If you think of it in terms of colour, shape and size, it might seem as though it has transformed as it has moved around the body. In EFT we call this 'chasing the pain' and you need to keep following the symptom around the body. Each time it moves and changes, give it a new set-up and reminder phrase. So a 'dull ache in the leg' may become a 'churning in the stomach'. Keep describing the new symptoms in a set-up and reminder phrase and following the sensations around the body whilst you tap until the symptom or issue resolves.

Test your Work

Always test your work to verify success. This can seem like an unnecessary step when the problem appears to have subsided. But testing the success will confirm to you that the problem really has gone away. You can test your success by vividly imagining the event.

Be Persistent

Some people have really quick shifts with EFT. Others take longer and need more persistence. The intention is to get the intensity of an issue down to a zero. Keep persisting until you do. Keep checking the SUDs level and repeat the EFT protocol as necessary.

Take Note of Cognitive Shifts

Cognitive shifts are when you have a change in your thinking about a past situation. When a cognitive shift occurs, memories or issues will be experienced in a different way. There will be evidence of a change in your belief system, which will be shown through statements such as:

- 'It happened.'
- 'It's over.'
- 'I'm safe.'
- 'I learned from it.'
- 'I'm ready to move on.'

Cognitive shifts are a great indication that the EFT process has worked, so when you notice your thinking and language changing in a positive way, you know EFT has been effective.

Resolve Aspects

You can use EFT to tap on the symptoms of an issue, such as the racing heart that accompanies anxiety. But the real work with EFT is to get to the root of the issue – why there is anxiety in the first place.

There may be a single life experience that has created the issue. If we keep anxiety as our example, it may be that one life trauma was so significant that it created an anxious condition that is now easily triggered by a variety of life situations. However, many issues are complex and there are multiple reasons why they are present. In EFT, these multiple reasons are known as *aspects*.

Aspects are all the different branches of a problem, and sometimes we have to resolve a number of these to get resolution of the main issue. Often we keep repeating the same patterns and attracting similar situations, which cause our issues to become more complex. So it is likely that there are lots of related life experiences on the same theme.

Let's take a spider phobia, for example. Perhaps the phobia started when we had our first experience of our mum screaming when she saw a spider. That would be one aspect. But there may also be related aspects such as the time someone put a spider down our back, the time we pulled our bed covers back and found a spider, the time we daren't go upstairs as there was a big spider on the landing, and so on. We may need to address each memory with EFT before the issue is resolved.

There can also be several aspects within the same memory. Let's go back to the spider being put down the back. There may be several peaks of emotional intensity around this memory. One could be seeing your classmate pick the spider up, the next might be when he started running towards you with the spider, the third could be him holding the spider in your face and the fourth might be when he dropped it down your back. Each of these different aspects may need to be resolved before the emotional intensity subsides. Each one would need a new set-up phrase to resolve the different feelings it created in your body.

Addressing all the different aspects will resolve the issue. So while the results of EFT are permanent, it can sometimes seem that an issue has returned if all the aspects have not been addressed.

If you find that a problem is not subsiding, you may have switched to a different aspect during the process. For example, if anxiety gives you a racing heart and a churning stomach, you may need to do the EFT process on each of these to clear the anxiety. But if you accidentally switch your focus mid-process from the racing heart to the churning stomach, your results will not be as effective, and it will seem as though you have not made progress. You need to stay with each issue separately and clear them one at a time.

Similarly, if you are working on a memory, for example being shouted at and sent out of class, you may need to work separately on the different aspects. These could include the impact the teacher's raised voice had on you, the embarrassment of being sent outside and your feeling of isolation as you stood alone in the corridor. Each aspect may need to be addressed individually in order to get the best results. Ensure that you create a new set-up phrase for each aspect and tap until the intensity has resolved.

Be Aware of the Generalization Effect

In some cases, resolving each individual aspect may not be necessary. There is a phenomenon in EFT known as the 'generalization effect'. What often happens is that when you resolve a number of memories along a similar theme, other memories can lose their emotional impact and no longer affect you. So if you have a series of memories along the same theme that give you a SUDs level of nine or ten, in resolving a small number of these memories you may find that you are able to recall all the memories without any emotional intensity.

And the Apex Problem

EFT often gets amazingly quick results. Sometimes it seems so quick and easy that the mind tries to find another explanation. When someone tries to explain away the results of EFT by suggesting it was something else that produced the results, it is called the 'apex problem'.

To overcome this issue, clearly state the initial problem, set out the desired outcome on paper and confirm that it has been achieved at the end of a session.

Advancing the EFT Techniques

Once you have a basic grasp of EFT, the following two techniques will help you work on specific issues and give you a good grounding for the Matrix Reimprinting Foundation Techniques.

Please note that if you have big traumas to address, you should read about these techniques for reference only *and either consult an EFT practitioner (preferably one who is also a Matrix Reimprinting practitioner if you intend to advance to Matrix Reimprinting) or attend an EFT/Matrix Reimprinting practitioner training course (see the* Resources section for further details).

Changing a Single Scene

Now you have a basic grasp of the EFT protocol, you can use it to change a memory you have from the past. It can be a single flash, image or scene from a memory. It can also be something that someone else said or something that you heard.

Choose a small issue, in other words something that is not greatly traumatic for you. But make sure it has some intensity for you, so that when you remember it there are some changes in your body or your emotions.

Step 1: Identify the Emotion

What is the emotion? Where do you feel it in your body? Follow the basic EFT protocol until there is no feeling around the emotion in your body. An example might be that you feel sadness in your heart. You would first check how sad you felt out of ten (the SUDS level). Then you would say the set-up phrase out loud three times while tapping on the karate chop point: 'Even though I have this sadness in my heart, I deeply love and accept myself.' Then you would tap around all the points from the top of the head downwards, repeating the reminder phrase: 'This heart sadness.' And you would continue until the intensity is zero.

Step 2: Check your Senses

Check the scene again. What did you see, feel, hear, smell, taste or think? Any of these senses may give you an emotional intensity and change your body chemistry. Examples include:

- Seeing blood which makes your toes curl when you remember it.
- Feeling fear in your legs when you weren't able to run.
- Hearing a scream which makes your heart race.
- Smelling burning which makes you feel sick to the stomach.
- Thinking, 'I just couldn't cope,' which makes your throat constrict.

Examples of set-up phrases for each issue include:

'Even though my toes curl when I see that blood, I deeply love and accept myself.'

'Even though I've got this fear in my legs...'

'Even though that scream makes my heart race...'

'Even though that burning smell makes me sick to the stomach...'

'Even though I couldn't cope and my throat is constricting...'

Work through every aspect of the scene until the impact is zero and you can remember it with no emotional intensity.

Changing a Whole Memory (Movie Technique)

Whatever life issue you are working on, you need to find the key events that relate to that issue. Your question should always be 'What's the earliest memory relating to this issue?' The above technique showed you how to work on a single image or scene and resolve all the aspects involved. But what if you have a longer memory with lots of different aspects, or peaks of emotional intensity? The most effective way of working with these in traditional EFT is the Movie Technique:

Step 1: The Memory

Identify a specific memory. It needs to be a single event.

Step 2: Movie Length

How long would the movie last? It needs to spread over a couple of minutes to a few hours in real time, within a single morning, afternoon, evening or night. If it spans several days or weeks, break it into several separate movies.

For example, Sasha used this technique with a client who wanted to work on a memory of her dog being put down. Her client said that the memory was one single event, but when the work got underway it turned out that there were actually three separate movies: the first was the day that the vet said the dog had to be put down, the second was a few days later when she took the dog for his last walk, and the third was the actual memory of the dog being put down. In some cases, working with the most intense memory will take all the emotional resonance out of the others, but make sure you break the memories into separate movies and work through each one in order to get the best results.

Step 3: The Movie Title

What would the title of the movie be? A common mistake here is to give it the title of a movie that already exists, such as *The Godfather*. Instead, the title needs to reflect the content of the movie, such as *Abandoned on the Beach* or *The Worst Thing That Ever Happened*.

Step 4: Assess your SUDs Level at the Movie Title

Check your SUDS level (intensity out of ten) at the movie title. Take the edge off the intensity. For example:

'*Even though I have this* Abandoned on the Beach *movie, I deeply and completely love and accept myself.*'

Do this until you can say the title and the intensity has reduced to no more than a two.

Step 5: Narrate the Movie

Start the movie before there is any emotional intensity. Narrate it out loud, stopping at any points of intensity and resolving each one separately with the EFT protocol. Use the same process that you used when changing a single scene, resolving any thoughts, feelings, body sensations, and so on. However, with this technique you will do this a number of times until all the different aspects are resolved.

Step 6: Check your Work

When you have finished, run the movie again in your mind, checking you have resolved the intensity. If there are any aspects that you missed or that still have intensity, tap in the normal way. Then replay the movie really vividly. Again, tap on any remaining aspects if there is still any intensity. The technique is complete when you can play the whole movie without intensity.

Practising the Techniques with Someone Else

You can either practise the techniques on your own or pair up with a partner. Often it is more effective to pair up with someone. If you choose to do so, the partner leads you in the process while tapping on themselves at the same time. They can also tap on you if you get upset.

- If someone is leading you, they will say your set-up phrase and you will repeat it after them, while you both tap on your own karate chop points. If you are working in this way, it is also preferable to split the set-up phrase into several parts, so that it is not such a long phrase to repeat.

- They then say your reminder phrase and you repeat it after them, while you both tap on your own points.

It is important that the words used are those of the person who has the issue. So the person who is leading the session listens carefully to what the recipient says about the problem and then feeds it back to them in a set-up statement, for example:

Recipient: *There is so much sadness in my heart when I think of him walking out of the door.*

Person leading the session: *What score would you give that feeling in your heart out of ten, one being 'It's barely there' and ten being 'It's as bad as it gets'?*

Recipient: *It's a seven.*

Person leading the session: *(tapping on their own karate chop point) Even though I have this sadness in my heart…*

Recipient: *(tapping on their own karate chop point) Even though I have this sadness in my heart…*

Person leading the session: *(still tapping on their own karate chop point) …when I think of him walking out of the door…*

Recipient: *(still tapping on their own karate chop point) …when I think of him walking out of the door…*

Person leading the session: *(still tapping on their own karate chop point) …I deeply love and accept myself.*

Recipient: *(tapping on their own karate chop point) …I deeply love and accept myself.*

The set-up phrase is carried out a total of three times in this way.

Person leading the session: *(tapping on the top of their own head) This heart sadness.*

Recipient: *(tapping on the top of their own head)* This heart sadness.

Person leading the session: *(tapping on their own eyebrow point)* He walked out of the door.

Recipient: *(tapping on their own eyebrow point)* He walked out of the door.

Person leading the session: *(tapping on the side of their own eye)* This heart sadness.

Recipient: *(tapping on the side of their own eye)* This heart sadness.

Person leading the session: *(tapping under their eye)* He walked out of the door.

Recipient: *(tapping under their eye)* He walked out of the door.

Continue in this way until the symptom has an intensity of zero.

• Then move on to the next aspect until all the intensity is resolved and the memory that you are working on can be recalled without a change in body chemistry.

CHAPTER 5

Matrix Reimprinting

As new information and research emerged, it was inevitable that new techniques would be created to meet our changing view of the world. There have been many advancements in our understanding of the Law of Attraction and quantum physics, but very few existing techniques work directly and intentionally with the unified energy field. However, Matrix Reimprinting does just that. It all began in Australia...

THE HISTORY OF MATRIX REIMPRINTING

In 2006, Karl was teaching EFT in Australia. While working on one of the course participants, he was making little progress, so he asked her, 'Can you see that little girl, your younger self, as a picture in the memory?' The participant replied, 'I can see her so clearly, I could tap on her.' In a moment of inspiration Karl encouraged her to tap on the little self in the memory while he continued to tap on her. She had an amazingly quick resolution of her issue and Matrix Reimprinting was born!

For the next couple of years Karl experimented extensively with the technique. At this stage it had no name and just involved the practitioner tapping on the client while the client tapped on their younger self in the picture while dialoguing with them to release the trauma.

Karl began to connect working in this way with the emerging research from the New Sciences and quantum physics. Already a leading specialist in working with serious disease using EFT, he had been applying the science of Bruce Lipton to his work for some time. What he started to realize more and more was that our negative life traumas, especially in the early years, formed our current beliefs. The part of ourselves that split off to protect us from the pain of the trauma was not only holding the trauma for us but also holding the beliefs about life that we created in that moment. And in turn these beliefs were affecting our biology.

Karl also began to realize that it wasn't only 'big T' traumas that created negative beliefs and disease. In fact, the 'small t' traumas that gave us the message that we weren't good enough, clever enough, special enough, pretty enough, bright enough, loved enough, and so on, could create more far-reaching negative core beliefs than the 'big T' events, especially in the early years.

He realized that to change the beliefs of his clients it wasn't enough to use EFT to release the information that the ECHO had taken on about the trauma. The picture itself had to be changed. This was not denying that the event happened, it was simply transforming the picture in the field, as the picture was what created the negative feeling in the body.

Karl also studied popular research on the Law of Attraction and began to realize that the pictures in the field very much related to this law. If you hold negative pictures of your life experiences in your field, you will keep attracting more of the same. As you continually resonate with them, you will continue to vibrate at that frequency and attract experiences of that frequency. As Karl started to help his clients and trainees to change the pictures in their fields, he was pleased to see that their life experiences started to become more positive too.

After listening to a talk by Rupert Sheldrake, Karl also saw how Sheldrake's work on morphic fields and morphic resonance fitted in with his own work. He was particularly fascinated by Sheldrake's assertion that morphic fields were habitual and were strengthened through repetition. He began to see clearly that we sabotage ourselves by repeating unsupportive behaviour due to the power of behavioural morphic fields. Furthermore, Sheldrake highlighted the possibility that memory was held in the Matrix, and this tied in with Karl's theory about ECHOs going into the field.

An idea along a similar theme came from Bruce Lipton in his DVD *Fractal Evolution*. Dr Lipton stated that cells didn't have the consciousness to hold memory, but the cell wall had antennae that tuned into the 'self' in the Matrix. This confirmed to Karl that ECHOs could be stored in the field. And eventually, he realized, our cells and DNA adapt to the misperceptions of these unconscious ECHOs in the Matrix. We label these changes as physical and mental dis-ease.

Karl also studied the research coming out of the HeartMath Institute and was particularly fascinated by how the heart's fields could be measured ten feet from the body in all directions. He started to realize that if the heart communicated with the Matrix in this way it could also be utilized to send out new pictures into the Matrix.

Matrix Reimprinting was also influenced by META-Medicine®, the diagnostic tool for pinpointing the exact emotional cause of a physiological illness. With confirmation from META-Medicine® that each disease was caused by a specific trauma, Karl realized that locating ECHOs and helping them resolve trauma at the time of the conflict would assist in the healing of physiological disease.

Further influence came from the work of trauma specialist Dr Robert Scaer and his research around the freeze response. Of particular significance was the fact that most humans do not discharge the freeze response. Dr Scaer also talked about 'trauma capsules' created during the moment of the freeze response.[1] This tied in with Karl's view that ECHOs were created at the moment of trauma.

At first Karl was calling the ECHO the 'inner child', as this term was one that many therapists were familiar with. However, when media producer Karin Davidson was over from the USA filming one of his trainings, she pointed out that this was an inappropriate term, since the dissociated parts existed in the Matrix and weren't always children. So the term 'Energetic Consciousness Hologram' was born.

Karl then developed the title 'Matrix Reimprinting'. *Matrix* was his preferred term for the unified energy field and, as imprinting is the system by which children take on the characteristics of their parents by observation and imitation, *Reimprinting* was recreating new programs in the place of old.

Having trained over 1,000 practitioners in EFT during his time as a trainer and EFT Master, Karl had built a community of practitioners who frequently returned for supervision and further training, and so, over the next couple of years, he was able to share his developments with them. He was used to getting brilliant feedback from his trainees about the effects of EFT, and life-changing experiences were commonplace. However, the results that his trainees were experiencing with Matrix Reimprinting were even more remarkable. Many of them were reporting that during almost every EFT session there was a call to use Matrix Reimprinting, and practically all their results were consistently phenomenal.

One such trainee was Sasha. Having overcome CFS/ME and bipolar affective disorder using Matrix Reimprinting, she was working intensively using Karl's technique in the field of serious disease and childhood trauma, and witnessing amazing results. Despite a vast array of qualifications and a varied career background, she put all her other disciplines aside to focus on Matrix Reimprinting. She recognized that as Karl's time was so devoted to innovating and training there was little time left to write about the technique, and so, after she had finished writing her first book, she made the suggestion that they should co-author this one.

At the start of writing, in July 2008, there was only one Matrix Reimprinting technique (Matrix Scene Reimprinting), but there are now two Foundation Techniques and an array of protocols for working specifically with trauma, relationships, phobias, allergies, and so on. In addition to helping to define and refine these protocols, Sasha has developed her own protocol on working with addiction. Other specialisms have also started to emerge. Sharon King has contributed the Matrix Birth Reimprinting protocol from her training in this area and others have started to follow suit. Matrix Reimprinting continues to develop and grow.

THE BASIC PRINCIPLES OF MATRIX REIMPRINTING

Matrix Reimprinting is grounded in popular psychotherapeutic theory about trauma. For trauma to occur all we need is a situation where we feel powerless and there is a threat to survival. This threat to survival is relative to our age and our ability to deal with the situation. For an adult, it may take a major event like a car crash or physical or sexual abuse. For a young child, being told by a parent that they are bad, stupid, ugly or lazy has the potential to traumatize.

At the moment the trauma occurs, if we can't fight or take flight, feel isolated and realize there is no way out, we simply freeze. Our chemical responses protect us biochemically from being emotionally and physically overwhelmed, and as our consciousness freezes, part of us splits off energetically. At this point, an ECHO is created.

When the ECHO splits off, it is held in the Matrix. It contains all the information about the traumatic event and that event is numbed out from our consciousness as if it never happened. But it lives on in the images of our subconscious and dictates our response to future situations. Similar events will trigger a similar response and so we suffer stress, anxiety, phobias, and so on, which affect our interactions in everyday life and eventually take their toll on our physiology.

A further problem is that it takes lots of energy to hold all this information in the Matrix, so as we age it gets more and more difficult for the ECHOs to hold these traumas at bay.

Another issue is that on a cellular level these pictures are real-life events happening now. Memories are only memories to the conscious mind. To the subconscious mind they are current events. You may want to ask yourself what 'current events' are keeping you from healing and happiness.

Matrix Reimprinting can release the energy of the trauma and bring about permanent healing through changing the pictures in the field. So if you have negative life pictures that are holding you in the past, you can change them for positive ones. Here is a basic outline of the main principles:

Working with ECHOs

The way we change the pictures is to work with the ECHOs that have been holding the trauma for us since the moment that the picture was created. In Matrix Reimprinting, the ECHO is the new client. So we thank them for holding on to the trauma for us and imagine tapping on them to help them release the trauma. At the same time, the points are physically tapped on our own body.

The outcome of the memory can also be changed by bringing in new resources, inviting someone else in for support or saying or doing what wasn't said or done at the time. We can also prepare the ECHO for what is about to happen.

This is not denying what happened, it is simply changing the old picture to affect wellbeing in the present. Neither is it planting memories. It is just replacing negative memories with positive ones. From a quantum physics point of view we have endless possible pasts and futures. So it is like tapping into a different past while still acknowledging the lessons learned from what we have been through.

Creating a New and Positive Picture

When all the stress and trauma of the incident has been released, a new and positive picture is created. The ECHO may go to a new place of their choosing or stay where they are but with a new and positive outcome. There are no rules here, but as a guide, if there has been severe trauma, the ECHO often chooses to go to a new location, such as a beach or a hillside. However, if the trauma has been something like falling over on stage, for example, the fact that the memory has been reimprinted with a positive picture of giving a great performance usually means that this is more appropriate for a new and positive picture.

Creating Community

When we make a new and positive picture, one of the aims is to create a sense of community for the ECHO. On his DVD presentation *Trauma, Transformation and Healing*, Dr Robert Scaer highlights the need to create bonding in order for trauma to heal. This is because of how the brain responds to trauma. When there is a threat, the anterior cingulate gyrus evaluates its severity. If it is not serious, it dampens the amygdala, which is the part of the brain that assesses the emotional content of a situation. This keeps the threat in proportion. When a person has experienced a great deal of trauma, their sense of threat is often out of proportion. But if we create a sense of bonding and the amygdala is inhibited, the traumatized brain can heal.[2]

So, in Matrix Reimprinting the ECHO is invited to create community in the new picture. It can bring in family and friends, respected figures, religious and spiritual figures such as Jesus, Buddha and angels, pets and animals, and so on, to create healing. In a vast majority of cases the client's older self is enough to create this healing.

Bringing the New Picture into the Mind

The picture is brought into the mind so as to reprogram the mind with the new information. We believe that this stage makes new neural connections in the brain and that this creates a healing effect. Childhood trauma burns out neural circuitry in the hippocampus to protect us from remembering, but these experiences can be regenerated, which is a process known as neurogenesis.[3] Neurogenesis also occurs when we experience new things, have experiences of excitement, wonder and awe, reach spiritual states or have strong positive emotions.[4] It is our belief that with Matrix Reimprinting, when we change the outcome of a memory and give an ECHO the chance to have new experiences, this creates neurogenesis too. Although this has not been backed up by experimentation at this stage, we are confident that when studies are carried out that detect changes in brain state, it will be shown that neurogenesis is taking place with Matrix Reimprinting. There is already a lot of related evidence of how we can influence our body with our mind in this way. The most comprehensive book on this subject to date is *How Your Mind Can Heal Your Body* by David Hamilton.

When we take the new image into our mind, we also intensify the colours in and around it. It has been said that colour is the language of the central nervous system, and heightening the colour in and around an image will intensify the way it is perceived by the senses. In Matrix Reimprinting, any positive emotions that are associated with the image are also highlighted so as to reprogram the emotional responses in relation to the image.

Sending the New Picture to the Cells

From the work of Bruce Lipton, we know that our cells are influenced by our thoughts. So we send the image to the body to say that the trauma is over. This reinforces the positive work we are doing with this technique. If there is a diseased organ that may be related to the trauma – for example, if the session started by working on a stomach ulcer and the trauma surfaced in relation to the ulcer – then the positive image is also sent to the diseased organ.

Bringing the Picture into the Heart

The new image is brought into the heart, and again the colours and the positive emotions associated with it are intensified.

Transmitting the Picture from the Heart

We saw in Chapter 2 that the heart is a powerful transmitter which communicates with the Matrix, so now the new picture is transmitted from the heart into the Matrix.

THE DIFFERENCE BETWEEN MATRIX REIMPRINTING AND CONVENTIONAL EFT

EFT, TFT and Matrix Reimprinting are all Energy Psychology techniques that involve the meridians. The difference is that while with EFT we clear the negative energy from past traumatic events, with Matrix Reimprinting we actually transform what happened.

Tapping on ECHOs

Though the tapping technique is the same, one of the main differences between traditional EFT and Matrix Reimprinting is that EFT doesn't involve working with ECHOs, whereas with Matrix Reimprinting the ECHO is the client. Traditional EFT also does not tend to view past memories as being held in the Matrix but in the body-mind.

Filling the Void

For a number of people, simply clearing the negative energy using EFT and not replacing it with anything positive can leave a void. Some EFT practitioners have developed visualizations to fill this void. Others have filled it with Reiki. For some, PSYCH-K® (an Energy Psychology technique used to reprogram the subconscious mind with positive beliefs) has been favoured. With Matrix Reimprinting there is no need to employ another modality to fill this void, as it is filled with the new picture.

THE BENEFITS OF MATRIX REIMPRINTING

The Matrix Reimprinting techniques are easy to use. They are also very gentle. They enable resolution of a whole range of traumatic experiences without retraumatization. They have further benefits as follows:

Resolving Core Issues and Instilling Positive Beliefs

With Matrix Reimprinting you can quickly find and resolve core issues. In traditional EFT, when someone expresses a belief such as 'I must be perfect to be loved', you find the earliest memories relating to this belief and resolve them. With Matrix Reimprinting you not only resolve the memories that contributed to the core issues, you also instil new supporting beliefs and experiences. This in turn transforms the current belief system.

Resolving Pre-conscious Trauma

Matrix Reimprinting also locates pre-conscious trauma, even trauma that occurred before the first six years. Very few therapies or practices have tools for working with pre-conscious memories, yet the research of cell biologist Bruce Lipton indicates that this is when most of the damage is done to our perceptions of self. With Matrix Reimprinting you can interact with yourself as far back as the womb to resolve pre-conscious trauma.

Producing Reframes and Cognitive Shifts

Another benefit of Matrix Reimprinting is that it commonly produces a change in perspective, known as a reframe, and a change in thinking, known as a cognitive shift. If you are working with this technique as a therapist, one of the great benefits is that most of the work comes from the client (although if they get stuck at any point, guidance is needed). As they lead the process, they decide what is best for them. As they have the power, they are much more likely to reframe the situation themselves or emphasize their cognitive shifts. As practitioners, we are well aware that these shifts indicate that resolution and therefore healing has taken place.

Forgiveness

Similarly, Matrix Reimprinting often leads to a place of forgiveness, particularly of the perpetrator of the traumatic experience. There are a number of schools of thought which believe that the purpose of any therapeutic intervention is to reach the point of forgiveness. This is not something to be forced or feigned, and there is often a sticking point in traditional therapeutic practices where a client will say they have forgiven their perpetrator consciously but will not have done so on a subconscious level. Matrix Reimprinting leads the recipient naturally to a place of true forgiveness.

Psychological Reversal and Secondary Gains

Matrix Reimprinting also elegantly locates psychological reversal (subconscious holding on to the problem). By interacting with the ECHO we can begin to understand exactly why they are holding on to a problem or issue which is keeping us stuck in an old pattern of thinking or behaviour (benefiting from a secondary gain).

Dissociated Clients

Another great benefit is that Matrix Reimprinting works on dissociated clients who have no SUDS levels (clients who have no feelings or emotions about issues that are still unresolved for them).

For an EFT practitioner this client group is one of the most challenging to work with. Matrix Reimprinting works perfectly with these people because when the client works with the ECHO the technique is even more effective when the client is dissociated (in other words, doesn't bring the feelings of the ECHO into their body).

Trauma Resolution

Matrix Reimprinting is very valuable in its ability to send a message to the body that the trauma is over. It ends the cycle where the trauma is constantly being replayed in the Matrix. This enables the body to respond in healthier ways and begin to heal.

Resolving the Irresolvable

With Matrix Reimprinting you can also resolve issues that have previously been irresolvable. This is particularly beneficial if you have lost family members or loved ones and not had a chance to say goodbye or resolve your differences. Using Matrix Reimprinting you can release the emotions around unresolved relationships and let go of the ties that hold you in the past.

The Law of Attraction

A further benefit of Matrix Reimprinting is that it utilizes the Law of Attraction. As mentioned earlier, when we have traumatic experiences and hold them in the Matrix, we continue to attract similar experiences. But once we resolve the trauma, we change our point of attraction and begin to draw more fulfilling and life-sustaining experiences to us.

The Tipping Point

When we collapse lots of images or memories in the field, there is a tipping point. Just as in the generalization effect in EFT (*page 63*), when we start to change the pictures in the Matrix, we sometimes only need to change a small number before similar pictures no longer hold any resonance for us. The positive pictures are many times more powerful in resonance than the negative pictures (just as your positive thoughts have a higher vibration than your negative thoughts). So, placing new pictures in the field can create a tipping point of attracting positive experiences in your life, even if you haven't changed all the negative pictures on the same theme.

PART III
Matrix Reimprinting Techniques
Rewriting your Past, Transforming your Future

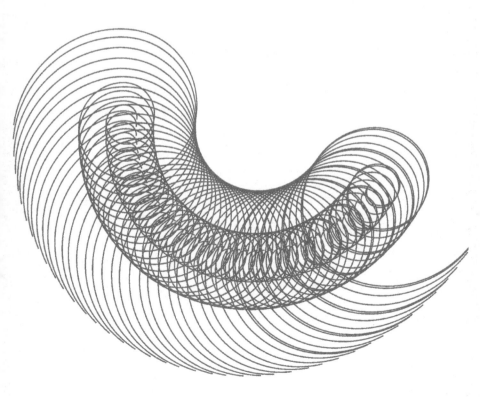

CHAPTER 6

Introducing the Matrix Reimprinting Techniques

There are two main Matrix Reimprinting techniques and a whole host of protocols for working with specific issues. You can use these techniques on yourself and on a relative, friend, colleague, associate or client. For the purpose of the instructions that follow, we will refer to the person that you are working on as 'the recipient'.

You do not have to be a trained therapist to use these techniques on others. However, please be aware that reading this book does not qualify you to use these techniques on others in a professional context and you will need to partake in a Matrix Reimprinting training course to be qualified to do so.

Also, please note that the techniques have been simplified into steps here so as to capture the essence of this work, but ultimately people are very individual and their issues do not always fit into these neat steps. So there are often many variations and refinements, which we will present in Chapter 8.

Most importantly, please be aware that if your recipient, family member or friend has deep-rooted emotional scars or very intense memories, it is important that you refer them to a Matrix Reimprinting practitioner rather than trying to work with them yourself. You must take full responsibility for your use of these techniques and exercise caution at all times in your use of them.

TECHNIQUES

Here is a brief summary of the Matrix Reimprinting techniques. Full instructions will follow in the next chapter.

Foundation Techniques

These include Matrix Scene Reimprinting, for transforming a single scene, image or flash of a memory from earlier in life, and Matrix Memory Reimprinting, for transforming a specific memory. These two Foundation Techniques form the basis of all the other Matrix Reimprinting protocols. You will need to learn and be confident with the Foundation Techniques before you use any of the other protocols.

Life Transformation Protocols

These include Matrix Core-Belief Reimprinting for transforming negative core beliefs, Matrix Life-Issue Reimprinting for transforming a current life issue and Matrix Law of Attraction Reimprinting for transforming your point of attraction.

Relationship Transformation Protocols

These include techniques for resolving past and present relationship issues. Matrix Relationship Reimprinting will resolve current relationship challenges and Matrix Resolution Reimprinting is for resolving negative relationships with people you are no longer in contact with.

Addiction and Habitual Behaviour Protocols

Addictions and habitual behaviour can be transformed using the Matrix Habit Reimprinting protocol. It can be used for all addictions, from chocolate to heroin.

Past-Life and Future-Self Protocols

Matrix Past-Life Reimprinting is for transforming memories which may arise from past lives. Matrix Future-Self Reimprinting is for learning from your future self and also for transforming fears of the future.

Birth and Early Years Protocols

Matrix Pre-conscious Reimprinting is used for identifying and transforming pre-conscious memories. Matrix Birth Reimprinting is for transforming negative birth experiences.

USING MATRIX REIMPRINTING ON YOURSELF

Matrix Reimprinting can be used as a self-help technique and is very powerful as such. However, please be aware that these techniques are intended for use on your own only with smaller issues and 'small t' traumas. Under no circumstances are you advised to work on intense memories, 'big T' traumas or highly stressful issues.

The best way to work on your own is to get some experience of these techniques from a practitioner or someone that knows Matrix Reimprinting well and then to continue working on your own afterwards.

The Benefits of Working on your Own

Working on your own is cost-effective, means that you can work on your issues as soon as they come up and is also empowering.

The Challenges of Working on your Own

You can make tremendous progress using these techniques on your own, but there can be a number of challenges:

- *Motivation issues*
  Sometimes it can be difficult to find the motivation to work alone. If you have a busy, fast-paced Western lifestyle, practising Matrix Reimprinting on your own may be something that always gets put to the bottom of your schedule.
- *Doing your own detective work*
  Sometimes we need another human being to help us out of the maze we have created for ourselves. The benefit of having a Matrix Reimprinting practitioner to help you resolve your issues is that they will ask you powerful questions you may not be able to ask yourself.

- *Your subconscious protecting you*
  Sometimes your subconscious mind will protect you from resolving your issues if it believes that there is an important reason for holding on to them.
- *Community*
  Bonding is important for the effective healing of trauma, and working with someone else creates a bonding effect.[1] If you don't want to work on others professionally but have lots of personal work to do, it may be to your advantage to train as a Matrix Reimprinting practitioner for your own personal development. These training courses are frequently attended by laypeople who want to learn Matrix Reimprinting for their own personal use and who continue to swap Matrix Reimprinting sessions with each other after the course.

Where to Start When Working on your Own

If you are working on your own you are advised to first learn Matrix Scene Reimprinting and practise transforming single scenes or images from your life. When you have become confident in doing so, then progress to Matrix Memory Reimprinting. With the two Foundation Techniques under your belt, you can then move onto the protocols that are relevant to your life situation.

If you are not sure what issues or memories to work on, ask yourself, 'What's not working in my life right now?' and then look for an early memory relating to this theme.

PRACTISING MATRIX REIMPRINTING ON OTHERS

The benefits of finding a partner to work with are that you keep each other motivated, talking about issues often helps to clarify and refine them, and you can guide each other through the process.

The challenges are that working with someone inexperienced may mean that you come unstuck when things aren't straightforward, and an untrained hand may be more likely to interfere with the process than guide you through it.

The following will give you some basic guidelines for using these techniques on others. Remember, if you are unqualified in them, only use them on others for minor issues.

Getting your Recipient's Permission to Tap on Them

You need to get permission to tap on the recipient before the session starts. If they are not comfortable being tapped on, the technique can still be carried out with you tapping on yourself and your recipient tapping on themselves throughout the process.

How to Tap on your Recipient

If you are carrying out Matrix Reimprinting on a recipient, sit opposite them at a 45-degree angle. Hold their hand in one hand, and with the other, tap on their points. Tap very lightly, approximately five to seven times on each point. As with EFT, it doesn't matter if you miss points out or tap the points in the wrong order. You can tap with either hand and on either side.

Where to Start If You Are Working with a Partner

If you are new to these techniques, we suggest you learn the Matrix Scene Reimprinting technique first and practise changing a single scene. Do this a number of times until you are confident. Then you can branch out into the Matrix Memory Reimprinting technique. Once you have got these two Foundation Techniques under your belt, you can work with the protocols that are relevant to your current life situation.

Working with an Experienced Matrix Reimprinting Practitioner

The benefits of working with an experienced practitioner are that you will be asked very specific and pointed questions that will help you identify and resolve specific memories, and the practitioner will be able to help you to overcome any challenges or blocks that you might face.

Practising Matrix Reimprinting over the Telephone

You can also practise Matrix Reimprinting on a recipient over the telephone. It is the same technique, except that you tap along with your recipient and they tap on themselves while imagining tapping on their ECHO at the same time. You will need plenty of practice face to face before you attempt this.

You may already be aware that some people are predominantly auditory (process the world through sound), some are predominantly visual (process the world through images) and some are predominantly kinaesthetic (process the world through feeling). These divisions are known as submodalities. Whatever your predominant submodality is, you can still carry out Matrix Reimprinting work on the telephone.

As an extremely visual person, Sasha was quite sure when she started her Matrix Reimprinting and EFT career that she would not be working by telephone. In fact, she had experienced an intense dislike of the telephone for most of her life! However, when her career took off both nationally and internationally, she had to make a concession and undertake telephone work. Interestingly, this is now her favourite way of working with Matrix Reimprinting. The sessions over the telephone are far more powerful and far-reaching than those face to face. Sasha enjoys hearing the extremely subtle changes in someone's voice, and the focus and concentration over the telephone leads to far more in-depth sessions. So if you are not keen to work over the telephone, particularly if you are a practitioner, do try it a few times before you dismiss it.

CHAPTER 7

The Foundation Techniques

The Foundation Techniques are Matrix Scene Reimprinting and Matrix Memory Reimprinting. All the other Matrix Reimprinting protocols are built around these two techniques, so a grasp of them will enable you to use them all.

If you are new to Matrix Reimprinting you are advised to read chapters 7 and 8 in full before you attempt these techniques on yourself or others. You may also benefit from reading Chapter 17, which shows Matrix Reimprinting in action, to give yourself an overview of the techniques before you attempt them.

Matrix Scene Reimprinting

Matrix Scene Reimprinting can be used on a single scene, image or short flash of a memory that you have, or your recipient has, from childhood or earlier life.

You, or your recipient, may already be aware of the image that you want to work on. You may have a flash of yourself as a child or earlier in life in a particular situation. If this is the case, bring the image to mind and use the following protocol. Later we will explore how to access a blocked memory and also find a memory relating to a current life issue.

The Basic Premise of This Technique

In this technique, you bring to mind a single scene or image of an early stressful or traumatic memory. As you tap on yourself, you imagine tapping on your younger self within the memory. That younger self is the ECHO. You introduce yourself to the ECHO, converse with them, find out what life messages they gained from this situation and help them to release the trauma of the memory. To assist in the process, you can bring in new resources or people, perhaps a trusted friend or relative, someone famous or a spiritual figure.

Once the situation has been resolved, the ECHO goes to a new place of their choosing such as a beach or meadow. They can also invite others in to create this new 'memory'. When they are in a good place, this new picture is taken into your mind. It is also sent to every cell in your body to let it know that the trauma is over. It is then taken into your heart and transmitted out into the field.

When the new picture has been sent into the field, the tapping is paused so that the old picture can be tested to make sure there is no negative resonance around the original memory. (We'll talk more in the next chapter about what to do if there is still negative resonance at this stage.) If the original picture has changed or holds no resonance, Matrix Scene Reimprinting is complete.

Throughout the process, you keep your eyes closed (if you are comfortable doing so) and carry out most of the work with the ECHO in silence. You need to give yourself time to carry out the change work.

Please note that although you might start with a single scene, it may lead on to a full memory, so you might start using Matrix Scene Reimprinting and end using Matrix Memory Reimprinting.

Matrix Scene Reimprinting: Working on your Own

Please remember to only use this technique on your own for 'small t' traumas. For intense and stressful traumas, please consult a Matrix Reimprinting practitioner.

Step 1: Set the Scene

Bring to mind a scene or image that you want to work with. Make sure that you are looking at yourself from the outside (known as being dissociated) rather than through your own eyes (known as being associated).

Step 2: Start Tapping

Close your eyes and begin tapping on yourself, using all the points (*page 57*). Tapping continues until Step 14, when you test the work.

Step 3: Step into the Picture

Imagine stepping into the picture as your current self.

Step 4: Meet the ECHO

Introduce yourself to your ECHO. You need to let them know who you are and explain that you have come from the future to help them feel differently about the situation. This is done silently in your mind.

Step 5: Thank the ECHO

The ECHO will often have been holding the trauma for a long time. Thank them for doing such a great job for you.

Step 6: Tap on the ECHO to Clear Negative Emotions

Ask the ECHO what they are feeling and where they are feeling it in their body. Then imagine carrying out the EFT protocol on the ECHO while continuing to tap on yourself.

For example, if the ECHO is feeling black fear in their heart, imagine tapping on their karate chop point while tapping on your own karate chop point. At the same time, say the set-up phrase out loud, for example: 'Even though you have this black fear in your heart, you love and accept yourself.' If the ECHO is a child, adapt the language of the set-up phrase to suit a child: 'Even though you have this black fear in your heart, you're still a great kid.'

Then imagine that you are tapping around all the points on the ECHO (while still tapping on yourself). Just as in traditional EFT, use a reminder phrase. So, sticking with the black fear in the heart, the reminder phrase would be 'This black fear in your heart.'

Continue this until the ECHO has cleared some of the intensity of emotion that they are feeling.

Step 7: Converse with the ECHO

Converse silently in your mind with the ECHO, asking what they learned about life from this situation. Check whether you are still running this lesson. For example, if the ECHO says they learned they were 'stupid', do you still feel stupid at times?

Step 8: Change the Memory

Ask the ECHO if there is anything they would like to do to resolve this situation. They can:

- bring in new resources
- change what happened
- invite somebody or something else in for help and guidance
- do what they didn't do or they wished they'd done in that situation

Change the image accordingly.

Step 9: Give the ECHO the Option of Going to a Different Place

When there is resolution around the original memory, ask the ECHO if they would like to go to a place of their choosing and create a new picture, for example a forest or the seaside. Going to a different place is the choice of the ECHO and isn't always necessary or appropriate.

Allow the ECHO to have a positive experience in the place of their choosing. They can bring in others of their choosing to create an experience of community.

Step 10: Change the Image in the Mind

When you have created a new and positive picture and the ECHO is in a good emotional space, bring the picture through the top of your head and into your mind. (It is only the positive picture that has been fully resolved that goes into the mind.)

Experience the picture through all your senses – what do you see, hear, smell, taste and feel? Name the colours around the picture and the positive emotions associated with it.

Allow all the neurons in your brain to connect with the knowledge that this is the new picture.

Step 11: Send a Signal to the Cells

Send a signal to every cell in your body that the trauma is over and that all is well. If there is an associated organ that is diseased (for example, a stomach ulcer), send healing to that part of the body as well.

Step 12: Take the Picture into the Heart

Next take the picture down into your heart, making the colours bold and bright and increasing the positive emotional intensity around the image. Tune back into the emotions you were feeling when you took the picture in through your mind, and also the colours in and around the picture.

Step 13: Change the Image in the Field

Now beam the image from your heart back out into the field. The heart picture goes in every direction, not just forward, as the heart's field radiates around the body and into the field. Give yourself time to experience the positive emotions that are part of this aspect of the technique.

Step 14: Test the Work

Finally, stop tapping on yourself. Come back to the present and open your eyes in your own time. Then close your eyes again and bring to mind the original image. If there is any intensity remaining, either clear it with conventional EFT or go back into the picture to resolve another aspect. However, it is most likely that the original image will have changed or disappeared.

Matrix Scene Reimprinting: Working with Another Person

You can also use this technique on another person. This is exactly the same as using it on yourself, except that you tap on them and they tap on the ECHO throughout. In summary:

- Ask them to bring to mind the image or scene they want to work on.
- Encourage them to describe what they are seeing. The important thing is to make sure that they are looking at the scene from the outside, not through the eyes of their younger self, the ECHO. In order to ensure that they are doing this, you can ask them a number of questions such as 'What are they wearing?', 'What do they look like?', etc.
- Encourage them to close their eyes, check you have permission to tap on them and then begin tapping using all the points (*page 57*).
- Ask them to step into the scene as their current self and introduce themselves to the ECHO. Let them explain why they have come and thank the ECHO for holding on to the trauma.
- Encourage them to ask the ECHO what they are feeling and where they are feeling it in their body. Then let them carry out the EFT protocol on the ECHO, using the set-up phrase

'Even though you have this [negative emotion], you love and accept yourself' or, if the ECHO is a child, '...you are still a great kid', while you continue tapping on them.

- They then imagine that they are tapping around all the points on the ECHO (while you keep tapping on them). Just as in traditional EFT, you use a reminder phrase and your recipient follows. So, with the black fear in the heart, the reminder phrase would be 'This black fear in your heart.' This is repeated as you tap on the recipient and they tap on their ECHO. Continue this until the ECHO has cleared some of the intensity of emotion that they are feeling.

- Encourage your recipient to converse silently in their mind with their ECHO, asking what they learned about life from this situation. Ask them if they are still running this lesson.

- Encourage them to change what happened, if appropriate, by bringing in new people and/or resources. The transformation work is usually done in silence. Explain to your recipient that you are going to give them time to complete this while you continue tapping on them and they continue tapping on the ECHO. Let them know that you are there if they need any assistance at any stage. Instruct them to let you know when this part of the process feels complete.

- When there is resolution, ask them to ask the ECHO if they would like to go to a new place (if appropriate).

- Bring the picture through the top of the head. Encourage them to experience the new picture through their senses. What do they see, hear, smell, taste and feel? Ask them to make the colours bright and identify the positive emotions they associate with the new picture.

- Ask them to send a signal to every cell in their body that the trauma has passed, and also to any organs or parts of the body that need healing.

- Ask them to send the picture to their heart. Invite them to tune into the positive emotions and feelings associated with it.

- Then encourage them to send the image out into the Matrix. Give them time to experience the positive emotions and instruct them to let you know when it feels complete.
- Invite them back to the present and encourage them to open their eyes in their own time. When you are sure they are in the present, ask them to close their eyes again and bring to mind the original image that they had of themselves. If there is any intensity remaining, either clear it with conventional EFT or go back into the picture to resolve another aspect.

MATRIX MEMORY REIMPRINTING

The Basic Premise of the Technique

This technique is similar to Matrix Scene Reimprinting, except that it allows you to work with a longer memory rather than a smaller scene or image. Just like the conventional EFT Movie Technique, the memory needs to be a single event with a number of peaks of emotional intensity within it. It also needs to span a short period of time, for example a few minutes, an hour, a morning, an afternoon or an evening, and to last for no more than ten minutes in total when you tell the story. If it spans several days or weeks, you will need to divide it into several memories, giving each one a separate title and working on them one at a time.

Matrix Memory Reimprinting: Working on Yourself

The usual precautions apply, and if you have deep-rooted emotional scars or memories with a very high emotional charge, it is always advisable to work with a Matrix Reimprinting practitioner to resolve these memories.

Step 1: The Memory

Bring to mind a specific memory that you want to change or work with. Ensure that it is a single event. Give it a title –

Abandoned on the Beach or *The Worst Day of my Life*, for example.

Step 2: Narration

Narrate the memory out loud or in your mind, starting before there is any emotional intensity. As soon as there is a point of emotional intensity, pause the memory.

Step 3: The Scene

Get a clear view of this particular scene. Ensure that you are looking at it from the outside (are dissociated). The younger version of yourself in the memory is the ECHO.

Step 4: Tap on Yourself

Close your eyes and begin tapping on yourself, using all the points (*page 57*). Tapping continues until Step 10, when you have resolved the first emotional peak.

Step 5: Meet the ECHO

Step into the picture and introduce yourself to the ECHO. Let them know who you are and explain to them that you have come from the future to help them feel differently about the situation. This is done silently in your mind.

Step 6: Thank the ECHO

The ECHO will often have been holding the trauma for a long time. Thank them for doing such a great job for you.

Step 7: Tap on the ECHO to Clear Negative Emotions

Ask the ECHO what they are feeling and where they are feeling it in their body. Then tap on them to clear the negative emotions, using the set-up phrase 'Even though you have this [*negative emotion*], you love and accept yourself' or, if the ECHO is a child, '...you are still a great kid.' Continue tapping on yourself as you do this.

Continue this until the ECHO has cleared some of the intensity of emotion that they are feeling.

Step 8: Converse with the ECHO

Ask the ECHO what they learned about life from this situation. Check whether you are still running this lesson. For example, if the ECHO says they learned they were 'unlovable', do you still feel unlovable at times?

Step 9: Prepare the ECHO or Change the Outcome

Ask the ECHO if there is anything they would like to do to resolve this situation. They can:

- prepare for what is about to happen
- bring in new resources
- change what happened
- invite somebody or something else in for help and guidance
- do what they didn't do or they wished they'd done in that situation

The transformation work is usually done in silence. Give yourself time to complete this while you continue tapping on yourself and on your ECHO.

Step 10: Continue with the Narration

Once the first emotionally intense peak of the memory has been transformed, stop tapping on yourself, open your eyes and continue with the narration.

Step 11: Clear Further Peaks of Emotional Intensity

Each time there is an emotional peak, pause the memory, close your eyes and begin tapping on yourself. Clear each individual peak in the same way by tapping on the ECHO and either preparing them for what will happen, changing the outcome of what happened, bringing in new resources or inviting in someone for support.

Do this until all emotionally intense peaks have cleared.

Step 12: Ask the ECHO If They Would Like to Go to a Different Place

When there is resolution of the full memory, ask the ECHO if they would like to go to a place of their choosing in the picture, for example a forest or the seaside. It is not always appropriate.

Allow the ECHO to have a positive experience in the place of their choosing. They can also bring in others of their choosing to create an experience of community.

Step 13: Change the Image in the Mind

When the ECHO is in a good emotional space and has a very clear and positive picture of this, bring the picture into your mind. Allow all the neurons in your brain to reconnect with the knowledge that this is the new picture. Experience the picture through all of your senses, intensifying the colours in and around it and the new emotions you associate with it.

Step 14: Send a Signal to the Cells

Send a signal to every cell in your body that the trauma is over and all is well. If there is a diseased body part which may relate to this memory, send healing to that part also.

Step 15: Take the Picture into the Heart

Take the picture down into your heart, making the colours bold and bright and increasing the positive emotional intensity associated with the image.

Step 16: Change the Image in the Matrix

Now beam the image from your heart out into the field in all directions. Take the time to experience the positive emotions that are part of this aspect of the technique.

Step 17: Test the Work

Finally, stop tapping on yourself. Come back to the present and open your eyes. Then close your eyes again and play the original memory in your mind. If there is any intensity remaining, go back into the memory to transform the unresolved aspect. However, it is most likely that the original image will have changed or disappeared.

Matrix Memory Reimprinting: Working with a Partner

The procedure for carrying out the technique on another person is almost exactly the same, except you tap on your recipient and they tap on their ECHO throughout. In summary:

- Ask your recipient to bring to mind a specific memory that they want to change or work with. Ensure that it is a single event. Ask them to give it a title.
- Encourage them to begin telling you what happened, making sure they start before there is any emotional intensity. As soon as there is a point of emotional intensity, pause the memory.
- Ask your recipient to describe this particular scene. Ensure

that they are looking at it from the outside (are dissociated) by asking them a number of questions such as 'What are they wearing?', 'What do they look like?', etc. The younger version of themselves in the memory is the ECHO.

- Get them to close their eyes, check you have permission to tap on them and then begin tapping, using all the points (*page 57*).

- Ask them to step into the scene as their current self and introduce themselves to the ECHO. Let them explain why they have come and thank the ECHO for holding on to the trauma.

- Encourage them to ask the ECHO what they are feeling and where they are feeling it in their body. Then they carry out the EFT protocol on the ECHO while you continue tapping on them. Continue this until the ECHO has cleared some of the intensity of emotion.

- Encourage your recipient to converse silently in their mind with their ECHO, asking what they learned about life from this situation. Ask them if they are still running this lesson.

- Encourage them to prepare for what is about to happen or change what happened, if appropriate, by bringing in new people and/or resources. The transformation work is usually done in silence. Explain to your recipient that you are going to give them time to complete this while you continue tapping on them and they continue tapping on the ECHO. Let them know that you are there if they need any assistance at any stage. Instruct them to let you know when this part of the process feels complete.

- Once the first emotionally intense peak of the memory has been transformed, stop tapping on your recipient, ask them to open their eyes and encourage them to continue with the narration.

- Each time there is an emotional peak, pause the memory, ask your recipient to close their eyes and begin tapping on them. Clear each individual peak in the same way as before. Do this until all emotionally intense peaks have cleared.

- When there is resolution, ask them to ask the ECHO if they would like to go to a new place (if appropriate).
- Ask your recipient to take the new picture in through the top of their head. Encourage them to experience the new picture through their senses. What do they see, hear, smell, taste and feel? Ask them to make the colours bright and identify the positive emotions they associate with the new picture.
- Ask them to send a signal to every cell in their body that the trauma has passed, and also to any organs or parts of the body that need healing.
- Ask them to send the picture to their heart. Invite them to tune into the positive emotions and feelings associated with it.
- Then encourage them to send the image out into the Matrix. Give them time to experience the positive emotions and instruct them to let you know when it feels complete.
- Finally, stop tapping on your recipient. Invite them back to the present and encourage them to play the original memory in their mind. If there is any intensity remaining, go back into the memory to transform the unresolved aspect.

CHAPTER 8

Refining the Matrix Foundation Techniques

What we have presented to you so far are the basic Matrix Reimprinting techniques. However, these are usually adapted to each individual recipient. As we are often working with long-standing emotional issues or traumas, the techniques don't always follow a simple or linear structure and there are sometimes complications in helping the ECHO to resolve the emotional disruption around the trauma. The following points will help you refine the techniques and also help you to address some of the challenges you may face when working in this manner.

Open Questions

This work is based on open questioning. Open questions are non-judging and designed to help the recipient both unravel their blocking beliefs and help the ECHO to resolve the emotional disruption they are feeling. Examples might include:

- 'What's your earliest memory relating to this issue?'
- 'What does she look like in the picture?'
- 'How is he feeling about what was said to him?'
- 'What did she learn about life that day?'
- 'Are you still running the same beliefs as her?'
- 'What does she want to say or do to change this?'

- 'Who does he want to bring in for support?'
- 'Is there any reason for her to hold on to that pain any more?'

This is not an exhaustive list of questions. The important thing is that it is the questioning that leads to the resolution.

The Importance of the Transformation Work Coming from your Recipient

It is important that the ideas for change come from your recipient and their ECHO. Sometimes when you first do this work with a recipient, they may need a few suggestions. But all the best ideas come from the recipient and you need to respect their views and feelings about changing the pictures. If you deny the ECHO the right to express itself in the way that is needed, there will be limited resolution. It is not your place to judge, only to allow.

You may occasionally get the feeling that you have a better suggestion, especially if you have a tendency to take over. But this work does not lend itself well to domination. As the practitioner you are just there as a guide. We can never truly know what is right for another human being, as our own judgements are coming through the filters of our own perceptions, which may be very different from those of our recipients.

There are also often occasions when the ECHO doesn't want to experience doing something differently. Sometimes they want to have the same experience, but with your recipient there to support them. For example, an ECHO may want to go through the same trauma to learn the valuable lessons from it, but this time with the recipient, a loved one, relative, friend, family member or spiritual figure present.

Helping your Recipient If They Get Stuck

With the above in mind, there may be occasions when your recipient gets stuck and doesn't know what the ECHO needs to do to change the situation. Your role here is to help them be creative. If you can, make several suggestions, as this still gives the power to your recipient. For example:

Recipient: *She's stuck, she doesn't know how to resolve this.*

Practitioner: *Do you have any suggestions?*

Recipient: *No, I'm not sure what the best way is either.*

Practitioner: *Does she want to walk away, confront her assailant or bring someone else in to support her? Ask her what would be best for her.*

Recipient: *She said that it doesn't feel right to walk away. She would be too scared to confront him on her own. She doesn't need to bring anyone else in, as I'm there with her – she wants me to support her.*

Practitioner: *Let her know that you are 100 per cent there for her. Keep tapping on her and ask her how she would like to proceed with your support.*

Using your Intuition

If your recipient gets stuck and you need to guide the process, the best way to help is with your intuition. There is an art with this work of keeping yourself out of the way and allowing your intuition to guide the other person. However, this is something that comes with practice and is not often within the realms of a beginner.

Your intuitive suggestions will feel as if they come from a place outside yourself, rather than from your own perceptions. They may even feel at odds with what you would normally suggest. The key is to remember that you are just a guide for the other person's journey, not the one making the decisions about the journey, so keep open to suggestions, even if they feel slightly odd to you, and always follow the recipient's lead.

Carrying Out the Transformation Work in Silence

It is vital that you give your recipient time to carry out the transformation work in silence. Do not talk over the work unless you are specifically asked to help or guide. In the silence, a tremendous amount of healing takes place. It is also important that you explain to the recipient what needs to occur, for example:

> **Practitioner:** *What does your younger self need to do in this part of the memory?*
>
> **Recipient:** *She needs to speak her mind. She needs to yell and tell him exactly what she thinks of him.*
>
> **Practitioner:** *Keep tapping on her. Just let me know when that part of the process feels complete for her, or if you need me at any stage. I'll keep tapping on you throughout. Just take your time.*

Occasionally, however, the recipient needs to speak out loud, particularly if the issue is one of being silenced or disempowered. So always let them know that they have the option of expressing themselves verbally.

The Recipient Saying the Set-up and Reminder Phrases on Behalf of the ECHO

Although the actual transformation work is usually done in silence, the recipient will speak out loud if they are doing set-up or reminder phrases on the ECHO. For example:

> **Practitioner:** *How is he feeling?*
>
> **Recipient:** *He is really anxious.*
>
> **Practitioner:** *Where does he feel that anxiety in his body?*
>
> **Recipient:** *It's in his chest.*
>
> **Practitioner:** *What colour is it?*
>
> **Recipient:** *Blue.*
>
> **Practitioner:** *OK, tap on your younger self on the side of his hand (practitioner taps in the same place on the recipient). As you do so, say, 'Even though you have this blue anxiety in your chest, you're still a great kid.'*
>
> **Recipient:** *'Even though you have this blue anxiety in your chest, you're still a great kid.'*

The set-up statement is repeated three times.

Practitioner: *OK, now tap around all the points on him, starting at the top of his head and working your way down. 'This blue anxiety in your chest.'*

Recipient: *'This blue anxiety in your chest.'*

Practitioner: *'This blue anxiety.'*

Recipient: *'This blue anxiety.'*

Practitioner: *'In your chest.'*

Recipient: *'In your chest.'*

The recipient keeps tapping until all the emotional intensity has resolved for the ECHO.

Practitioner: *How is he now? Is it coming down a bit?*

Recipient: *Yes, he's calming down.*

Saying the set-up phrases out loud on behalf of the ECHO helps them to clear the energetic disruption around the issue.

The Age Range of ECHOs

Just to clarify, although much of this work is about getting back to a point in early childhood where unhelpful beliefs were formed, ECHOs can be any age. For example, if a 60-year-old person has a bad fall, there will be a 60-year-old ECHO that needs resolution. ECHOs can also be formed in utero, so there is no age limit in either direction.

The Possibility of a Healing Crisis

As with any therapeutic work, sometimes Matrix Reimprinting brings about a healing crisis (intensification of symptoms before they resolve). This is another reason why bigger issues are best handled by a Matrix Reimprinting practitioner. We have found that healing crises are rarer in Matrix Reimprinting than they are in other techniques, but be aware that they can occur.

Refining Matrix Scene Reimprinting and Matrix Memory Reimprinting

The following pointers will help you to further your results with these two Foundation Techniques, whether you are working with someone else or on your own. Please note that the following is mainly written from the perspective of working with someone else. Much the same applies when working on your own, although, as we have already stated, there are times when working on your own is not going to bring the same results.

Ask the Recipient to Close their Eyes

It is not always appropriate for the recipient to close their eyes. Some prefer not to and can actually picture the scene better when their eyes are open. So if this is more comfortable for them, encourage them to keep their eyes open.

Ensure the Picture is Being Viewed from the Outside

It is crucial for the success of Matrix Reimprinting that the picture is viewed from the outside, which is known as disassociation. This is because the ECHO is the real client in this work, and we need to be dissociated from it so that we can truly help it to get resolution. If your recipient is associated – in other words, viewing the picture through the eyes of their ECHO – ask them to step out of their body so they can see their younger self in front of them. For example:

Practitioner: *Can you see your younger self standing there in your memory?*

Recipient: *Yes, she's standing all alone.*

Practitioner: *What is she wearing?*

Recipient: *A red dress. She's carrying a school bag.*

Practitioner: *What does she look like?*

Recipient: *Sad. My head is hanging down.*

Practitioner: *Let me just check. Are you in your body or out of your body?*

Recipient: *Oh, I am her – I'm looking through her eyes.*

Practitioner: *OK, can you separate from her so that you are looking at her? Step out of her body and stand opposite her.*

Recipient: *Yes, I can see her clearly now.*

Another thing that you can do to help the recipient disassociate is invite them to come back to the room, open their eyes and get a good sense of being there by feeling the contact of their feet on the floor. Then they can close their eyes and imagine walking slowly towards the picture, first seeing their ECHO from a distance and then moving in closer.

Similarly, if you are doing this work on yourself, ensure that you are looking at an image of your younger self.

Ensure the ECHO Knows Who your Recipient Is and What They Are Doing There

It is important that the recipient introduces themselves to the ECHO and explains that they have come from the future to help them let go of the pain they are feeling, for example:

Recipient: *She's confused, she doesn't know why I'm here.*

Practitioner: *Let her know that she's safe. Tell her you've come from the future because you've found a really great way of helping her to feel differently. Just check she's OK with that.*

Recipient: *Yeah, she is fine now. In fact she is really pleased that I'm here. She's been alone for a very long time.*

Practitioner: *Reassure her that she isn't alone any more and that you are here to help.*

Equally, when working on yourself, it is still important to introduce yourself to the ECHO and let them know why you are there.

However, once you start to do a lot of this work with your ECHOs, the need to introduce yourself will diminish and you will find that the ECHOs already know who you are.

Thank the ECHO

It is important to thank the ECHO. They may have been holding on to the trauma for a long time and it takes a lot of energy to do so. They have been shielding you or your recipient from the pain of the trauma, and it is vital they are acknowledged for this. The acknowledgement of the role that they have played is an important part of the healing.

Tap on the ECHO as Soon as Possible

The key is to tap on the ECHO as soon as possible, so the first few steps before this should only take a moment. The ECHO is likely to be in distress, and this distress will resolve when the tapping starts, so bear this in mind when you begin the process. As with conventional EFT, the tapping is where the changes take place.

What If the ECHO Won't Let your Recipient Tap on Them?

Sometimes the ECHO will be resistant to being tapped on. In this case you can let your recipient know that others can be brought in to aid the process, but the decision as to who would be the best to help must be made or agreed upon by the ECHO. You can frame this by saying something along the lines of 'Is there someone else who can assist this process and help your younger self to feel safe in this situation? You can bring in anyone your ECHO chooses, including friends, trusted relatives, teachers or guides.' The role of those who are brought in is to help the ECHO get to the point where they can be tapped on by your recipient. There needs to be an interaction between your recipient and their ECHO so that resolution can take place for both.

Sometimes it is a matter of using persistence. In one very early Matrix Reimprinting session Karl spent almost an hour getting the ECHO to the point where she could be tapped on. The ECHO – a small child of around six – spun around and around in order to avoid the recipient tapping on her. Eventually she was coaxed into standing still.

But it was a very slow process, with the ECHO first having to experience the points being touched lightly before trust was established.

If you are working on yourself and your ECHO is resistant to being tapped on, you may need a Matrix Reimprinting practitioner or someone skilled at using this technique to guide you through the resistance.

Katie and the Phantom

When Karl worked on Katie, she wasn't immediately able to tap on her ECHO. This is because when she tried to do so, the ECHO had a phantom in front of her who wouldn't let Katie near. In fact, the phantom had been Katie's imaginary friend in childhood – someone she had created to help her cope with the trauma she'd been through.

Karl encouraged Katie to ask her ECHO what she got from the phantom. The ECHO replied that it gave her love and attention and played with her. When Katie asked her ECHO, 'Wouldn't you like love from both of us?' the phantom stepped aside. It was no longer needed, as Katie herself was able to give her ECHO the love that it had provided.

Making Sure the Recipient Wants Resolution for the ECHO

The objective of Matrix Reimprinting is for both the recipient and the ECHO to gain resolution. However, occasionally the recipient does not want resolution for their ECHO. Sometimes the ECHO learned a behaviour strategy from the trauma that the recipient is not ready to change. This is an issue which would need to be resolved by a Matrix Reimprinting practitioner rather than a beginner. The objective is for the trauma to be resolved and the recipient to find new resources and strategies that serve them better. Sometimes a relationship needs to be built between the recipient and the ECHO for resolution to occur.

When the ECHO and Recipient Are at Odds with Each Other

ECHOs and recipients are not always initially able to work together to resolve the emotional intensity of a trauma. Sometimes the ECHO will be resistant to your recipient (or you, if you are working alone). When the little girl mentioned above kept spinning around and didn't want to be tapped on, she was asked why. She replied, 'I don't want her [meaning the recipient] to touch me – she looks like my mother!' Her mother was part of the problem. To resolve this, the recipient had to explain to her younger self that she wasn't her mother but her own self who had come from the future to help her. With this outlined, she was able to accomplish the tapping.

More unusually, the recipient can feel resentment towards the ECHO. This sometimes happens in abuse cases where the recipient still feels some form of responsibility for the act that took place, or blame towards their younger self. It is common in these cases for the recipient to use very strong and derogatory language towards their ECHO, and this particular work needs to be carried out by a qualified and experienced Matrix Reimprinting practitioner.

If you are qualified to deal with a case such as this, the intention, as with all therapeutic work, is to get the recipient to a place of forgiveness with their ECHO. Of course the ECHO hasn't done anything wrong, and the realization of this by the recipient is the ultimate aim. However, do not force this. You will need to build bridges between the recipient and the ECHO.

There are a number of things you can do here, depending on the nature of your recipient. One is to attempt to speak to the recipient's 'higher self', if this is a term that resonates with them. A phrase which often works is something along the lines of 'With all the knowledge and the wisdom that you have now, and drawing on your higher, core or true self, what would you say to any child who found themselves in a situation like this?'

If this doesn't build a bridge, you can ask your recipient to call upon someone else to help them bridge the gap in the situation. Encourage them to keep their eyes closed with the ECHO still in view and ask them who they would call upon to help resolve the differences between them and their younger self. Outline that it can be friends, loved ones, ascended masters, religious figures (ones they have positive connections with), beings of light, angels or anyone else that they have respect for. Some answers will be simple and earthy: 'I want to bring my brother Tom in. He's a good bloke and very accepting.' Others will be more spiritual: 'I want to call upon the angel of love as I can only feel anger when I look at my younger self.' Again, the answers come from your recipient, and you need to respect their standpoint. If you love working with angels but your recipients are earthier in nature, you will not help the situation by limiting their choices and trying to influence their decisions, so always go with what is right for them.

When your recipient has selected someone to help them, ask them how that person can help bridge the gap between them and their younger self. If they are very resistant to this bridge being built, you may need to step in with a suggestion, but first see if the attempt for the resolution can come from the recipient.

If you do need to step in, this is part of the process that can become very creative, and as always there are no definitive answers as to how this can be done. Sasha's preferred method is to invite the other being to tap on the ECHO and the recipient simultaneously, creating an energetic link between the two (of course, you are tapping on your recipient's physical body the whole time this is occurring). When your recipient releases their negative feelings towards the ECHO, you can then suggest that the ECHO and the recipient touch hands in the picture, while the helpful person or being is still tapping on both. When you have reached a point where this is comfortable, you can suggest that the recipient taps on their ECHO. This stage does not need to be rushed and may be a session in itself if long-standing abuse issues have occurred.

If you have been working on your own and you have strong feelings of resentment towards an ECHO, you are advised to consult a Matrix Reimprinting practitioner to help you get resolution.

What If the ECHO Doesn't Want to Let Go of the Pain?

Sometimes an ECHO or recipient will want to hold on to the pain that they are experiencing. Time and again both Karl and Sasha have heard their clients say things such as 'He wants to hold on to the pain because if he lets go of it, it will be letting the person who attacked him off the hook' or 'If she lets go of this now, then her abuser will have got away with it.' You need to let your recipient know that holding on to pain in this way is like taking poison and expecting someone else to suffer. For example:

Recipient: *He doesn't want to let go of the anger just yet. He wants to hold on to it.*

Practitioner: *Is the anger serving a purpose?*

Recipient: *Well, if he lets go of it, it's like forgiving his uncle. He's not ready to do that.*

Practitioner: *Let him know that he is letting go of the anger for you and him, not for his uncle. Just reassure him that it is for the good of both of you.*

Talk to the ECHO in an Appropriate Age Language

It is important that the recipient speaks to the ECHO in the language appropriate for their age. So if the ECHO is five, then your recipient speaks to a five-year-old.

If the ECHO is pre-speech, perhaps in utero or in the first few years of life, the recipient needs to find a way to communicate non-verbally. This gap is usually bridged quite easily with a simple instruction, for example, 'Can you see your younger self there? OK, find a way to communicate with him that he understands.'

The same goes if you are working on yourself.

Use the Name That the Recipient Had at the Time of the Trauma

It is important to note that if your recipient has changed their name, they should use the name that they had at the time of the trauma to talk to their ECHO. For example:

Practitioner: *Can you see little Chris standing there? Just tap on him and start talking to him. By the way, were you called Chris or Christopher in those days?*

Recipient: *I was actually Christopher, come to think of it.*

> **Practitioner:** *OK, tap on little Christopher and let him know who you are and why you are here.*

Talk to the ECHO in the Recipient's First Language

If you are working with a recipient whose first language is not the one you are using for the session, you can suggest that they talk to their ECHO in their first language. Both Karl and Sasha have worked with a number of clients whose ECHOs did not understand them when they spoke in their current language but understood when a language adjustment was made.

What If the Recipient Is Still Running the Same Life Messages That the ECHO Gained from This Situation?

A vital part of this work is to ask your recipient to check with their ECHO what life messages or learning was gleaned from this situation. The answers are usually indicative of core beliefs that the recipient is running in the present moment or has been running throughout their life. So if the recipient replies that the message they gained was 'I have to be perfect to be loved', 'I'm stupid', 'I'm worthless' or any other destructive or self-sabotaging belief, check with them to see whether they are still running it.

Recipients are often astounded to make the link between their present viewpoint and the situation of the ECHO, and this in itself can be tremendously enlightening. There are sometimes tears of recognition or relief when a lifetime of behaviour is explained away by one early experience.

> **Practitioner:** *And what is the life message that you got from this situation?*
>
> **Recipient:** *The world's a dangerous place.*
>
> **Practitioner:** *Do you still believe that now on some level?*
>
> **Recipient:** *Yes, I never go out on my own after dark. I always think danger lurks just around the corner. I had no idea it all stemmed from this incident.*

A phrase which was created by Gary Craig in his work using conventional EFT is often appropriate: 'Are you still listening to that seven-year-old child?'

You might follow this with something along the lines of: 'And would you take the advice of a seven-year-old now?!'

It is important to note that this phrase is intended to lighten the intensity of the session, so needs to be delivered with an appropriate tone of humour.

If you are doing this work on yourself, take a moment to reflect on the life messages that your ECHO learned in this situation and whether or not you are still running them.

When working on someone else, there is often an opportunity to get a different perspective here (known as reframing), and if it seems right you can also ask your recipient if there were any positive life lessons gained from this situation. If your recipient used excellent coping strategies, for example, then this can be indicated to the ECHO when your recipient converses with them silently:

Practitioner: *What else did you learn that day? Were there any positive outcomes?*

Recipient: *Actually, I was really strong that day. Even though it was painful, I actually gained a lot of independence from this situation. I can see that now.*

Practitioner: *Let her know how strong she was.*

Similarly, if you are working on yourself, you can take a moment to reflect on any positive life lessons that were learned or any excellent coping strategies that your ECHO showed.

Changing What Happened

How often in a situation have you wished that you had behaved differently? How many times have you kicked yourself for not saying or doing something that you would dearly love to have said or done? How many times have you regretted, mulled over or waded through the same situation over and over again, holding on to the past in pain and anguish? What is more, have you any idea how destructive it is to your physical and emotional wellbeing when you do this?

'Just let go' is something you may have heard time and time again, but often this is very challenging, especially when your subconscious mind is playing the memories over and over again. Conventional EFT has brought many people great relief on this front, but even when the memories are resolved and don't hold any emotional charge for us, the pictures are still the same. Often they fade from our memory, but they still remain in the field on some level. So what if you could replace these pictures with new and supportive images? How would that change your health and wellbeing?

Remember that this is very different from pretending that something didn't happen. It's like creating a different past while honouring and acknowledging the past you have gone through. What is your past, after all, but a series of memories filtered through your own perceptions? Everyone remembers events differently, as they are all remembering through the filters of their own perceptions. So you can change your memories without denying them. Here are some suggestions on how you can do this:

Bring in New Resources

The list of resources you can bring in is endless, and can include anything that will help the ECHO to play the situation out differently. Some of Sasha's favourites have included bringing in a magic carpet so that the recipient can escape from the situation, putting up a glass window so the recipient can deal with the situation from a safe distance, using a light-sabre in order to feel safe and protected, creating lightning bolts from the ECHO's fingers in order to scare their attacker away, and bringing in teddy bears to help them feel comforted.

Your recipient will have all the resources that they need to resolve the issues, because they will have been trying to resolve them subconsciously since the trauma. Sometimes this is even reflected in their career choice, for example the young girl who feels that she was unfairly judged becomes a high court magistrate or the young boy that was never listened to becomes a university lecturer.

Sasha and the Matches

It was bringing in new resources that helped Sasha resolve bipolar affective disorder on the first EFT practitioner training that she attended with Karl. The issue that she was working on was one of some inappropriate photographs being taken of her earlier in life. Although she had subsequently managed to obtain the photographs and burn them, they were still imprinted on her mind. What Karl did was to give her ECHO a box of matches and allow her to burn the photographs.

As Sasha's ECHO burned the photographs, an amazing thing happened: Sasha flipped out of the bipolar depression she was in. This was incredible for her as usually such a depression could last for days or even weeks. So at first it seemed that Matrix Reimprinting was a really handy way of enabling her to flip out of a bipolar depression. However, as the weeks and months passed and her mental health stabilized, it became apparent that resolving the trauma had resolved the condition.

In fact you can see a live session where Karl Dawson and the head of META-Medicine®, Richard Flook, resolve a bipolar depression on the META-Medicine® and EFT DVD (see Resources).

Invite Someone in for Guidance

As well as inviting someone else in for support if your recipient's ECHO is resisting being tapped on or if your recipient and ECHO are at odds with each other, you can also bring in another being to support your recipient as they change the memory or situation. Again, these can be anyone of their choosing. Often recipients come up with a figure that resembles someone of great personal or spiritual power. They may say, 'I'm not sure who this person is but they look like Mother Teresa' or 'He's a young version of Gandhi.'

Although the choice of being needs to come from the ECHO, it is sometimes helpful to prompt them by letting them know the vast range of beings available to them to support this work. Sasha's preferred method of doing this is to give them a list, for example, 'Is there anyone else who they would like there to support them? This could include a trusted friend or relative, a figure from TV, a pop star, a superhero, an angel, a spiritual figure, or anyone else that they choose.'

The choices are often age-specific – younger ECHOs often choose children's fictional characters, grandparents or dogs. Teenage ECHOs may be more likely to bring in superheroes, pop stars or respected teachers or peers, while older ECHOs will bring in family members, trusted friends, spiritual figures or angels. Sasha's favourite example of this came from one of her trainees, a very peaceful and loving gentleman, whose 14-year-old ECHO brought in Mr T from *The A-Team*!

The being that comes in to guide the situation often brings resources with them. This is where your recipient and their ECHO can be really creative. Some examples are St Michael, whose sword has cut the energetic connection between the recipient and an attacker, a trusted grandparent who has brought a light to bring an ECHO out of a dark situation, and a fairy godmother who has brought a net to cover the gang of children that were taunting the recipient. The list is endless and as always, comes from the ECHO.

Allow the ECHO to Do What They Wished They Had Done

This is perhaps the most empowering part of the session, especially if your recipient has experienced the freeze response during their memory. It is also highly therapeutic if they have experienced any physical, sexual or emotional abuse and not been able to express their anger and rage.

Jacob and the Stick

Jacob is black and during his childhood he had experienced some racial hatred. On one occasion he had been taunted by a group of white supremacists who had spat at him and called him names. When it came to what his ECHO wanted to do to redress the balance, he chose to beat his assailants with a stick. It was only by doing this that he could

---

> *re-empower himself and release the negative emotion that he had been holding for so long.*

There have been concerns from a small number of Matrix Reimprinting trainees that allowing the ECHO to express themselves in this way is promoting violence. If you are a spiritual and peace-loving being, this part of the technique may contradict everything you believe in. Furthermore, it seems to contradict the fact that even just thinking an angry thought compromises the immune system. However, if we take a closer look at this aspect of the technique, we can begin to understand that it is sometimes necessary for the ECHO to dispel the negative energy or the freeze response in this way. They have been holding on to these emotions for a long time and sometimes need to express rage before they can reach a point of peace and forgiveness.

Another thing to consider is that if the ECHO wants to retaliate with violence, it is likely that they have wanted to do so since the incident occurred. By giving them a short moment in which to express this, they can redress the balance.

If you have very strong views against this, then please honour your recipient's wishes and do not try and inflict your views on them. To reach a place of peace there sometimes needs to be a strong release of anger first.

Going back to Jacob and the stick, this session took place on Karl's EFT practitioner training. After the session the question was raised by one of the group members as to whether giving Jacob a stick was an appropriate action. The important point to consider here is that Jacob's ECHO needed that stick to re-empower himself. It is important to note that we are not re-enacting the rage by allowing ECHOs to release in this way. Instead, we are allowing them to respond with their instincts, which are often based on how they feel as children who have been disempowered by adults or their peers. Allowing the ECHO this release means that your recipient will return to a more peaceful place in the present, without the negative energy of the ECHO in their field any more.

What If the ECHO Wants to Kill Someone?

On extremely rare occasions, the ECHO may say that they want to kill an attacker or perpetrator of abuse. This has only occurred a small number of times in the history of the technique. On one occasion, a recipient wanted to kill the nurses who weren't able to save her mother from cancer. As the anger in this situation was out of proportion, the best question to this recipient would have been: 'So when was the first time you remember feeling so angry that you wanted to kill someone?' That would then have been the memory that would have been worked on, as that would have been where the core issue started.

On other occasions, young ECHOs have wanted to kill their sexual abusers. It is worth noting that when this has taken place, they have often wanted to then send them somewhere for healing. So it was not a true death that they wanted at all, just a release in the only form their young ECHO could understand.

What If the ECHO Wants to Bring Back to Life Someone Who Has Died?

Occasionally the ECHO will want to do this and this was a stumbling block in the early Matrix Reimprinting work, as we puzzled over the ethics of bringing to life a dead person or pretending that they had not passed on. However, Karl began to consider the possibility that ECHOs and spirits existed in a similar dimension. So if an ECHO wants to bring back someone who has passed away, the protocol is to ask them if they can create a place where they can be with that person any time they need to.

Create a New Picture

When there is full resolution, ensure that it is only the new and positive picture that gets taken into the mind through the top of the head. The picture needs to be one without anger, violence, frustration or resentment. It needs to be peaceful and loving.

Remember, because community creates healing, it is also preferable that others have been invited into the picture with the

ECHO. Their original image has usually been one of fear and isolation, so the opposing image needs to be one of safety and community.

Open the Eyes Before Replaying the Original Memory

Whether you are doing this work on yourself or others, it is important to open the eyes and come back to the present before you test the work. This gives a clean break and allows a more objective assessment when testing the work. Otherwise, the work you have done and the testing that follows may all blend into one. So open the eyes first.

Replay the Original Memory

When you have completed the Matrix Reimprinting work, it is vital you test the results by attempting to play the original memory. One of three things is likely to happen:

1. *The most common is that when your recipient tries to play the old memory, they are only able to play the new one. This experience is often a delightful (but sometimes quite stunning) one for the recipient, especially if they have been playing the old memory in their minds for a number of years. They may ask you, 'Will this last?' You can reassure them that it will.*

2. *The second most common event is that when your recipient goes to play the old movie, there is nothing there. If there actually is a blank space, it may be appropriate to ask your recipient what they would like to fill it with. You may then choose to repeat the steps of taking a beautiful and positive image down through their minds, into their hearts and out into the field.*

3. *The third and least likely thing to happen is that there is some intensity remaining around the memory. Resolve this by going back into the points that need changing with further Matrix Reimprinting work. Remember you can go back into the field as many times as you need to until the intensity has cleared.*

FURTHER REFINEMENTS FOR MATRIX MEMORY REIMPRINTING

Due to the fact that Matrix Memory Reimprinting involves some extra steps, there are a number of further considerations when using this technique:

Start the Memory at a Safe Place

Your recipient needs to start narrating the memory at a safe place, before any intensity has occurred. If they start at a point of high intensity, they are likely to go into fight or flight and bring the trauma of the memory back into the body. If they start before the intensity, you can go in gently and keep them calm. This will help you to get the best results.

Choose the Right Point to Stop the Memory

After you have used Matrix Memory Reimprinting a number of times, you should get a sense of where to stop the memory and go into the Matrix. It is usually the first point of major intensity. You can stop the memory several times, or you may just need to stop once.

When to Send the Picture into the Field if You Stop in Multiple Places

If there is more than one key point of intensity and you have to stop the memory in a number of places, only send the final image back out into the field.

If after sending the image into the field and testing the work you find that there is still some intensity, go back into the Matrix and resolve the remaining aspect. Once you have, you can either send a new picture out into the field or take the part of the ECHO from the newly resolved aspect to the new image in the field.

FURTHER REFINEMENTS IN USING MATRIX REIMPRINTING ON OTHERS

These will help you to get better results when you use these techniques on others.

Who or What is This Really About?

When someone presents a recent issue that they are angry about and you begin to work on it with either Matrix Scene Reimprinting or Matrix Memory Reimprinting, there is a really valuable question that you can ask your recipient: 'Who or what is this really about?'

The thing is that much of the current emotion is likely to be related to earlier life experiences, particularly experiences in early childhood. So, current issues usually lead us back to earlier, sometimes seemingly unrelated memories along a similar theme.

One way to identify these is to check what the feeling is around the current event and find out where that feeling first came from. If something occurred recently that made the recipient feel abandoned, for example, you question would be: 'What is your first or earliest memory of feeling abandoned?' This can be a great way to find out how and why themes have developed.

Often a recipient will bring something up and then say 'Oh, but it can't be that, it seems so insignificant.' However, if the subconscious is tuning the recipient into a memory, it is almost certain to be related, however small the issue may seem. Remember, the subconscious doesn't know the difference between something that is happening now and something that happened a long time ago – it has no perception of time. So issues that arose in childhood are still very real and pressing to your subconscious, and need to be resolved so that you can feel happy in the present.

One ECHO Leading You to Another ECHO

You can ask the ECHO that you are working with to take you back to an earlier time where the same theme or issue occurred. If there are likely to be multiple memories around the same theme that the recipient can't remember, then the ECHOs that you have already found and worked with can lead you to others. So when you have worked on a memory and got the ECHO to a safe place, sent out a new picture and tested the work, ask your recipient to enter the new picture and ask the ECHO to take them to a related memory.

Here is an example of Sasha's:

Shirley at the Surgery

Shirley, a lovely mature lady with a 'heart of gold', worked in a doctor's surgery. It was opposite a centre for recovering heroin addicts and the reception staff were under strict instruction only to give the toilet key to patients within the practice. This was because on a past occasion someone from the centre across the road had overdosed on heroin in the surgery toilets.

During a busy period, Shirley was working on the reception desk on her own when two men entered the surgery and asked for the toilet key. They insisted they were patients. There were children in the queue and one of the men was becoming particularly agitated about gaining access to the toilet. Under pressure, and with protecting the children in mind, Shirley relented and gave him the key.

Tension built for her as the man was in the toilet for some time. Then his friend went to check on him and began shouting that he had overdosed on heroin. There was a huge commotion as doctors, nurses and ambulance staff fought to save the man's life. He was eventually resuscitated and was coherent when he left the surgery.

Shirley's confidence in her ability to make a decision under pressure was severely knocked by this incident, and she considered leaving her job. During a one-to-one session we used Matrix Memory Reimprinting.

First Shirley went back and tapped on herself on the issue of handing the key over. On conversing with her ECHO, she realized that she had made the right decision, as she had had the intention of protecting the children in the queue.

The next point of emotional intensity in the memory was the moment she heard that the man had overdosed. One of her core issues was that she felt responsible for others. While imagining tapping on her ECHO at the reception desk, I asked the ECHO to take her back to her earliest

---

memory of feeling responsible for others. Initially the memory was one when Shirley was in her late thirties and was ignoring a phone call from her alcoholic mother. She tapped on the ECHO in the memory and conversed with her to reassure her that she was not responsible for her mum. The phone tone changed from a shrill and jarring sound to a more melodic tone and it did not hold any emotional intensity for her. A feeling of calm and peace came over her. At this time she was not able to access an even earlier memory from childhood which made her feel responsible for her mum, but we made a note that there might be future work around this.

We went back to the memory in the doctor's surgery and Shirley returned to tapping on the original ECHO. The next point of intensity was when the doctors and nurses rallied round. I asked Shirley to check with her ECHO what messages she was giving herself at this point. She replied, 'I can never get it right' – another core belief. Tapping on the ECHO, I suggested that the ECHO took her back to her earliest memory of never getting it right. This time she was six years old and standing there as her mum listed all the things that she had done wrong. An angelic child who always tried to please her mum, Shirley was nevertheless told how much of a failure she was throughout her childhood. She got permission to tap on her ECHO, and as she did she entered into a dialogue with her. She reassured her that she was a beautiful and lovely child and that it was her mum that was at fault. Her ECHO was carrying a sense of isolation in her body which was resolved with the tapping.

After the intensity had resolved, Shirley's ECHO wanted to go to the beach. She wanted to spend time with Shirley and experience love and reassurance. I asked Shirley to check if her ECHO would like to meet others who loved Shirley now, such as her son, her grandson and her daughter-in-law, or her friends. However, she just wanted to be with Shirley, and experience her love, like the love of a parent, one to one. When this felt complete we took the picture into Shirley's mind and heart and projected it back out into the field.

I then asked Shirley to return to her ECHO in the doctor's surgery and see if she still felt that she could never get it right. There was a pause and a rush of emotion from Shirley. 'No,' she replied. 'I did get it right because my actions saved his life. If he had gone somewhere else and overdosed, there would have been no one to save him.'

On playing the original memory, she found no intensity remained at all. Instead she felt a sense of compassion for the man who had overdosed. She had spent several weeks agonizing over her decision, but now she recognized it was the best one she could have made at the time. She also resolved to raise in a staff meeting the issue of how to handle people who insisted on having the key and the protocols that needed to be put in place to ensure staff safety.

Shirley loved working at the surgery, and now this incident, rather than shattering her confidence, had given her a renewed sense of positivity about her work.

Getting Resolution for an Earlier ECHO

Sometimes you need to get resolution for an ECHO in an earlier memory before the ECHO in a current memory can get resolution.

Jane and the Beach

Jane had an issue of feeling unlovable. The first memory that surfaced was when she was lost on the beach when she was seven years old. Her ECHO felt that the fact that her mum and dad had allowed her to be lost meant that they didn't love her.

Karl worked with Jane's ECHO on the beach, but she was resistant to resolution. Suddenly an earlier memory surfaced where Jane had been left alone when she was two years old. It felt more appropriate to resolve this memory first, and Jane's two-year-old ECHO was made to feel loved and reassured.

> *When Jane returned to her ECHO on the beach she was smiling and had resolution. In fact, she viewed the situation differently now and said she wasn't on her own for long. The new picture was sent out into the field and Jane felt much more lovable in the present.*

So, if you are having trouble getting resolution for a current ECHO, check that there is not an earlier memory along the same theme that needs resolving first. If you do this, though, be sure to return to the ECHO that you started with. Jane's seven-year-old ECHO didn't need further resolution, but this is not always the case. Sometimes you have to go back and forth to several memories before resolution is gained. Because of this, the work with Matrix Reimprinting is not always linear. The more complex work which goes backward and forward in time is, therefore, better in the hands of a Matrix Reimprinting practitioner.

What If Someone Can't Visualize an ECHO?

There are a number of people who are not able to visualize their ECHOs at all. When working with these recipients (or working with yourself if you fall into this category), it is fine to just get a sense of the ECHO rather than a clear picture. As a practitioner working with someone in this category, your language would change slightly. For example:

Practitioner: *Can you get a clear image of your younger self back then?*

Recipient: *It's not a clear picture, it's really hazy.*

Practitioner: *But there's something there? More of a sense?*

Recipient: *Yes, I can definitely sense him.*

Practitioner: *OK, introduce yourself, let him know who you are. Get a sense that you are tapping on him. Can you feel that even though you can't see him?*

Recipient: *Yes, I think so.*

Practitioner: *OK, keep that sense of him there in front of you throughout.*

Always adapt the techniques to suit yourself, if you are working alone, or the person that you are working with.

Finding a Blocked Memory

Blocked memories tend to be the most traumatic ones, so it is unlikely that you will be looking for one as a beginner in this technique. Therefore this section has been included mainly for the benefit of practitioners.

You can find a blocked memory with the Matrix Recall Technique (*page 136*) or Matrix Pre-conscious Reimprinting (*page 179*). You can also ask the recipient to get into the energy of the blocked memory. Where do they feel it in their body? What colour is it? What shape is it? When they have done so, begin tapping on the feeling, being open to them tuning into a flash of a memory.

Once there is a flash of a memory to work with, go into the image as usual, tap on the ECHO to bring their emotional intensity down and then ask the ECHO to take you through the rest of the memory. Sasha's way of doing this is to put the ECHO in a really safe place first and put lots of protective mechanisms in place by asking the ECHO what would make them safe. Once they are in a safe place they can then take the recipient through what happened. Every time Sasha has used this method she has always uncovered the blocked memory, even in cases of abuse memories which have been blocked since the first couple of years of childhood.

CHAPTER 9

Life Transformation Protocols

The three Life Transformation protocols are Matrix Core-Belief Reimprinting, Matrix Life-Issue Reimprinting and Matrix Law of Attraction Reimprinting. This chapter also contains an extra technique, the Matrix Recall Technique, which helps you to tune into memories related to core beliefs or life issues.

MATRIX CORE-BELIEF REIMPRINTING

We've already highlighted that your core beliefs affect your health, your attitude to life, your behaviour, your interactions with others and just about every thought or feeling that you have. So how about being able to quickly and effectively release your negative core beliefs? This is easily achieved with Matrix Core-Belief Reimprinting.

This work is best carried out with a partner, as examining your core beliefs in this way can have a tendency to make you feel low until they are resolved, particularly if you have a multitude of negative core beliefs. So only start this work when you are in a good frame of mind and, as always, consult a Matrix Reimprinting practitioner if you have a host of deep-rooted negative core beliefs to resolve.

Step 1: Select a Core Belief

First of all, select the core belief that you want to work with. If you are aware of your self-limiting core beliefs, pick one of them. If you are not aware of them, take a look at the list below and pick the one that resonates with you most:

- 'I'm unlovable.'
- 'I'm flawed.'
- 'I'm insignificant.'
- 'People must think well of me.'
- 'I'm hopeless.'
- 'Life is hopeless.'
- 'I must be in control.'
- 'I can't do it.'
- 'I'm not capable.'
- 'I'm bad.'
- 'Something bad will happen.'
- 'The world is a dangerous place.'
- 'People will take advantage of me.'
- 'People are too sensitive.'
- 'People are out to get me.'
- 'It's not fair.'
- 'I'm unforgivable.'
- 'Something must change for me to be OK.'
- 'I'm helpless.'
- 'I must be perfect to be loved.'
- 'I'm not good enough.'

Please note, this is not a definitive list, so if you have one that resonates with you more, use that.

Also, if you are working one to one with a client in a professional context, you don't have to show them a list of core beliefs in order to do this work (although it is OK to do so, especially if you are working with someone whose issues aren't obvious). Generally you will hear the beliefs in your client's language and how they speak about themselves and others. You can sensitively ask questions such as 'Let me just check with you – are you running the belief that the world is a dangerous place?' If you have a good relationship with your client, they will usually be immensely relieved when you identify a core belief that they had not consciously realized that they were running, and even happier when you help them to resolve it.

You may need to work through a number of these beliefs and it is advisable to pick one at a time and work with it until it is resolved.

Step 2: Determine the VOC Level

Once you have identified the core belief that you want to work with, rate it on the Validity of Cognition (VOC) level as a percentage. The VOC level is a way of determining how much something is a problem for you right now. By determining this, you can then chart your progress, because as you start to resolve different memories on this theme, the VOC level will reduce. For example, 100 per cent would be 'I totally believe this to be true for me' and 10 per cent would be 'This is only a slight problem for me.' Make a note of your score.

You may have a whole host of memories that you need to work on in relation to the belief. Each one is likely to reduce the VOC score. Sometimes, a single memory is entirely responsible for a belief and collapsing that memory may collapse the belief altogether. Other times you may work with a memory which brings the VOC level down by, say 2, 5 or 10 per cent.

However, do not underestimate the power of reducing the VOC level by even a tiny amount. Each reduction will change your point of attraction, make you feel better about yourself and reduce the power of that negative belief for you.

Step 3: Matrix Recall Technique

You may know the memories that you need to work with in relation to your destructive core belief. If you do, use either Matrix Scene Reimprinting or Matrix Memory Reimprinting to work through them. Each time you have resolved a memory, make a note of your VOC level. It should reduce every time you clear a related memory.

If you don't know which memories to work on, try the Matrix Recall Technique (which has been adapted from the S-L-O-W EFT technique by Silvia Hartmann) as follows. First of all, use the belief that you are working on as a global set-up statement, tapping on the karate chop point three times as you say:

'Even though [limiting core belief], I totally love and accept myself.'

For example:

'Even though I must be perfect to be loved...'
'Even though something must change for me to be OK...'

Next, close your eyes. Tap on one point for a number of minutes as you repeat the reminder phrase silently and occasionally in your mind. For example, if your set-up phrase was 'Even though something must change for me to be OK...' you would silently repeat 'Something must change for me to be OK' every now and again with your eyes closed, while tapping on one point, such as the crown, for a couple of minutes. Then move to the next point. Continue this until you tune into a relevant memory.

Step 4: Resolve the Memory

Once a relevant memory has come to mind, once again use either Matrix Scene Reimprinting or Matrix Memory Reimprinting to work through it.

Step 5: Recheck the VOC Level

Each time you have resolved a memory, make a note of the change in the VOC level. It should reduce every time you clear a related memory.

Step 6: Repeat the Process

Repeat steps 3 to 5 as many times as you need to until the core belief that you have been working on has a VOC level of zero.

Sasha has found that core-belief work has liberated her, many of her clients and her workshop attendees from destructive beliefs they have had for years. While writing this section, it made her smile (almost with disbelief!) that only a couple of years before, when Karl first introduced her to core-belief work, she was still running the belief that she was unlovable at 80 per cent. She needed to clear a number of memories from past relationships, which included being with someone for several years who wasn't able to verbalize his love for her and with someone else who told her, 'I do love you, just not enough.' Of course, as most of these beliefs generated from childhood, she also needed to use Matrix Reimprinting to give her younger self the experience of having some quality time with her father, whose alcoholism had meant that he had not spent any quality time with her as a child. With these new 'memories' in place, the belief that she is not lovable has not resonated since. And of course, this has had a massive impact on her present-day relationship with her partner and also on how she feels about herself in general.

MATRIX LIFE-ISSUE REIMPRINTING

This technique is used when you are not reaching your full potential in a given area of your life.

Step 1: Choose a Life Issue

Take a look at the list below and identify which area of your life is not working to its full potential right now:

- family and relationships
- money
- home and environment
- work and career
- leisure and fun time
- socializing
- spirituality
- creativity

Step 2: Determine What's Not Working

So what's not working for you in this particular life area? For example:

- If it is money, is it that you spend it too quickly, you can't seem to make enough or you've always got debt?
- If it is relationships, are you unlucky in love? Do you always pick an unsuitable partner? Are you self-devaluing in your relationships?
- If it is spirituality, are you blocked spiritually? Do you see yourself as separate from the universe? Are you so spiritually oriented that it's difficult to keep your feet on the ground?

Step 3: Give your Life Issue a VOC Level

Giving the issue a VOC level (see *page 135*) will help to determine your progress. So, out of 100 per cent, how much is money a negative issue for you, 100 being a totally negative issue and 10 being a slightly negative issue?

Step 4: Find Early Memories Relating to This Theme

Your life issues, whatever their nature, have been determined by your life experiences. So, as with all the Matrix Reimprinting work, your task is to identify which experiences created your issues and resolve them with Matrix Scene Reimprinting and/or Matrix Memory Reimprinting.

So, to continue with money issues as an example, what was your family's attitude towards money while you were growing up? What did you learn about money and from whom?

You may have memories along this theme. If you don't, use the Matrix Recall Technique (*page 136*).

Step 5: Resolve the Related Memories

Resolve each related memory on this theme until your VOC level is zero and you have no negative emotional intensity around this theme.

MATRIX LAW OF ATTRACTION REIMPRINTING

This is not a protocol but a process. Earlier we highlighted how the Law of Attraction teaches us that the pictures in our fields attract more of the same into our lives. So, from a Matrix Reimprinting perspective, changing the negative pictures in our fields changes our point of attraction.

Gary Craig, the originator of EFT, understood the importance of working with all our past negative memories in order to change our health and wellbeing in the present. He created a process called the Personal Peace Procedure, which involves working on one memory per day with the EFT Movie Technique until all our destructive and negative life memories are cleared of emotional intensity. This is an extremely powerful process which has helped to transform the lives of many thousands of people.

With Matrix Reimprinting we have taken it further. Instead of just clearing the original memories, we actually replace the past memories with new ones, creating supportive pictures in our field. This dramatically alters our point of attraction, which is why Karl has renamed this process Matrix Law of Attraction Reimprinting.

If you don't know where to start with Matrix Law of Attraction Reimprinting, we suggest that you make a list of everything that is not working in your life right now and clear the related memories, using Matrix Scene Reimprinting (*page 91*) and Matrix Memory Reimprinting (*page 98*). Remember, you can use the Matrix Recall Technique (*page 136*) if you are having challenges finding related memories.

CHAPTER 10

Relationship Transformation Protocols

The Relationship Transformation protocols include Matrix Relationship Reimprinting and Matrix Resolution Reimprinting. These two simple protocols will powerfully transform your past and present relationships.

MATRIX RELATIONSHIP REIMPRINTING

Matrix Relationship Reimprinting is a protocol which is designed to help you resolve current relationship issues.

Step 1: Identify the Relationship That You Want to Work With

Is there a relationship that isn't working in your life right now? Bring a person to mind that you are having relationship difficulties with. This can be a partner, boss, colleague or friend.

Step 2: Identify How Intense your Conflict Is

Use the VOC level (*page 135*) to identify how much this conflict is an issue for you, with 10 per cent being only a slight issue and 100 per cent being a major issue. Use this level to measure your progress as you work through the protocol.

Step 3: Identify Who the Conflict Is Really About

The conflict is rarely about the person who is triggering you. It is usually about someone who triggered you in your earlier life. So your work here is to trace back to your earlier or earliest memory of when you had this feeling. Ask yourself the following questions:

- 'Who does this person remind me of?'
- 'What feelings do they trigger in me?'
- 'Where do I feel those triggers in my body?'
- 'When was the first time I remember feeling this way?'

If you tap on yourself as you ask yourself these questions, you are likely to tune into a memory.

Step 4: Resolve the Early Memories on This Theme

Resolve earlier memories which are related to the feeling that you have, either using Matrix Scene Reimprinting (*page 91*) or Matrix Memory Reimprinting (*page 98*).

Step 5: Test the Work

Test the work by bringing the person to mind, or spending some time with them. What is your VOC level now? Does it rise in certain situations with this person? What do those situations remind you of? Keep unravelling until you can be with the person with little or no triggering.

Matrix Resolution Reimprinting

Matrix Resolution Reimprinting is a simple technique for changing the way you feel about unresolved relationships with people who are no longer in your life. These can include people who have passed away, people with whom you have had a physical relationship and are

142

no longer in contact, and people with whom you have had a conflict in the past. It is specifically designed for people who are no longer in your life but with whom you still have some connection due to there being unresolved issues between you.

Step 1: Choose the Person

Bring to mind the person from the past whom you would like to work with.

Step 2: Choose a Specific Moment

Recall a specific moment in time which represents the unresolved issues that you have with this person.

Step 3: Step into the Picture

As your current self, step into the picture and begin tapping on your younger self. Let them know that you are there to help them feel differently about the situation.

Step 4: Allow your Younger Self to Express their Feelings

Advise your younger self that this is an opportunity for them to express themselves in the way they wished they could have done at the time. This can include speaking their mind, having an emotional outburst, saying goodbye or any other intervention that feels appropriate. Allow time for this to take place.

Step 5: Take your Younger Self to Another Place

They can create a new picture either with the person with whom there was an issue, or without them, whichever feels appropriate.

Step 6: Send the New Picture out into the Field

Take the picture through the mind, around all the cells of the body, into the heart and into the field as normal.

Step 7: Test the Work

Look at the original picture and test to check that it doesn't hold any negative resonance. If it does, go back into the Matrix and continue to express yourself until the resonance is clear, or alternatively, go to a different moment in time with the same person.

Eric and his Boss

Eric had worked as a school inspector and headmaster for a number of years. In one high-flying position he had worked for a particularly negative and domineering boss, who had seriously undermined him and a number of his colleagues. He worked with Sasha to resolve his feelings around this former boss, who had now passed away.

Sasha: *OK, so at what point do you want to go in and speak to your former boss, Eric? Where do you feel that resolution is needed the most?*

Eric: *At the point where I accidentally went to the wrong place for a meeting. When I went to her office to let her know that I had made a mistake, she said, 'If you do that again, I will kill you.'*

There is a lot of emotion in Eric's voice at this point.

Sasha: *Can you see younger Eric there now, when he has been told that she will kill him if he makes that mistake again?*

Eric: *Yes.*

Sasha: *Step into the picture. Let him know who you are and why you are there. Start tapping on him. Is he OK with that?*

144

Eric: *Yes, he's fine.*

Sasha: *Let's just bring his intensity down a bit before he says what he needs to say. Where is he feeling the emotion in his body?*

Eric: *It's dark red dread in the pit of his stomach and it's spinning.*

Sasha: *Tap on the side of his hand and repeat after me, 'Even though you have this dark red spinning dread in the pit of your stomach, you love and accept yourself.'*

Eric repeats and taps on his ECHO using the set-up and reminder phrase until the intensity reduces.

Sasha: *OK, what does he want to do now?*

Eric: *He didn't stand up for himself at the time, so now he wants to tell her how he feels.*

Sasha: *Do you want to do this silently or out loud, since he was silenced back then?*

Eric: *Silently is fine.*

Sasha: *OK, take your time.*

Sasha continues to tap on Eric as he goes through a range of visible emotions, shaking at times.

Eric: *OK, he's told her how he feels. He got really angry with her, actually.*

Sasha: *Does anything else need to happen, Eric?*

Eric: *No, it feels complete. He's said what he needed to say.*

Sasha: *Where would he like to go now, younger Eric?*

Eric: *There's a really peaceful place in Ireland he'd like to visit. It's tremendous there – really tranquil.*

Sasha: *OK, take him there.*

Eric takes his ECHO to Ireland, creates a new picture in his mind and sends a signal to all the cells in his body to let them know that the conflict is over. He then takes the new picture into his heart, intensifies it and sends it out into the field.

Sasha: *Right, now test the original picture.*

Eric: *It's fine.*

Sasha: *What were the words she said to you? 'If you do that again, I will kill you.' Is that exactly how she said it?*

Eric: *Yes, and it doesn't do anything to me now.*

Sasha: *No dark red dread in the pit of your stomach?*

Eric: *Nothing. It's completely clear. Thank you – I've been carrying that one for years!*

Ella and her Ex

Ella was in a loving relationship, but her previous relationship had not ended well. She had wanted to confront her partner at the time about how things were, but he hadn't come round to her house and she hadn't had the chance to express how she felt.

She often obsessed about the end of this relationship, so Karl worked on her using Matrix Resolution Reimprinting. She tapped on her ECHO while her ECHO expressed her unresolved feelings. This enabled her to release the trauma around the end of the relationship.

Several days later, she saw her ex in the street and was able to walk past him without any of her previous feelings. What's more, things improved in her current relationship, as she was no longer holding the traumatic image of the end of the previous relationship in her field.

CHAPTER 11

Addiction and Habitual Behaviour Protocols

Sasha created the Matrix Habit Reimprinting protocol in response to her lifetime challenges with addiction. She overcame drug, alcohol, caffeine and smoking addictions in her late twenties, almost a decade before she created these protocols. However, she was still challenged by lighter addictions such as chocolate and sugar until she created them. Matrix Habit Reimprinting can help you to overcome all kinds of addiction, from chocolate to coffee, food, the internet, shopping, sex, alcohol, tobacco, cannabis, cocaine, heroin... It can also be used to transform negative habitual behaviour or self-destructive behaviour.

The Matrix Habit Reimprinting protocol is a process, and if you have deep-rooted addictions or long-standing destructive forms of behaviour, then it is highly unlikely that you will release them in one session. You will also need commitment to carry out this protocol, and it is recommended that you do some work on yourself seven days a week for 21 days for a minor addiction, and for three to six months for a major addiction. If you are overcoming drug or alcohol dependency, or have deep-rooted destructive psychological problems, it is recommended that you work with a Matrix Reimprinting practitioner who is also qualified in working with your issues.

Please also note that you have got to *want* to give up the addictive substance in order for these techniques to be effective. Sasha worked with people who were half-hearted about giving up their addictive substance to test whether the protocols would work despite a lack of enthusiasm or motivation. The answer, so far, has been no. So, as with all the addiction work, the desire has got to be there in the first place. And that desire has to come from the individual who is giving up the substance, rather than their family or loved ones.

So, how does Matrix Habit Reimprinting work? It is based on the understanding that addictions have their root in underlying emotional issues. Whether it is chocolate, coffee, alcohol, cannabis, cocaine or heroin, the addictive substance is generally used to make a person feel better. So the real work is to determine why they don't feel good in the first place.

Sasha has trained a number of alcohol and substance misuse workers in Matrix Reimprinting. They all echo her sentiments. It is not the substance but how it is used to block the emotions that is the real issue.

One outstanding worker in this field is one of Sasha's trainees, Brett Moran. He has used Matrix Reimprinting extensively with his clients and had some excellent results. The scope of the research that Brett and Sasha are putting together is too great for this book alone, so will form a follow-up book at a later date. You can also learn more information about this work on a specialist training course with Sasha and Brett. In the meantime we can share that these techniques have been tested with the most challenging addictions and have proved to be very effective.

MATRIX HABIT REIMPRINTING

This technique is in three parts. It involves transforming previous life traumas, changing the images of yourself in your field as a user of the substance or performer of the habitual behaviour and then creating a new field for yourself in relation to your addictive behaviour.

Step 1: Choose the Habit

First choose the habit you would like to change. This can include any substance and also any form of addictive, self-destructive or self-sabotaging behaviour. You are advised to only change one at a time, as otherwise you will create too much pressure on yourself and are thus less likely to succeed.

Step 2: Rate the Validity of Cognition (VOC) Level

Before you start, rate the VOC level (*page 135*) to determine how much the habit or behaviour is a problem for you currently, with 10 per cent as only a minor issue and 100 per cent as totally dominating your life.

Step 3: Use Conventional EFT to Manage the Cravings

If you are not yet familiar with conventional EFT (*see Chapter 4*), learn it and use it to manage your cravings. Tap on the symptoms that the cravings bring in the body as soon as they start to surface, for example:

'Even though I've got this burning in my chest because I need to get wrecked...'

'Even though I've got this churning in my stomach because I need a drink...'

Also, determine an emergency point – one that feels really beneficial when you tap on it. It can be any of the tapping points. If you have a severe craving, tap on this point until it reduces in intensity. Don't concern yourself with set-up phrases or reminder phrases at this stage – these are there to help you stay tuned into the problem and if you are in a severe state of craving, you are most definitely tuned into the problem. When you have reduced the intensity you might want to then do some conventional EFT with set-up and reminder phrases around what you are feeling.

Step 4: Resolve Life Traumas

The first part of this protocol involves resolving all life traumas. This might take some time but is an important part of the process, as the feelings from the life traumas are likely to be what you are trying to block in the first place. Please remember that if you have intense, heavy or 'big T' life traumas, you will need to work with a practitioner to resolve these. If you have 'small t' traumas, use Matrix Scene Reimprinting (*page 91*) or Matrix Memory Reimprinting (*page 98*) to resolve them.

Be sure also to resolve any stressful or traumatic life memories around the time that the addiction started.

Step 5: Reimprint the Original Habit

The second part of the protocol involves reimprinting the origin of the habit and all the previous pictures you have associated with it. This means changing images throughout your life of, say, using the substance. Make a timeline of the addiction, including when it started, and any significant memories around you using the substance along the way. Then reimprint these pictures. For example, if you have memories of the first time you used a drug, go back into that image using Matrix Scene Reimprinting and change the picture so that you refuse the substance and find a different coping strategy. Remember, we are not denying who you are or the journey you have been on, we are simply creating new images for your subconscious and your field, so that you can start to respond differently.

Then go through all the associated memories that you have of using this substance, particularly those where your use of it was at its worst, and change the outcome of those memories. You may, for example, put new pictures in your field of you refusing drugs when previously you took them, making healthy food choices when previously you made less healthy ones, or being centred in a relationship when previously you were possessive. If this is a long-term issue, this may take some time.

If you can't remember all the images due to using for years, just take several images from each year that you have been using and transform these. If you are a practitioner or are fairly advanced in using these techniques, you can work ECHO to ECHO (*page 126*), asking each ECHO to take you back further and further to relevant memories.

Please note that if you are having difficulty accessing memories then you can use the Matrix Recall Technique (*page 136*) to help you tune into them. Use a set-up phrase such as 'Even though I can't remember what happened when I was out of it, I totally love and accept myself.'

Step 6: Clear the Field of the Addiction

The third part of the protocol includes a five-minute daily field-clearing exercise that you will need to repeat seven times per week for three weeks to six months, depending on the severity of your habit. You will need to have completed steps 4 and 5 (resolving life traumas and reimprinting the original habit) before you move onto this part of the process. This is because you need to have cleared some of the negativity from the old field before you start tuning into a new one.

This step is an important part of your transformation, as the more we repeat a pattern of behaviour, the stronger its morphic field becomes. This is particularly true with addictions, as the substance evokes strong emotions which make the field stronger each time you repeat the behaviour. You can start to understand why your addiction may have been so challenging to break. Not only is the substance creating a chemical craving in your cells, but each time you repeat the behaviour you are reinforcing the field. So the Field-Clearing Technique will help you tune into a more supportive and positive field.

It is not only the field that is strengthened by repetition, it is also the neural connections in your brain. Like the muscles in your body when you exercise, the more often you repeat a thought pattern, the more you strengthen your neural connections and make that thought pattern habitual.[1] You have probably experienced this many times with negative thought patterns. However, by repeating the Field-Clearing Technique daily you will begin to experience this with positive thought patterns.

Field-Clearing Technique

This technique was put together by Sasha and combines Matrix Reimprinting with Neuro-Linguistic Programming (NLP), along with some teachings from a number of other Energy Psychology techniques. You will need to practise it daily for a minimum of 21 days – there is a lot of research that suggests that it takes 21 days for new neural connections to form in the brain – and for three to six months if you have severe addiction issues. Much of the leading-edge research in addictive behaviour suggests a 90-day programme for changing behaviour.

You already know the habit that you don't want, so what do you want instead? If you are an overeater, you may want to eat in a more balanced and healthy way. If you are a drug user, you probably want to be clean. If you are habitually untidy, you probably want to be tidy and organized. So your first step is to identify the complete opposite of your behaviour. Then use this as your set-up phrase while tapping on your karate chop point:

'Even though I haven't always [positive behaviour], I totally love and accept myself.'

Repeat this three times, for example:

'Even though I haven't always had a healthy diet...'

'Even though I haven't always been clean...'

'Even though I haven't always been tidy and organized...'

Keep your eyes closed for the remainder of the technique (if this is comfortable for you). Tap using the following sequence:

- Tap on the top of your head as you say: 'I haven't always [*positive behaviour*].'
- Tap on your brow as you say: 'I want to always [*positive behaviour*].'
- Tap on the side of your eye as you say: 'I choose to always [*positive behaviour*].'
- Tap under your eye as you say: 'I love to always [*positive behaviour*], because...' and then list all the reasons why you want to behave in that positive way, either in your mind or out loud.
- Tap under your nose. As you do, ask yourself what your life would look like if you behaved in that positive way. Either verbalize or bring to mind all the positive images you associate with that behaviour.
- Tap on your chin. As you do, ask yourself what you would hear if you behaved in that positive way. What would you expect to hear others saying about you? And what would you be saying about yourself? You can say these statements out loud if it helps you to resonate with them more.
- Tap on your collarbone. Ask yourself what action you would need to take in order to regularly behave in this positive way. Either verbalize the actions or just bring them to mind.
- Tap under your arm. Ask yourself how you would feel if you frequently or constantly behaved in this positive way. Allow the feelings of the positive behaviour to move through your whole body.
- Tap on your thumb. As you do, choose one image that you associate with the positive behaviour. Be sure that you are in the image and take this image into your mind.
- Tap on your first finger. As you do, with the image in your

mind, picture all the neurons in your brain reconnecting to make this image your reality.

- Tap on your middle finger. As you do, send a signal to every cell in your body that the positive behaviour is your new reality.
- Tap on your fourth finger. As you do, take the new image into your heart.
- Tap on your little finger. As you do, make all the colours around the image really strong and bright, and get in touch with all the positive emotions that you associate with the image. Experience the image through all your senses.
- Tap on your wrist. As you do, send the new image out into the field. Spend a minute or two doing this so there is a very strong sense of the new image out there.
- Tap on the karate chop point. As you do, bring to mind all the things you are grateful for in relation to your new behaviour. You can list these silently or out loud. Finish with a dance of gratitude, either in your mind or in reality, in order to seal the new belief with positive emotions!

Thank you to David Hamilton, author of *How Your Mind Can Heal Your Body*, for the inspiration on ending a positive exercise with a dance of gratitude, as joy and fear cannot exist in the same space at the same time.

Here's an example:

- Tapping on the karate chop point: 'Even though I haven't always exercised three to six times per week, I totally love and accept myself.' *Repeat three times.*
    With eyes closed:
- Tapping on the top of the head: 'I haven't always exercised three to six times per week.'
- Tapping on the eyebrow: 'I want to always exercise three to six times per week.'

- Tapping on the side of the eye: 'I choose to always exercise three to six times per week.'
- Tapping under the eye: 'I love to always exercise three to six times per week, because it gives me more energy, I like being fit, my mind is clearer when I exercise and I like having a fit body.'
- Tapping under the nose: 'It looks like every day at 5.30 p.m. I go to my studio and do some cardio or some weights. It looks like I have a fit and toned body. I also see myself carrying out tasks with more energy.'
- Tapping on the chin: 'Other people say that I look really fit and healthy. I say that I enjoy my toned body and enjoy having lots of energy.'
- Tapping on the collarbone: 'The action I need to take is to ensure that I have arranged my schedule so that I have created enough time to exercise, and also that I need to have eaten well in the afternoon to have enough energy.'
- Tapping under the arm: 'I feel strong and energized when I exercise three to six times per week. The strength is in my heart and I can feel it radiating around my body when I get into the feeling space of that energy.'
- Tapping on the thumb: 'The one image that I associate with exercising three to six times per week is me on a treadmill looking really fit and healthy.' *This is taken silently into the mind.*
- Tapping on the first finger: *Silently in my mind I can picture all my neurons rewiring as I see myself on the treadmill.*
- Tapping on the middle finger: *Silently in my mind I send a signal to every cell in my body to let it know that I exercise three to six times per week.*
- Tapping on the fourth finger: *Silently in my mind I take the new image into my heart.*

- Tapping on the little finger: *Silently in my mind I imagine a strong white light around the image and I feel the strength and energy associated with it in my heart.*
- Tapping on the wrist: *Silently in my mind the image is sent out into the field, with the new colours and emotions associated with it.*
- Tapping on the karate chop point (*out loud*): 'I am grateful for: having all the equipment I need to work out, having a partner who sometimes works out with me, knowing what to do to get fit, having the energy to work out.'
- Finishing with a dance of gratitude.

Sasha Working on Herself

After over a decade in the personal development industry I had experienced my fair share of overcoming destructive behaviour. I had released dependency on both recreational and medical drugs, alcohol, cigarettes and caffeine, as well as a whole host of destructive relationship patterns. Some habits, though, no matter how hard I tapped, affirmed, reprogrammed or just plain old tried, were not so easily released. I understand now that this was because their fields were strong and I simply didn't know how to consistently change them.

When I started writing this book I was struggling with my eating habits and my exercise habits. Since my early teens I had followed a three-week cycle of healthy eating and moderate, consistent exercise then a three to six-week cycle of being haphazard in my eating choices and undisciplined in my exercise patterns.

Every time I was following a positive and healthy routine, I would be convinced that I had 'cracked it this time'. About three weeks in I would decide that I was disciplined enough to have a bar of chocolate, and before I knew it, I was attached to a chocolate drip and buried under a mountain of cake! The problem was compounded by the fact that these very foods had such a detrimental effect on my health. Being highly sensitive physiologically, I found that sugar had a similar biological effect to cocaine, and trans fats left me feeling fatigued and listless. Lack of exercise very quickly took its toll on my body and I would soon experience severe energy dips that would lead me back to the start of the cycle and I would repeat the whole process.

I began by going back to when these patterns started – my early teens – and doing Matrix Reimprinting with my younger self to help her find confidence from within, as opposed to feeling that she needed to be obsessive about the way she looked and adhere to rigid diet and exercise regimes. I worked through all the memories on diet first and then all the memories on exercise. As I had previously resolved all my trauma issues from this period, I did not need to carry out Part 1 of the Matrix Habit Reimprinting protocol. For Part 2 of the protocol, in the place of sporadic exercise patterns, I went through each year of my life and visualized myself working out consistently three times a week, tapping on and transforming the images of myself as a sporadic exerciser. I did the same for eating. Any images I had of myself out of shape, I replaced with images of myself with good levels of fitness. I also helped my younger self identify her underlying emotional reasons for eating junk food, which were her way of showing herself love, but also of sabotaging herself.

I then practised the Field-Clearing Technique for three weeks, doing two separate field-clearing exercises, one for diet and one for fitness. As I am very visual and creative, I also made image boards of what my positive goal looked like, complete with things that others might say about me and things I would say about myself. This is not a necessary part of the process but was something I enjoyed doing.

The results I experienced were phenomenal. Very quickly I believed in myself as a consistent exerciser and healthy eater. It was as though my field almost instantly changed. However, what I found was that if I stopped using the Field-Clearing Technique in the first week or so, I would remain tuned into the new field for a while but then would find myself back in the old field. So, bearing in mind the recent developments in psychology which say that it takes 21 days for new neuron connections to form in the brain, I repeated the Field-Clearing Technique seven times a week for three weeks. By the second week, I knew I didn't need it any more, but I decided to continue to the third week, just to make sure. After the third week I had a very strong and consistent healthy eating and exercise pattern – something that I had been trying to achieve for over 20 years without reliable results. My field had totally transformed.

On occasion, when life got really hectic, particularly when I was finishing this book while travelling, the field became disrupted again. What I realized was that I was actually blocking some of the stressful emotions that I was feeling during this hectic period by reverting back to negative habits. As soon as I cleared the related memories and did the Field-Clearing Technique for several days, I was able to easily tune back into the new field.

Please note, you can also use the Field-Clearing Technique for goals you want to achieve or things that you want to attract into your life. If there are no traumas or stress-related memories that are blocking the goal or no negative habits to clear, you can just go straight to the Field-Clearing Technique and form a new field for your goal. This is a very powerful technique for manifesting, and it works well if you are familiar with the Law of Attraction and manifestation. Carry it out for 21 days and then let it go.

You can also use the Field-Clearing Technique to aid you in transforming illness, disease or allergies. We will discuss allergies further in the next chapter and disease in Chapter 15.

Billy's Control Issue

Practitioner: Brett Moran

As a Matrix Reimprinting addictions specialist, I have had numerous opportunities to share Matrix Reimprinting and EFT with drug and alcohol users who are trying to resolve their addictions. I previously worked in a drop-in centre for recovering addicts and was often limited to a small number of sessions with my clients due to funding. I therefore didn't always have the luxury of long-term intervention. In this case study I only carried out Part 1 of the three-part intervention, but still saw amazing results. So this shows just what can be achieved in three sessions.

Billy came to me with an issue around smoking cannabis. He had started to become concerned that his tolerance level was high and he was extremely dependent upon it. He informed me that he had been smoking skunk weed (an extremely strong form of cannabis) for over ten years and while at university his intake had been extremely high.

He had not come to me for Matrix Reimprinting or EFT and knew nothing about them. He had come to me to start the process of setting goals, targets and a care plan, which was part of my role as a key worker. However, as he was extremely anxious, I was initially keen to help him settle with EFT. For the first session we simply helped him to reduce his nerves and to feel more comfortable about approaching his issues. I felt that this was paving the way for future Matrix Reimprinting work.

A week later Billy returned and informed me on arrival that he felt at ease about that day's session. He was still smoking as much cannabis as he had been previously, as we hadn't addressed anything other than his nerves about the session. What had changed was that he really wanted to address his drug issues, which he admitted were really making him depressed. I informed him we would begin with more tapping and we started off with the issue of feeling depressed and frustrated.

We completed several rounds of conventional EFT on these topics. However, as I carefully listened to Billy's language I noticed that he was playing a theme about not being in control of his feelings. My feeling was that there was a time in his life when he felt that he had lost control and this was still playing out in his subconscious. I began asking questions such as: 'How long have you not been in control?' and 'When was the first time you felt you lost control?'

Billy's SUDS level was extremely high, but it took a while to get him into a specific memory. We continued to tap on the feeling of being out of control for a while and it turned to sadness. Once we started tuning into the emotion behind it, I knew we were getting somewhere. I asked Billy where this was and how it felt. He described it as a dark sinking feeling in his heart that hurt him when he thought about it. So I asked him when he had first felt like this. He went back to a situation where he was playing football as a child and was laughed at for doing something wrong. He said that he could not control his emotions back then and ran off the pitch.

We began Matrix Scene Reimprinting. Billy introduced himself to his ECHO, explained why he was there and began tapping on him. 'Even though you had all these emotions and felt that you couldn't control them, you're still a great kid.' 'Even though you felt silly and embarrassed and could not control your feelings...' 'Even though you ran off and felt that you weren't in control...'

We reimprinted the picture, asking his younger self what he wanted to do and how he wanted to do it. His ECHO replied that he did not want everyone to laugh at him and did not want to make the mistake in the first place. So we replayed the original memory but without the mistake.

When this was complete, I asked Billy if he and his ECHO wanted to stay where they were or go to a different place of their choosing. Billy chose to take his ECHO to a football stadium at the time when England beat Germany 4–0. He brought some friends and his brother into the scene and they all watched the brilliant match together. When it felt complete, this new picture was sent out into the Matrix.

Although we reimprinted this picture and did some really positive work, I knew there was more to be done around being laughed at, not being in control and losing power, but we came to the end of the session. However, Billy informed me that he was eager to come back the following week.

Upon his return I informed him that if he was really serious about giving up smoking cannabis then he would need to do some tapping while at *home and back out there in the real world. I work with a lot of clients with severe issues, traumas and addictions, and motivation is often low, so I feel if they are prepared to work on themselves at home then they are prepared for change. Billy was prepared to work on himself and informed me that even though he was still smoking he had used EFT on other situations over the past week. I showed him how to use it specifically for craving.*

After our introduction we picked up where we had left off the previous week. We tapped around some of Billy's issues and feelings which related to smoking cannabis, using appropriate humour to shift some of the negative energy that he was feeling. This helped us get straight to the point. As I tapped with Billy I asked him what size bags he bought his skunk weed in. There are various measurements such as 'a ten bags' worth', 'an eighth of an ounce', and so on. He told me his ideal size, so I asked how he felt about being controlled in circumstances where he had to buy a smaller bag. Straightaway we were back into his feelings of not being in control and losing his power, which triggered sadness, frustration and anger.

With a few more rounds of tapping and intuitive questioning we pinpointed a feeling of anger deep in his heart. I asked Billy to remember the first time he had felt this feeling. It took some time to tune into a memory, but eventually we found ourselves back in the school playground. His so-called friends had bullied him, pulled down his trousers and pants and proceeded to take photos of him. The perpetrators included girls and boys and it was severely humiliating for Billy.

Billy stepped into the picture at the point where one member of the gang was sitting on his chest while others were taking his pants down and further people were taking photographs. He needed to get his ECHO out of that situation straightaway, so he froze the picture and freed his ECHO, while beginning to tap on him.

Billy needed to retaliate with some violence to redress the disempowerment that he felt. Of course I do not condone violence in the real world, but on some level Billy had been retaliating with violence in his subconscious ever since this event had occurred, so he needed to release this. So he did what he wished he had done all those years ago: he retaliated physically. He also told his so-called friends that what they had done was wrong and what he thought of them for abusing him in that way. His adult self was there the whole time and he felt the need to also tell them that he understood that they were just kids and sometimes they didn't think before they acted. Billy's ECHO felt fine about this being communicated, as it was done after he had released the anger.

After smashing the camera into millions of pieces and throwing away the film, Billy felt that the picture was complete and I knew he was ready to go to a more positive place of his choosing. This time he chose a beautiful beach resort in the sun with different friends and sent this new picture in through his mind and out through his heart into the universe. He tested the old picture and it had transformed completely. That concluded our session.

I didn't see Billy for a few weeks after that, but did get a text message from him informing me that life was really great and that he had stuck to his quit date and not smoked any skunk weed since.

And last week I was halfway through writing this case study when who should walk into the office but Billy! He had a big smile on his face and was looking a lot calmer. He informed me that life was really good and although there were still many things he would like to work on, his skunk addiction was under control. He told me that over the last month he had only had a few puffs of a joint and it had tasted really horrible and he had not gone back to actively smoking. From my experience of working with this client group, that is an incredible result, given that we only had one session of conventional EFT and two sessions of Matrix Reimprinting. I'm sure we would not have achieved the same results with willpower alone.

What's more, Billy had been using the tapping in his everyday life. He was tapping in moments of stress and he informed me that he now had a *much more positive take on life. There was also a new woman in his life and he felt more confident and comfortable than he had done previously in female company.*

My personal conclusion is that Billy has conquered far more than just his addiction. He has also got back his confidence, his self-esteem and his sense of control. One of the most amazing things I have found with this case and other similar cases is that we empower the client to achieve what they desire. The clients I work with who are overcoming addictions are always seeking instant gratification from a substance. They use the substance to get rid of a feeling or emotion. So the substance is only the surface issue. Matrix Reimprinting and EFT help them get to the underlying core issues – the reasons why they are using the substance in the first place. Billy was a prime example of this and I am delighted by his progress.

Brett's contact details can be found in the Resources section.

CHAPTER 12

Specialist Resolution Protocols

The Specialist Resolution protocols are designed to target specific life issues. They include Matrix Trauma Reimprinting for transforming severe trauma and post-traumatic stress disorder (PTSD), Matrix Phobia Reimprinting for transforming phobic responses, and Matrix Allergy Reimprinting for releasing allergic reactions.

MATRIX TRAUMA REIMPRINTING

A variation on the Matrix Memory Reimprinting technique is Matrix Trauma Reimprinting. This technique is for working on extremely traumatic memories such as rape, child abuse, torture, war memories, disasters, tragedies, and so on. It is also the most effective technique to use for post-traumatic stress disorder (PTSD).

Please note that you cannot use this technique on yourself and it is vital that you only use it on others if you are a qualified Matrix Reimprinting practitioner with experience of working in this field.

For Matrix Trauma Reimprinting, the Matrix Memory Reimprinting technique is followed (*page 98*), but with one important adjustment. Instead of starting at the beginning of the memory and working through to the end, with this technique you start at the end, after the trauma has taken place. Work with the traumatized ECHO after the event, and when you have taken some of the intensity off the end of the memory it is then easier to go into it and work through it sequentially, clearing the intensity from each peak.

A reminder here, though: if the memory spanned days or weeks, you will need to break it up into several memories and work with them one at a time. In a case such as this, if you are not sure where to begin, start with one part of the memory and work through the rest in whatever order your client presents them.

When working with severe trauma and PTSD, it is advisable not to start with the most intense memory, unless your client is keen to do so. It is best to give them an experience of working through and resolving a less intense memory before the larger ones are tackled. This gives them confidence in the technique and builds bridges.

If there is no conscious memory of the trauma, see how to work with a blocked memory: refer to the Matrix Recall Technique (*page 136*) or the Matrix Pre-conscious Reimprinting (*page 179*) if the memory is from the early years.

We would like to again reinforce that if you have gone through severe trauma or are experiencing PTSD, it is imperative that you work through your memories with someone who is experienced and qualified. Do not, under any circumstances, attempt this work on your own, as one of two things may happen. The first is that you could make your symptoms worse by retraumatizing yourself, as the tapping often tunes you into aspects of the memory that you have blocked or forgotten. The second is that you may not be able to get to the relevant points to clear the intensity around the memory, as your subconscious and your ECHOs may be doing a very good job of protecting you from what happened. However, please be reassured that you can reach a point of peace working with a Matrix Reimprinting practitioner, however dramatic and devastating your life experiences have been.

MATRIX PHOBIA REIMPRINTING

Phobias occur because our subconscious remembers a stressful or traumatic moment in our life and triggers the fear response again when the subject of the phobia subsequently shows up in our life.

Phobias are just the subconscious trying to protect us. So we are usually afraid of dogs because a dog bit us. We are usually afraid of spiders because we saw someone else scream (often a close female relative) when one appeared. There is always a reason why we have these fears, based on our life experiences, and we can change the subconscious responses without the pain of Exposure Therapy (making someone face up to their fear).

Conventional EFT is extremely successful in releasing phobias. With it you can work with the symptoms of the phobia and also with early memories that created it. The success of the phobia work is usually tested first by looking at a picture of something related to the phobia (for example, a snake) and then looking at it in real life. Matrix Phobia Reimprinting takes the work a step further. It is a very simple process that achieves profound results.

You are advised to carry out the phobia work with a partner rather than on your own. If you are extremely triggered by your phobia, you will need to work with a Matrix Reimprinting practitioner to resolve it.

Step 1: Select a Phobia

Choose a phobia that you want to work with. It can be anything.

Step 2: Reduce the Intensity

Usually just the mention of the fear will create an intensity. Use conventional EFT to reduce this to a SUDS level of about three.

Step 3: Reimprint the Origin of the Memory

If the recipient can remember the first time that they had a phobic response, you will work with this memory. If they can't, use the Matrix Recall Technique if the memory is blocked (*page 136*), or Matrix Pre-conscious Reimprinting if the memory is from early childhood (*page 179*). You can also work from ECHO to ECHO (*page 126*), finding the most recent memory of a phobic incident, tapping on that ECHO and asking to be taken back to the earliest memory where this was an issue.

Once you get to the original memory, use either Matrix Scene Reimprinting (*page 91*) or Matrix Memory Reimprinting (*page 98*) to transform the reaction to the phobia. However, do not take the ECHO to a new place in your mind at this point, and do not send a new picture out into the field just yet either. These steps will come after you have tested the work.

Step 4: Test the Work through the ECHO

The ECHO tests the phobia for you. So when they are in a good space and have released all their original fears, get them to hold the snake, or look over the edge of a high building, or stroke the rat, or whatever it is they feared doing. If there is still emotional intensity, tap on them or bring in new resources until they have released all their fears.

Step 5: Create the New Picture in the Field

Once the ECHO is no longer showing any signs of phobia, create a new picture of them existing comfortably with the thing that they feared. This could be a picture of being in a confined space for a claustrophobic or being in the same space as a spider for an arachnophobic, for example. Send this new picture out into the field.

Step 6: Clear any Related Memories

Next check if there are any related memories where intensity needs to be cleared. For example, if the original trauma was when Mum screamed at a spider, a further trauma might be when someone put a spider down the recipient's back. Ask the recipient to bring to mind any further traumas that might have been created, and repeat the above steps. Please note that clearing the intensity around the original trauma may mean that subsequent traumas have no negative emotional resonance, so this step might not be necessary.

Step 7: Test in Real Life

When all related memories have no resonance, test in real life, first with a picture, then with the real thing if possible.

MATRIX ALLERGY REIMPRINTING

Allergies are complex and can stem from an overly acidic body condition and also a reduction in the flora of the gut, which can be compromised by a poor diet and antibiotics. However, they can also be emotional in nature. Like phobias, they are the result of the body reacting to something that it misperceives as dangerous. What tends to happen is that if a person is eating something at the time something stressful happens, the body associates that food with danger or stress and starts rejecting it as dangerous. A couple of examples are a lady who developed an allergy to oranges from eating them when she discovered her father had died and another lady who had an allergy to cheese which related back to when she was really unhappy at university and used to eat cheese all the time. Over the years Karl and Sasha have helped many clients and EFT trainees to resolve their allergies using EFT and Matrix Reimprinting. You can read an example of this on page 242, where a life-threatening coffee allergy is resolved in a 30-minute session.

The other thing about allergies is that they have very strong fields. These are often fear-based, so what starts as a minor allergy can become more and more intense each time you have an allergic reaction, as the mind sends messages to the body that the substance is harmful, and the severity of the allergy can become worse and worse.

Furthermore, allergies can be linked to beliefs. Sasha had over 20 allergies when she started her journey with EFT and Matrix Reimprinting. In fact, when she first went to train with Karl in EFT, she had to stay at a self-catering apartment rather than in residence with the other trainees, as she wouldn't have been able to attend had she not brought her own food.

If your allergy is totally emotional in nature, it can easily be resolved with Matrix Reimprinting. If it is physiological in nature – for example, if you have an overly acidic condition or compromised gut flora – you can still use these techniques to resolve any negative memories about severe allergic reactions and this may reduce your symptoms.

Please note, if you have anaphylaxis (severe and life-threatening allergic responses), do not attempt these techniques without the assistance of a qualified and experienced Matrix Reimprinting practitioner, as tapping into the related memories can recreate the symptoms of the anaphylaxis.

Step 1: Identify the Allergy

Identify the allergy that you wish to work with. If you have more than one allergy, just work on one at a time. It can be food- or substance-based, pet-based, chemical-based, and so on.

Step 2: Identify your First Memory of the Allergy

If you can remember the first time that you had an allergic response, work with this memory. Also work with any traumatic or stressful memories from around this period.

If you can't remember your first allergic reaction, use the Matrix Recall Technique (*page 136*) if the memory is blocked, or Matrix Pre-conscious Reimprinting (*page 179*) if the memory is from early childhood. You can also work from ECHO to ECHO (*page 126*), finding the most recent memory where you had an allergic reaction, tapping on that ECHO and asking to be taken back to the earliest memory where this was an issue.

Step 3: Reimprint the Original Memory of the Allergy

Once you find the original memory, use either Matrix Scene Reimprinting or Matrix Memory Reimprinting to release the intensity of the allergic reaction. Ensure you tap on the ECHO until the recipient has released the original allergic reaction.

Next recreate a new memory, where the ECHO ingests or comes into contact with the allergen, which no longer causes a reaction.

Send a peaceful and positive image of the ECHO with the previous allergen through the mind, to every cell in the body (an important step, so take your time with this one), to the heart, and then out into the field.

Step 4: Reimprint any Further Stressful or Traumatic Memories around the Allergy

If there are further memories around the allergy, such as intense allergic reactions, special events missed because of allergic reactions, memories of days spoiled because of allergic reactions and so on, reimprint them in the usual way.

Step 5: Consider Clearing the Field

Sometimes the above steps are enough to prevent the allergy from recurring. However, sometimes you will need to clear the field of the allergy as well. It is useful to use the 21-day Field-Clearing Technique (*page 152*) with the set-up phrase 'Even though I haven't always been able to eat/drink/inhale/touch [*the allergen*], I deeply love and accept myself.'

For example:

'*Even though I haven't always been able to eat oranges, I deeply love and accept myself.*'

Step 6: Test the Work

It is not advisable to test the work in the usual way. The suggestion is to test the work as the allergen occurs in life, rather than to go specifically looking for it. If you are using the Field-Clearing Technique, definitely don't test the allergen until after the 21 days. If it is an item which brings a severe reaction, definitely do not test at all.

CHAPTER 13

Past-Life and Future-Self Protocols

The Past-Life and Future-Self protocols include Matrix Future-Self Reimprinting for working with fears of the future and also learning from your future self, and Matrix Past-Life Reimprinting for working with past-life ECHOs.

MATRIX PAST-LIFE REIMPRINTING

If you are already working with past-life issues, or if they arise, then it is possible to use Matrix Reimprinting to address them. Karl and Sasha both have a personal view about past-life work, believing that there is enough to work with in this lifetime without going back to previous lives and that working on yourself can become a bottomless pit if you keep continuously going back. It would seem that themes from past lives, if unresolved, will occur again in this lifetime anyway, so it is just as beneficial to work with and resolve them in this lifetime.

However, this is just Karl and Sasha's personal opinion and they respect those who carry out past-life regression. Furthermore, they have both worked with a number of clients who have presented past-life issues during therapeutic sessions, as they both have a policy of working with whatever presents itself. So if past lives come up then it is fine to work with them, and if you already work them anyway, Matrix Past-Life Reimprinting will enhance your tools for working with yourself and clients.

Step 1: Identify the Image or Memory

Bring to mind an image or memory of yourself from a past life that you would like to change.

Step 2: Step into the Image

Work in the usual way: introduce yourself to the ECHO, explain who you are, tap on the ECHO and ask how they felt in the given situation.

Step 3: Determine the Life Learning

What was the life learning from this situation? Check whether you are still running it.

Step 4: Get Resolution

Release all the negative energy around the image or memory. Bring in new resources if necessary and allow things to play out differently according to the ECHO's needs.

Step 5: Create a New Picture in the Field

Take the past-life ECHO to a new place of their choosing. Take the new picture in through your mind, around your cells and out through your heart.

Step 6: Test the Work

Check the original memory or image to determine whether the resonance has changed. Go back to Step 4 if there is more work to do.

MATRIX FUTURE-SELF REIMPRINTING

Matrix Reimprinting is not confined to what has happened in the past. You can use it to shape your future. There are a number of ways that this can be done.

First, you can use Matrix Reimprinting when you have fears about the future.

Reimprinting a Negative Future Image

Have you ever played an imagined movie about what you fear is going to happen, over and over in your head? Sometimes we rehearse destructive futures, which is only reinforcing our point of attraction for negative encounters. However, fearing the future is so socially acceptable in Western culture that it has become a norm. All too frequently we ask ourselves 'What if...?' and then play out possible negative outcomes.

If you haven't noticed yourself or others doing this, try an experiment. Spend next week casually observing how common negative future-focusing is in both your own life and the lives of those around you. Listen in on buses, at work or on the television. You may be quite surprised by how frequent this kind of behaviour is.

So, if you find yourself imagining the worst, use Matrix Memory Reimprinting (if it is a specific imaged event with a beginning, middle and end) or Matrix Scene Reimprinting (if it is just a single image), and change the imagined scene or picture to a more supportive and positive one.

You can also ask your future self to take you back to an early memory which reminds you of this fear, and this can be a good way of accessing memories around themes that were not previously accessible to you. For example:

Jenny: *I keep picturing it over and over again: my boyfriend Paul leaving me.*

Sasha: *Have you got a clear image or scene that comes to mind when you do?*

Jenny: *Yes, it's the same thing every time. Paul's walking away with his head down and I'm curled up in a ball, crying.*

Sasha: *OK, tapping on your karate chop point, repeat three times after me: 'Even though I can see Paul leaving me, I totally love and accept myself.'*

Jenny: *That's brought an overwhelming panic in my chest.*

Sasha: *What number would you give it?*

Jenny: *It's a ten.*

Jenny taps with Sasha to bring it down to a two.

Sasha: *OK, can you see the future image of yourself curled up in a ball?*

Jenny: *Yes.*

Sasha: *Step into the image. Let her know that you have come to help her feel better, and if she's OK with it, begin to tap on her. Ask her what's going on.*

Jenny: *She says she's not good enough, that's why Paul's left her.*

Sasha: *Ask her to take you to an earlier memory, one that reminds you of this situation.*

Jenny: *I can't believe it – she's taken me to when I was 14 and I was rejected by a guy named James after two weeks. I haven't thought about that for years.*

Sasha: *Ask her if it's OK for you to tap on her. Let her know you've come from the future to help her feel better. What is she feeling?*

Jenny: *A dark sadness in her heart.*

Sasha leads Jenny through several rounds of 'Even though you have this dark sadness in your heart...' while Sasha taps on Jenny and Jenny images tapping on her younger self.

Sasha: *Now ask her what she needs.*

Jenny: *She wants a boyfriend who stays with her for a while. She keeps getting dumped after a few days or weeks.*

Sasha: *Does she want a new boyfriend? Ask her who she'd like to be with.*

Jenny: *There's this really cool guy, Jez. She'd like to be with him.*

Sasha: *Is it OK to let that play out?*

Jenny: *Yes.*

Sasha: *Let me know when she's happy.*

Sasha continues to tap on Jenny whilst Jenny allows the new scene to unfold.

Jenny: *Yeah, she's had some great times with him.*

They send the image of them together into Jenny's mind and out through her heart, and back out into the field. The original memory of being rejected by James is tested and has been replaced by being with Jez.

Sasha: *OK, now you have that picture of her with Jez, tap on her and ask her if there's anywhere else you need to go.*

Jenny: *She's taken me back to when I'm six years old. My dad's just walked out on my mum.*

Sasha leads Jenny through a session where she taps on her younger self while her dad stays and resolves issues with her mum, rather than storming out. Jenny had assumed that they were arguing about her because she wasn't good enough. The new images are sent out into the field in the usual way.

Sasha: *OK, back to your future self.*

Jenny: *Oh, that's amazing. She's sitting face to face with Paul, having a conversation. They both look really animated.*

Sasha: *Can you get the original image back where she was crying and Paul was leaving?*

Jenny: *No, it's not there! It's completely disappeared!*

So our fears of the future are usually fuelled by our experiences of the past, and allowing our fearful future selves to take us back to the moment these experiences came about can help us to resolve them.

From a quantum physics point of view, there are endless possible futures open to us, and by reimprinting a positive future, we are more likely to move towards and attract it.

Learning from a Positive Future Image

Another powerful technique is to visit a positive future self and ask them what it is the recipient needs to do to create a positive future. This is an excellent technique to use if someone is overcoming long-term illness or serious disease and needs to work out what they need to do to get better.

The technique involves picturing a positive future self, stepping into that image, and the future self tapping on you as you are now and letting you know what needs to be done to transform.

Jonathan and the Golden Key

Jonathan had been ill for 20 years. Sasha had worked with him on a number of his life traumas and some great progress had been made. In one session she suggested he went to meet his future self, who was healed, to ask what he needed to do in the present to get to where that future self was.

Jonathan did this and his future self tapped on him while he told him what he needed to do. He said that he needed to learn patience, to accept his situation and to stop fighting the illness.

The future self gave Jonathan a golden key and they walked through a golden door together. That door was the beginning of the journey to health.

This session was not the end of Jonathan's healing journey and there was still a lot of work to be done, but visiting his future self gave him hope that he could be healthy in the future and was an important part of his healing journey.

CHAPTER 14

Birth and Early Years Protocols

Matrix Reimprinting can be used to transform pre-conscious memories (memories from your early life of which you don't have any conscious recollection) and to reimprint the entire birth process. Matrix Pre-conscious Reimprinting is used to work with traumas that took place in the womb, during birth and in the early years. In addition to this, Matrix Birth Reimprinting is used to specifically reimprint the birthing process.

MATRIX PRE-CONSCIOUS REIMPRINTING

This protocol is used when you have no conscious memory of a specific event but have a sense or some knowledge of something that has happened to you. It includes a vast array of things that may have occurred in the womb or in pre-conscious or early childhood. It may be an event that someone else has told you occurred, such as a very early childhood operation or the loss of a close relative at an early age. For some people it is more of a sense of what happened in the womb or early childhood, and can include: feelings around not being wanted in early childhood, early arguments between parents, family traumas or tragedies which were perceived by the baby emotionally but not understood, and the mother drinking, smoking or taking drugs while the baby was in the womb. Such events leave disruptions in the field and cause an imprinting of beliefs. Matrix Pre-conscious Reimprinting can transform these.

Step 1: Determine the Issue

Determine the issue, for example:

- 'I was not loved as a small child.'
- 'My father died when I was a baby.'
- 'There was a great tragedy in my family when I was a tiny baby.'

Step 2: Tap Globally on the Issue

Begin with a couple of rounds of your recipient tapping on themselves using a global set-up statement, for example:

'Even though I was not loved as small child, I totally love and accept myself.'

'Even though my father died when I was a baby...'

'Even though there was a great tragedy in my family when I was tiny...'

This should start to bring some of the energy or emotion around the issue in from the Matrix.

Step 3: Identify the Energy around the Issue

Ask the recipient where they are holding the energy in their body around this issue.

- Where do they feel it most?
- What colour, shape or sound is it?
- What texture is it?
- What is it made of?

If the feeling is very intense for the recipient, they may have associated with an ECHO already. If they have, instruct them to step out of the ECHO and look at the picture from the outside, then proceed to Step 5.

Step 4: Access the Pre-conscious Memory

As the recipient tunes into the energy in their body, ask them to go back to their earliest memory of it. What can they see, sense or hear? If in utero, there may be a sense of being in the womb, colours, feelings or emotions. If the memory is after your recipient was born, there may also be voices or sounds, smells or tastes. Ask them to fully describe what they see, feel or hear.

Step 5: Instruct your Recipient to Begin Tapping on their ECHO in the Memory

Instruct your recipient to let their ECHO know that they have come from the future to help them let go of the stressful feelings they are experiencing and check that they are OK to be tapped on. If the ECHO is pre-speech, your recipient will get a sense whether it is OK to tap on them. The foetus in utero can be tapped on in your recipient's imagination in the same way that the ECHO of a child can be tapped on. Instruct your recipient to begin tapping on their ECHO as you tap on them.

Step 6: Determine What the ECHO is Feeling

Instruct your recipient to ask their ECHO what emotions they are feeling. Again, if the ECHO is pre-speech, your recipient will usually get a sense of it without the ECHO needing to talk. Ask the ECHO what colour the emotion is, and then instruct your recipient to begin tapping on their karate chop point as you tap on that of your recipient. Carry out conventional EFT on the ECHO. For example:

'Even though you have this black sadness in your heart, you totally love and accept yourself.'

'Even though you have this red anger in your chest...' etc.

Continue until the ECHO has released the feelings.

Step 7: Bring in New Resources

Instruct your recipient to ask their ECHO what they need in order to feel differently about the situation. If they feel unloved, they may need to either bring in some love from elsewhere or invite someone in to heal their parents so that they can then give the ECHO the love that they need. If the ECHO feels unsafe, they may need an angel or a spiritual figure to help them feel safe, or they may simply need to be wrapped in a comfort blanket or be given some strength from an external source. These are just examples, and as with all the Matrix Reimprinting work, the answers will come from your recipients.

Encourage your recipient to continue to tap on their ECHO as you tap on them throughout the process. The transformation work is usually carried out in silence throughout.

Step 8: Take the ECHO to a Different Place (if appropriate)

The usual step of taking the ECHO to a different place may not be appropriate for the foetus in utero, but it is still appropriate for children in pre-conscious memories. The foetus usually does not want to be removed from the womb, but the important aspect of this work is that the energy in the womb has changed. So if the colours were dark and the emotions were negative at the start of the work, you need to get to the point where the womb feels like a safe and nurturing place to be.

The pre-conscious child can go to a place of their choosing, as in the Matrix Scene or Matrix Memory Reimprinting techniques.

Allow them to choose a place which feels safe and emotionally supportive, such as a cot, a play pen, their mother's arms, snuggled up to a family pet, etc. This could equally be a place from a fairy tale or a story.

Step 9: Change the Images in the Mind, Cells, Heart and Field

When the ECHO is in a good emotional space, send the image in through the mind, around the cells, into the heart and out into the field as normal.

Step 10: Test the Work

Test the work by checking the original issue – for example, ask your recipient to say 'I was not loved as a small child' and determine if this still has a negative resonance. There may be more pre-conscious memories around the same issue, so continue to process until the statement no longer has a negative resonance.

John's Operation

Sasha worked with John over the telephone. At 45, he had found out four years previously that at 18 months he had undergone a hernia operation. This had taken place in the 1960s, when there was limited understanding of the needs of children in surgery, and for John, it had been a very traumatic experience. He had been strapped down both during and after the surgery and his parents had had very limited access to him. His mum reported that his screams had rung around the hospital and it had been very distressing for all involved.

Although John had not been aware of what had happened to him, he felt it explained a lot about his behaviour and feelings throughout life.

He was an experienced EFT practitioner and had previously attempted to address this memory with conventional EFT, but he could not access any emotions associated with the memory. He did, however, have a dull ache in his groin and a sense of a 'frown' on his forehead when he thought about what had happened.

In order to help him access the memory, I suggested that he tapped on the dull ache in his groin. He described it as a 'black emptiness'. He was very quickly able to connect with the helplessness and despair associated with the pain.

I asked him to go back to the time when the pain originated and he soon got a very clear image of himself at 18 months old. His younger self was strapped to a hospital bed in terror. While tapping on himself in current time, John tapped also on his 18-month-old ECHO. The ECHO was experiencing a black terror around the head and face and also around the groin area, and John could also feel this terror. John tapped on himself and his ECHO for some time. The fear soon turned to rage and it became clear that the way to release this was to free John's ECHO from the straps that were holding him down. He chose his father to come in and release him. At this point John and his ECHO were outraged, and I encouraged John to continue tapping on his ECHO as they both released the pent-up anger and frustration that they were experiencing.

One of the issues for John's ECHO was that he was silent in expressing his rage, so we tapped on 'Even though you can't be heard' and this released the blockage that John's ECHO was experiencing around vocal expression.

We asked the ECHO if he would like anyone else in the room with him and he chose an angel to be there and protect him throughout. He also wanted his mother there and we spent some time in the company of the angel and his parents while tapping to help him release the 'shell-shocked' feeling that he was experiencing.

The lesson that John had taken from this situation was that 'People aren't safe' and although he was a very outgoing, warm, people-centred person, he felt he still ran this belief on some level. We tapped on the 'People aren't safe' energy in the heart area of his ECHO.

When the intensity was released, John took his ECHO to a beach, where he built sandcastles and enjoyed a sense of playfulness and freedom. The image was projected back out into the field in the usual way.

On testing the work, John still had some sadness when he saw his younger self in hospital. We tapped for a few rounds on the sadness and then John reported feeling peaceful about the image. However, I had a sense that there was something still to resolve. We had reached the end of our allotted session, so I asked John to report back to me in the next 48 hours, just to check on the outcome.

Following the session John had a number of interesting experiences. First, a sense of rage welled up in him which was very intense. As he lay down and tapped, he experienced a physical sense of trauma release and his whole body trembled uncontrollably. This anger continued to well up for the next 24 hours. On discussing this later, we concluded that he hadn't given his ECHO enough time to fully express his rage after he had been strapped down.

Coming from a family where strong emotions were seen as inappropriate, John realized he had calmed his ECHO and himself, rather than allowing the rage to be fully expressed. He had thus taken into himself the energy that the ECHO had been holding for him for so long.

A few days later I took John back to the image of the younger self there on the bed and he found that the ECHO was still strapped down and extremely angry. He said he looked like a cartoon caricature of an angry face. He tapped on him and at the same time spoke to him gently and reassuringly. He told him that he had every right to be angry and that what had happened to him was wrong. He told him he could express his anger any way that he wanted for as long as he wanted, and that he would be there for him.

His ECHO tore away the straps and screamed and thrashed for some time. John encouraged him and reassured him the whole time.

After this, John's ECHO was bewildered, so we tapped on the black, bewildering energy that was held in his face. We also invited the angel to return. John explained to his ECHO, as he would to one of his own children, that the people were trying to make the pain better for him. When he had given his ECHO lots of love and reassurance, and all the energy around the memory was resolved, the ECHO chose to go to the swings with John and the angel.

After spending some time on the swings, John said that both he and his ECHO felt content, but they were both disconnected from source. He brought in all the people that had ever loved him and they surrounded him and his ECHO, while bathing them in bright light. However, John and his ECHO still could not access the love that these people were giving them. He felt there was a blockage in the forehead which was a black energy disconnecting them from source, and the angel was chosen to remove this while we tapped simultaneously. Once it had been removed, John and his ECHO were able to feel the love of those around them, and this image was transmitted through the mind and heart and back out into the field in the usual way.

John felt a tremendous sense of peace and connectedness after the session, and when he looked at the image of himself in the hospital bed, it had totally changed and his ECHO was sitting up on the bed looking calm.

MATRIX BIRTH REIMPRINTING

As well as transforming pre-conscious memories we can also reimprint the whole birth experience. This protocol was created by Sharon King, and came out of her training in a cross-section of healing modalities, including various techniques which incorporated birth and the early years. She combined this with Matrix Reimprinting to create a new way of transforming our birthing experience.

Sharon delivers workshops showing how our birth stories affect our lives in the present. In her work she highlights how conception, our time in the womb, our birth and the first six years are such a critical time, and how our belief systems are formed during this time. There is also a whole host of scientific research behind the importance of natural birth and mother–child bonding.

With the Matrix Birth Reimprinting protocol all the issues around birth and bonding can be addressed and transformed. Other issues around birthing, such as adoption, the loss of a child, infertility, pregnancy, traumatic childbirth memories, and so on, can also be addressed.

The Science behind the Matrix Birth Reimprinting Protocol

Research has shown that the pregnancy and birth experience affect the development of the child and also the development of the brain. During pregnancy the mother's perception of the environment is chemically communicated to the baby through the placenta. The baby is also affected by the experiences of the father. This is brilliantly demonstrated on the Bruce Lipton DVD *Biology of Belief 'Lite'*, where a camera shows a baby jumping with shock in the womb when its parents start arguing.

During pregnancy, the brain goes through a series of developments. In the first trimester, the reptilian brain is formed, which is associated with learned behaviour. In the second trimester the limbic brain is formed, which is associated with emotion. In the third trimester, the neocortex is formed, which is associated with language and thinking. During the first year after birth the prefrontal cortex is formed, and this is responsible for the civilized mind of the child.[1] It is shaped by the child's environment and life experiences.

Chronic or continuously held emotions affect the development of the brain, both in pregnancy and beyond. If the mother is living in fear then the foetus will develop a larger reptilian brain than normal, with a stronger sense of survival. Fight and flight will also be more easily triggered and the attention span will be compromised, because the child will be constantly scanning the environment and looking for danger. Concentration will therefore become impaired and intelligence affected. The child is more likely to become a violent teenager.

On the other hand, if the child grows up in a loving and supportive environment then the development of the prefrontal cortex and neocortex is likely to create a higher level of intelligence.

If a baby comes into the world unloved or unwanted, it is likely to have a large number of negative core beliefs from an early age. These beliefs can include 'The world is not a safe place', 'I'm not wanted', 'I'm not good enough,' 'I'm unlovable', 'I'm worthless', 'I'm unworthy' and 'I don't want to be here.' These beliefs continue throughout childhood and adult life and can lead to problems such as depression, childhood and adult suicide, aggression and violence, abuse, feelings of disconnection and separation, mental disorders, high anxiety and worry, as well as eczema and skin problems.

The Ideal Birthing Experience

In her groundbreaking documentary *What Babies Want*, Debby Takikawa outlines the vital elements of the birthing process that have been lost in our sterile and clinical Western birthing procedure.

After birth, the bonding instinct awakens the cingulate gyrus in the baby. This is part of the limbic system and is involved with emotional formation and the control of aggressive behaviour. A number of things awaken and nurture the cingulate gyrus, such as breastfeeding, being held, eye contact with the mother and hearing the mother's voice. However, there is only a small window of time for this to happen naturally after birth.

An ideal birth should take place in the home with the family around and a feeling of support. The father or another family member should be there to receive the baby and place it in the mother's arms. There should also be eye contact and bonding with the mother. If you were born in the West, the reality of your birth is likely to have been a very different story. But with Matrix Birth Reimprinting you can recreate a whole new birthing experience and release the trauma of your birth.

How the Matrix Birth Reimprinting Protocol Differs from the Foundation Techniques

There are some key differences between Matrix Birth Reimprinting and the Foundation Techniques of Matrix Scene Reimprinting and Matrix

Memory Reimprinting. The first is that when reimprinting a person's birth using this technique, there is a step which includes checking if there are any issues from past lives that need to be resolved. As stated in Chapter 13, we do not usually look for these, but in Sharon's work developing this protocol, she deemed it to be a necessary step. Given the great results and feedback that she gets from using this protocol with others, her opinion is highly respected on this matter, so working with past lives has remained part of the process.

There is also a second difference that again contradicts one of the key principles of Matrix Reimprinting. Although all the work with the ECHO is carried out in the womb in a dissociated state as normal (tapping on the ECHO from the outside), when it comes to the actual rebirthing of the ECHO, the recipient associates with their ECHO (is inside the body of the ECHO and sees the world through their eyes). The ECHO and recipient then experience the birthing process together, in an associated state.

When Sasha and Karl first witnessed Sharon working in this way, they were fascinated by the protocol, but not sure that it was necessary to associate with the ECHO for the rebirthing process. Lots of lengthy discussions followed between the three of them. Sharon explained the science behind it. Her belief was that in order to activate the chemicals in the brain that were likely not to have been activated by the previous traumatic birth experience, the recipient needed to be associated with the ECHO. Karl and Sasha disagreed, feeling that if the ECHO was holding the trauma, reimprinting the birth of the ECHO would be sufficient to trigger this chemical reaction in the recipient. They were already both very familiar with the chemical changes that take place in the body of a recipient when their ECHO heals a trauma.

Sasha followed this discussion with experiment and spent the next few months using the Matrix Birth Reimprinting on anyone she could get her hands on! What she found was that it seemed that Sharon was right about association being necessary in the birth reimprinting process. Without it, the results were not so powerful. So although it contradicts the foundations of Matrix Reimprinting, association with the ECHO has remained part of the protocol, as it is results we are interested in rather than following rigid formats.

The Matrix Birth Reimprinting Protocol

You need to be a Matrix Reimprinting practitioner to carry out this technique on someone, but it is included here for information and reference.

Step 1: Finding an ECHO in the Womb

This technique is easiest to use if there is some knowledge of what happened in the birthing process. There is a lot more skill involved if there is no knowledge of the birth but a sense that the birth contributed to some of the negative feelings a person is having in the present.

If there is no knowledge of the birthing process but a feeling of separation, isolation or abandonment, then the recipient tunes into that feeling. The practitioner then asks a series of questions to trace the feeling back to the womb. For example:

Practitioner: *Did you have that feeling five years ago?*

Client: *Yes.*

Practitioner: *How about ten years ago?*

Client: *Definitely.*

Practitioner: *Was it present in your early twenties?*

Client: *I think so. Yes, definitely.*

Practitioner: *Your teens?*

Client: *Yes.*

Practitioner: *When you were ten?*

Client: *Yes, it was.*

Practitioner: *How about when you were five?*

Client: *Definitely.*

Practitioner: *Do you remember feeling it when you were two?*

Client: *Yes.*

Practitioner: *Did you feel like that in the womb?*

In the hands of a skilled practitioner this line of questioning often leads the client back to the ECHO in the womb. At this point, the client often associates with the ECHO. It is not helpful to do so at this stage, so encourage the recipient to get a clear sense of themselves outside the ECHO, as association is only necessary towards the end of the protocol.

Alternative ways of finding the ECHO in the womb are working ECHO to ECHO (*page 126*), using the Matrix Recall Technique (*page 136*) or Matrix Pre-conscious Reimprinting (*page 179*).

Step 2: Tap on the ECHO in the Womb

Once there is a picture of the ECHO in the womb, the recipient imagines tapping on the ECHO. The idea is to transform how they feel about being in the womb. Examples can include changing the shape or size of the womb to give more space, making the womb safer or tapping on any anxiety that the ECHO might have.

Step 3: Determine the Life Themes

It is useful to find a way of communicating with the ECHO to check what life themes are running. For example, if the ECHO is picking up stress, anxiety, the fact that they are not wanted and so on from the mother, they may be feeling unworthiness or a sense of not belonging, even at this early stage of life. Help them to release the feelings they have by tapping on them.

Step 4: Visit Past Lives

Check if the life theme has been running in previous lives. There may be flashes of memories or images from past lives.

If there are, use Matrix Scene Reimprinting or Matrix Memory Reimprinting to resolve them.

Step 5: Recheck the ECHO in the Womb

Return to the ECHO in the womb. Check if there is anything else that needs to be done to help them feel in a good space.

Step 6: Let the Client Associate with the ECHO

When the ECHO is in a good space to enter the world, the client becomes associated with them (sees the world through their eyes).

Step 7: Reimprint the Birth of the ECHO

The client/ECHO experiences the rebirthing process. At this point, the practitioner only taps on the client if any negative emotions arise. Otherwise the rebirthing process is carried out as a guided meditation without tapping. It is suggested that the baby is placed on the mother's tummy to rest after the birth and the mother or father helps the baby to move up to the breast, then, once feeding, the baby makes contact with the mother through the five senses, particularly eye contact.

Step 8: Send the New Picture into the Field

In the usual way, take the new picture of the birth in through your mind, send it around your cells, take it into your heart and send it out into the field.

Step 9: Test the Original Feelings or Pictures around the Birth

When they are ready, ask your recipient to open their eyes and come back to the present. Test the work in the usual way by bringing to mind pictures or feelings of the birth. If there are any unresolved aspects around the birth or being in utero, go back in and resolve these in the usual way.

Step 10: Check for Issues Arising in the First Six Years

In this or future sessions, check if there is any further work needed on the first six years.

Refining Matrix Birth Reimprinting

As with all the Matrix Reimprinting techniques and protocols, this work is led by the client and ECHO, and if there is any stage that does not feel appropriate to them, it is their prerogative to skip it or adapt it.

There are lots of far-reaching considerations for this technique. For example, sometimes an ECHO and client wish to be born of their foster mother. Other times an ECHO and client have refused the breast, as they know they are going to be given up for adoption and it doesn't feel right for them to bond with the mother in this way.

Caroline's Birth Traumas

Practitioner: Sharon King

Caroline had two lovely boys, Luke and Jamie, and was 34 weeks pregnant with her third child at the time of our session. She had had traumatic births with both her sons. Both had been very slow labours which had had to be induced. Both had needed numerous medical interventions. Caroline and both her boys had been left shocked and traumatized. She had struggled to breastfeed either of her boys, which made her feel a failure. She feared that the third birth was going to be as traumatic as the first two.

We started the session working with and releasing the belief and fear around the third birth and then we worked on the birth of Caroline's first son, Luke. She was able to clearly connect with the ECHO of herself at

---

that time. There was a lot of fear and feeling of being powerless due to not knowing what was happening and not being able to control everything that was being done to her. I asked her if she would like to invite somebody in to help her feel safe and secure. An angel appeared to her and with its help we were able to work with Caroline's ECHO. As we tapped, we explained to the ECHO what was happening. We tapped on the sound of the baby's heartbeat on the monitor, which kept dipping, causing more anxiety; this turned into the lovely relaxing sounds of waves on a beach.

Towards the end of the birthing process Caroline had felt that she was nearing the birthing stage, but the midwife had told her she had only been 6cm dilated 15 minutes before and so there would be at least two more hours of strong contractions. This had led Caroline to have an epidural, though it turned out that she had been 10cm dilated and could have given birth without it. We tapped on her frustration and anger because she missed experiencing the actual birth and also for the belief that people miss things so cannot be trusted.

Once we had worked with the ECHO to release all the emotions around this event, we were able to take Luke and Caroline back through the natural birth experience the way it should have been. Caroline was able to tap on Luke's ECHO before the birth to prepare him for his journey and to let him feel how much she loved him. She showed him the lovely young boy he is right now and we then guided him into the world with the angel and Caroline's husband there to assist with the process. Caroline felt the bonding process happen when Luke was placed on her and he went straight to breastfeeding.

Caroline was then drawn to working on her own birth experience. She worked with her ECHO while still in her mother's womb. She felt stuck and didn't want to come out. Her mother had also been induced and Caroline was picking up on the fear. We tapped on the ECHO for her fear and feeling of being stuck and also worked with her mother on her fear. She asked for her own mother to come in to help. Caroline's ECHO showed her what had happened at the birth. There had been a lot of people in the room and a sense of panic. We tapped and released these feelings and with the angel's help we reimprinted the birth. Caroline was then given time to bond with her mother.

However, she still had a feeling of isolation from after the birth, when she had been put in an incubator for two weeks. During this time her mother had been with her during the day but had had to go home at night to be with her brother. The nurses had fed Caroline with the milk her mother had expressed for her. We once again tapped on Caroline's ECHO for her feelings of abandonment and we explained to her the reason why her mum had to go home. Caroline wanted the angel to stay with her so she felt protected.

We then moved forward to Jamie's birth and were both surprised to find that there was not much to work on, as most of the negative emotions had been cleared with Luke's birth. We worked on the memory of Jamie's experience of having his head twisted by the midwife. We tapped on his ECHO to release the shock and reimprinted his birth. Caroline then breastfed him while telling him all about his big brother waiting to meet him at home.

We then went into the future to when the new baby, Archie, was born. We visualized an easy birth while continually tapping. Caroline spoke to Archie and told him all about his brothers and how much she loved him. She showed him the positive experience of being born. We saw that the whole process was natural and the right people were there to assist if needed. Caroline's husband, Paul, was there, as was her consultant, and of course the angel.

After that session Caroline's husband noticed a shift in her. She was now so relaxed about the forthcoming birth that it changed the dynamics of the whole family. Archie was born almost exactly as we had visualized. The only medical intervention Caroline needed was help to break her waters, and she was happy for this to be done. She was also back on her feet almost immediately after the birth and was able to breastfeed Archie without any problems. He is a very happy, relaxed and peaceful baby.

Due to working on her time in the incubator, Caroline no longer has a panicky feeling when her husband has to work away from home. She also has a strong sense of completion because she has finally been able to have the birthing experience she dreamed of.

Sharon's contact details can be found in the Resources section.

CHAPTER 15

Working with Long-Term Illness and Serious Disease

We have included a section on working with long-term illness and serious disease here as a guide to working with major physical health issues. This is not a protocol, but some important information for either working with this client group or working on yourself.

When working with serious disease it is important to note that although you may have heard of many one-hit wonders with Matrix Reimprinting, EFT or other Energy Psychology techniques, recovery from long-term illness or serious disease is very rarely instant, and can be a long journey which often encompasses a variety of issues and challenges.

When Sasha recovered from CFS/ME, she had miraculous results with her symptoms and made great progress in a short space of time. But to fully resolve the illness took almost a year from the start of her journey with Matrix Reimprinting and EFT. She also used a multi-dimensional approach including a change in diet, dietary supplementation, lymphatic massage and another Energy Psychology technique known as PSYCH-K®.

The key to working with long-term illness and serious disease is persistence and patience. Those recovering from disease conditions need to commit to a daily practice of these techniques and also to integrate them with a balanced lifestyle including an alkaline diet, quality drinking water, adequate rest, exercise appropriate to the condition, dietary supplementation, regular sleep, avoidance of alcohol and recreational drugs, adequate sunlight and a reduction in stress.

It is also important to note that as practitioners of Matrix Reimprinting we never heal anyone, we create opportunities for people to heal themselves. It takes commitment for a person to take responsibility for their own health, and it can sometimes be a long and frustrating journey. Some people do not want to make that commitment. That is their choice and their path, and we cannot heal them. Others may say they want to make the commitment, but not put in the work required for self-healing. There are various reasons why this happens and we will address some of them below. However, for those who are prepared to make the commitment, the good news is that with these techniques excellent progress is often made.

It is also important to note that encouraging a person to take responsibility for their health is different from blaming them for the disease. With the knowledge from META-Medicine® and information from the New Biology, it is easy to see how disease states are caused by life stresses, traumas and beliefs. But this is relatively new information rather than common knowledge and is intended to enlighten people about their current condition, rather than make them feel blamed for where they are.

Considerations for Long-Term Illness and Serious Disease

The following questions highlight common challenges which arise when a person is recovering from a disease condition. Not all the challenges will apply to everyone, but if you are working with someone overcoming a disease, or if you are overcoming one yourself, work through the following questions to determine which ones are blocking recovery.

Has the Condition Been Medically Diagnosed?

The first place to start is with a medical diagnosis. It is important that the condition is sufficiently diagnosed (although you can still use Matrix Reimprinting if you are awaiting the diagnosis).

Is Medication Being Used?

You may have your own beliefs about medication. In the West we have an over-reliance on it and a tendency to look outside ourselves for healing, rather than looking within. While some medication, for example Thyroxine to control the thyroid, is certainly necessary, our medical system is dominated by a pharmaceutical industry that is driven by profit.

Whatever your views about medication, if you are practising these techniques on someone else in a professional context, *you are not legally permitted to advise people to reduce or stop taking their medication.* You must work alongside medical intervention rather than in place of it. What may happen is that a need for medication reduces when you begin this work. For example, some diabetics who have worked with these techniques have reduced their need for insulin significantly. So it can be important to advise recipients that they should visit the doctor to check if they need to reduce their medication, or keep a check on your levels if you are doing this work yourself.

Conventional EFT can be used on side-effects, withdrawal symptoms and other issues around medication (though in the first instance a doctor should always be consulted about these). For example:

'Even though these tablets make my stomach churn, I deeply love and accept myself.'

'Even though my heart is racing from stopping the tablets...'

Please note that some medications interfere with the meridian pathways and can make it difficult to carry out Matrix Reimprinting.

What Are the Disease Symptoms?

One place to start working is with the disease symptoms. Of course, the real work is to get to the underlying issues of why the disease manifested in the first place, but working with symptoms is a great place to start, as it can yield immediate results, or at least make the symptoms more manageable. The best way to work with symptoms is to use conventional EFT, for example:

'Even though I have this blood clumping, I deeply love and accept myself.'

'Even though I have this low thyroid...'

'Even though I have a slow metabolism...'

'Even though I have these low blood sugar levels...'

You are advised to tap on symptoms at least ten times per day if you are recovering from a long-term illness or serious disease.

You can also work with the symptoms more creatively through metaphor, particularly if there is physical pain. Using metaphor will help you or your recipient to notice specific changes and if pain or symptoms are changing, moving, decreasing, etc.

Simply describe the pain in terms of shape, colour, size, material, texture, sound, and so on, for example:

'Even though I have this acid running down the back of my legs, I deeply love and accept myself.'

'Even though I have this deep blue spinning circle in my chest...'

'Even though I have this barbed wire in my back...'

Describing the symptoms through metaphor will also keep you or your recipient interested when having to tap on the same issues long term.

Are there Negative Beliefs about Recovery?

Sometimes negative beliefs about an illness, perhaps passed on by the medical system, prevent healing. The body is listening, particularly if your belief system places a lot of faith in the Western medical model. So, if you have been given a glum prognosis by a GP, use Matrix Memory Reimprinting to transform the memory. Matrix Reimprinting can also be used to clear the shock around diagnosis, as Sasha shows here:

Clearing Saskia's Diagnosis

I had worked with Saskia on numerous occasions when she was recovering from cancer. She had taken a multi-dimensional approach to her healing and EFT and Matrix Reimprinting were just two of the myriad techniques that she used to recover. I was delighted when she announced she had made a full recovery.

Several months later, she booked a session with me. Although in great health, she had never worked on the shock of the diagnosis and occasionally was racked by an old fear of the cancer returning.

In the session she talked of the run-up to the diagnosis. She described cancer as being 'in the air' for that eight- to twelve-week period. This description gave me a very strong sense that when she said 'air' she actually meant 'field'. I asked her to bring to mind a picture of herself in the period that was the run-up to the diagnosis. When she did, I asked her to describe her field. She felt that it was filled with grey smoke. We used creative visualization while tapping on her earlier self. She imagined the smoke being sucked away by an angel with an industrial vacuum cleaner! We needed to take the image of her out into the open air for this to take place.

Next we invited a shaman to cleanse her aura and for it to be filled with a pink aura-cleansing mist. This took a short while and there was a very powerful sense from both of us that she was clearing her field. This image was sent out into the field through her mind and heart.

Following this, we worked on the ECHO from when she received the phone call that she had a tumour. She had been alone on the couch at

---

home, funnily enough, sitting in exactly the same place that she was for the session, as we were working on the telephone. She tapped on the ECHO created by the trauma and allowed her to release the shock around the memory. She also resourced a close friend so that she didn't have to be alone for the news. She took her ECHO to the future, showing her that she made a complete recovery. And she also filled her field with the pink healing mist from the first picture.

The next memory was the following day – the first time Saskia saw the gynaecologist and was actually diagnosed with cancer. Again she tapped on the ECHO, surrounded her with healing mist and took her to the future to see that she had returned to health.

When I asked Saskia what she needed, her reply was that she wanted to be surrounded by all the people who had contributed to her healing journey. We took her ECHO out into the woods and her friends, therapists, associates and family surrounded her in a circle. The intensity of the work was palpable and we sent a very positive image of this circle back out into the field. This was a very important session for Saskia and she was finally able to release the shock of the diagnosis.

After this session, it became clear to me that it was important to do this for all our clients who had had a shocking diagnosis. Previously I had often worked on the run-up to the condition, but for serious disease it is vital to clear the actual fields on the run-up to the condition and also to clear the energy around the diagnosis.

When Did the Problem Start and What Was your Life Like at That Time?

From a META-Medicine® perspective, this is the most important question. META-Medicine® shows us that there is always an emotional contributing factor to a physical illness. Were there any significant traumas leading up to the condition? These traumas may have been triggers to the condition.

Make a timeline of the problem (a line on a page indicating when the problem started and also when there were various peaks in the problem) and use Matrix Scene Reimprinting or Memory Reimprinting to resolve any issues or traumas leading up to the start of the illness.

You can also book a META-Medicine® diagnosis to pinpoint the cause of your condition so you know which traumas to resolve. *(For more on META-Medicine, see the Resources section.)*

Are There Accompanying Issues?

Long-term illness is often accompanied by a whole host of emotional issues. These can include feeling devalued, as you are not able to contribute financially, having financial fears, feeling socially isolated, having lowered self-esteem due to loss of status, and so on. You can tap on the feelings themselves using conventional EFT. But the real work is to get to the root of why you are feeling this way. Obviously, some of these concerns may represent very real issues to you, such as loss of living accommodation, loss of income and so on. However, there may be issues around how you are handling this. Ask yourself the following questions:

- 'Is there any excessive emotion about these issues?'
- 'Am I going into patterns learned in my earlier life?'
- 'Are there specific memories which relate to my earlier life?'

If you find specific memories, resolve them in the usual way with Matrix Scene or Matrix Memory Reimprinting. Use the Matrix Recall Techniques (*page 136*) to help you tune into any relevant memories.

What Are your Negative Core Beliefs?

Core beliefs can contribute to ill-health or disease. Use the Matrix Core-Belief Reimprinting to resolve these (*page 133*). Addressing and overcoming negative core beliefs is a key component to any healing journey.

For example, when Sasha was recovering from CFS/ME, she found that she was running the core belief 'The world is a dangerous place.'

This belief was affecting her physiology. One of the symptoms of CFS/ME is an overactive hypothalamus-pituitary-adrenal axis (HPA axis). If you recall from Chapter 3, the HPA axis is linked to our stress perception and triggers adrenaline. When Sasha resolved related memories that had taught her that the world was a dangerous place, her physiology changed. The HPA axis, usually on red alert due to perceiving dangers in the environment, began to function normally, due to a change in perception, and thus she started to recover.

Are There Blocking Beliefs?

Blocking beliefs can prevent you from healing. They include beliefs such as:

- 'I am being punished for something in a previous lifetime.'
- 'God would heal me if he really loved me.'
- 'The doctor said I would always be on medication.'
- 'I have attracted this illness to overcome it for others' benefit.'
- 'I'll never get well.'
- 'This type of injury doesn't ever heal.'
- 'I know John Smith had this illness and he only got worse.'
- 'I'm being punished.'
- 'I don't deserve a healthy body.'
- 'I've attracted or manifest this illness to learn some cosmic lesson.'
- 'This illness somehow protects me or others.'

Once again, where did these beliefs come from? What did you learn about life that made you believe this to be true? As with all of this work, get back to the root of this belief, which has come from your life experiences, and reimprint those experiences with the Foundation Techniques.

Is There a Conscious Vow?

Sometimes a vow that someone has made will be making them sick. For example, 'I will never leave my wife because my children always come first.'

If such a vow has been made but is conflicting with an individual's core self or spiritual path, it can lead to sickness. Ask the following questions:

- 'Why was this vow made in the first place?'
- 'What belief about life and my role in it was I running to make a vow such as this?'
- 'When was this belief formed?'

Again, transform related memories using the Matrix Scene or Memory Reimprinting.

Is There a Conscious Conflict?

Similar to a conscious vow, a conscious conflict may also be contributing to disease. For example, 'I'll never leave this job as it gives me stability and security, but I really want to do something that is more in line with my spiritual beliefs.'

Again, if you are going against your core, it could be making you sick. Resolve these conflicts in the same way as the conscious vow above.

Are You Sabotaging your Success?

Many people who have serious diseases are behaving in a self-sabotaging way which prevents healing. This can include eating foods which aggravate the condition, pushing themselves when they need to rest, putting earning money before healing, and so on. As always, you are looking for why this is happening and resolving related beliefs through transforming previous memories.

Is There a Benefit to Remaining Sick?

Often with long-term illness or serious disease there are subconscious reasons for remaining ill. These are known as primary or secondary gains. Please note that this is a sensitive topic and it is important to emphasize that as primary or secondary gains are subconscious, there is no blame here.

A primary gain is when the illness serves a fundamental life purpose so the body remains in illness to continue serving this purpose. For example, Karl once worked with a client who had CFS/ME. She had become ill at the start of a relationship and her partner had stayed with her because of the illness. He had become her main carer. Through working with her and allowing her to release some of the trauma that made her feel that she needed a carer, Karl found she was able to release the illness and also move on from the relationship. It wasn't that the illness was all in her mind; it was that her traumas and fears were changing her physiology to a disease state.

A secondary gain is when the illness fulfils a purpose on some level, but this is not the main reason for being ill. Examples include the fact that the illness is the only time someone gets rest or attention, or the fact that there may be some benefits or insurance which come from being ill. When the underlying stresses and fears are resolved with Matrix Reimprinting, a person is often able to release and move through the subconscious secondary gains that keep the body in a disease state.

If you are a therapist, this is an extremely sensitive issue to raise with your client. Do so only when you have built great rapport and when you have worked with your client for some time. The key is to explore the possibility of primary or secondary gains in a light and investigative manner, rather than to alienate your client by sounding accusatory. A few good questions to lead into primary or secondary gains are:

- 'If there was an important reason for keeping this illness, what would it be?'
- 'If this illness went away tomorrow what would you have to do that you don't like doing?'

Things to Remember When Working with Long-term Illness and Serious Disease

If you are a practitioner working with long-term illness and serious disease, don't try and save people. Instead, give them the tools to heal themselves.

Some aren't ready to go on that journey. Do not take this personally and make it about you. Just support in the best way you can if they are ready to make the journey and let go if they aren't. We can never really know what someone's spiritual or life purpose is, and it may not be their time to heal – there may be more they need to learn from the illness before they recover.

On this note, if you are working with this client group, insist on homework. They need to tap around ten times a day minimum using conventional EFT and to commit to resolving several memories a week using Matrix Scene or Memory Reimprinting. If they won't, it is wise not to work with them. Both Karl and Sasha have worked extensively with this client group and have only seen great results when the client is willing to work on themselves.

Also, make it clear to your clients that they may feel worse before they feel better. Sometimes resolving issues with Matrix Reimprinting can mean that there is temporarily more tiredness as the body releases and adjusts. This does not mean Matrix Reimprinting is not working. It simply means that the body needs rest to heal and change.

Jack's Wardrobe

Jack had been experiencing ME for 20 years. An incredibly positive individual, he had for some time taken responsibility for his own personal healing journey and had tried various therapies, including EFT, the Lightning Process and PSYCH-K®. Despite extensive work on himself, he still had ME and described himself as 70 per cent recovered.

After Sasha had a discussion with Jack, it became apparent that he had experienced various traumas in childhood and that although he had worked extensively on his condition, these traumas had not been touched upon. He had been put up for adoption at a very young age, due to being born out of wedlock in a Catholic community, and had also experienced trauma as a child in the Second World War. He worked on all of these in turn over a number of sessions with Sasha.

Next Jack worked on his memories of being ill in childhood. He could picture himself lying in a bed at 12 years old, being told by the doctor that he was not thriving and needed more affection. Sasha and Jack asked his ECHO to take them back to an earlier memory where he needed affection.

He took them back first to a five-year-old and then a three-year-old Jack – a very isolated and neglected little boy who desperately needed love and affection and had been passed from pillar to post for much of his young life. Jack remembered, however, that when he had been with one family there had been a lovely sheepdog there. His three-year-old ECHO chose to go to the beach with this dog. This ECHO also felt he would like a brother, a sister and a father figure, and he played with them on the beach before taking the new memory into his mind and his heart and sending it out into the field. It was a very powerful and emotional memory and Jack physically changed as the picture was sent into the field.

He completed a similar exercise for his five-year-old self, creating a picture of the family with the lovely dog once again. However, at the end of this memory, Jack's ECHO also wanted to know that he could visit the family with the dog anytime. He rather movingly created a porthole in the life of little Jack – a wardrobe similar to the one in the children's story The Lion, the Witch and the Wardrobe. *Jack's ECHO was reassured that at any time he wanted to, he could step through the wardrobe door and be with his 'new family'.*

When Jack returned to his 12-year-old ECHO, who had been lying in bed, he was now sitting up. To complete the session, his ECHO wanted healing from his new family. The new father, brother and sister entered the scene. They all laid their hands on Jack and gave him healing. Jack's ECHO also needed to know that things were going to be alright in the future. So Jack took him forward in time to show him his successful careers. He also took his new family along so that they could be proud of him.

Although Jack still had much healing to do, clearing the trauma from his early memories and creating a porthole through which his younger ECHO could experience consistency was an important part of his journey.

CHAPTER 16

Positive Life Experiences and Guiding Stars

So far we have presented the popular therapeutic model, which presupposes that at conception we are a perfect template that gets spoiled by various life traumas. As therapists we look for the issues that we need to fix. We search for our life traumas, birth traumas and pre-birth traumas, even past-life traumas. While we have shown that resolving trauma is relevant for changing our beliefs and transforming our health, there is also another aspect of working with our life issues that often gets overlooked: our positive life experiences.

Obviously, positive experiences are fundamental to a happy existence. But what happens when we have an experience that is so positive that we spend the rest of our life trying to recreate it? Those perfect moments in time are known as 'guiding stars' and are examined in *The Advanced Patterns of EFT* by Silvia Hartmann. We will explore them briefly here as they can be fundamental to understanding and resolving destructive behaviour patterns.

GUIDING STARS

Sometimes we have a moment in life that is utterly perfect and we reach a state of pure bliss. There is nothing wrong with feeling such profound love, profound connection and profound happiness. The problem is when that moment creates an effect similar to an ECHO and part of our consciousness becomes locked in space and time. Then we feel we need to recreate all the circumstances around the event in order to get us back there. Ultimately, the subconscious is trying to get back to a state of bliss and has our best interests in mind. But the path to that bliss can be very destructive and have far-reaching consequences.

Because this behaviour is automatic, we usually don't know why we are doing it or how it originated. We very rarely say, for example, 'Ah, I am trying to recreate the perfect moment I had with my father when he showed me love when I was seven.' Instead we might find ourselves saying, 'I don't know why I keep acting this way with men. It just feels automatic. No matter how hard I try to stop it, I keep repeating the same pattern.' So our guiding stars can account for our unexplained behaviour.

Guiding Stars and Vibrations

We create guiding stars because we are vibrational beings. We resonate at a vast number of different frequencies, depending on our surroundings, what is happening, who is involved, and so on. There will be moments in your life when you feel a perfect resonance with all that surrounds you. In that moment, everything will be vibrating at a frequency that feels perfect to you. And if that moment creates extreme bliss, a guiding star may be formed.

To understand this, imagine that you have just heard a particular musical chord and it really resonated with you. In fact, it filled you with a feeling of bliss unlike any you had ever experienced before. It created a moment of transcendental beauty and in that moment you felt that everything was perfect.

If it took place when you were hearing Beethoven's Fifth Symphony at the Albert Hall, you might go back to the Albert Hall when the same orchestra was playing, under the same conductor, and sit in the same seat, with the same friend sitting next to you, in order to recreate that feeling. But you'd have to recreate every single one of the circumstances in which you heard the chord to recreate the feeling. That would include the environment, the instruments, the passion with which those instruments were played, the person that was sitting next to you when you heard the chord, and so on. It would be impossible to match all of these variables. Also, you would have changed since that moment and would be likely to be vibrating at a totally different frequency too. The experience could be perceived as exactly the same by your conscious mind, but your subconscious would pick up the differences. This would then lead to disappointment and further pursuit of the original event.

This is very much like what happens when we have that perfect guiding star moment – we keep subconsciously trying to recreate the circumstances of the event, at the expense of living in the present.

Revealing a Guiding Star

The shock that can accompany the revelation of a guiding star can be devastating. When a person realizes that their whole life has been dedicated to recreating a past event, they can become extremely depressed. If you discover a guiding star in your own life, you are advised to tap on yourself using EFT to bring down any emotional intensity and then consult an experienced Matrix Reimprinting or EFT practitioner who has an understanding of working with guiding stars.

If you are a Matrix Reimprinting or EFT practitioner and you suspect that your client might be running a guiding star, approach the topic with extreme caution and make sure you have plenty of time in the session or afterwards to deal with the emotional consequences that it may create for your client.

For more information on the consequences of revealing a guiding star, consult *The Advanced Patterns of EFT* by Silvia Hartmann.

Examples of Guiding Stars

Many examples of guiding stars can be seen in day-to-day life (although you are advised not to point these out to people, as doing so can have far-reaching consequences).

One example is that of a young woman who was the daughter of an alcoholic going on to marry another alcoholic. The guiding star was the moment when her father, coming home drunk from the pub, sat her on his knee and told her for the first and only time that he loved her. She continued trying to recreate that moment by having intimate relationships with other alcoholics.

A similar example is given by Silvia Hartmann in *The Advanced Patterns of EFT*. Her client ate strawberry ice-cream by the bucketful and resisted using conventional EFT to tap on her cravings. Her guiding star had been created when at seven years old her father had bought her a strawberry ice-cream on the beach and put his arms around her. She had had little contact with him, as he was always working, and this was the only time in her entire childhood that she felt he loved her. As a result she continued to try and recreate that moment.[1]

A further example is that of a sportsman who won his first competition on a school sports day and spent the rest of his life trying to emulate that feeling by chasing the gold medal.

Guiding stars are also often prevalent in drug users. Often the first hit is so significantly powerful that a person will continue to use the substance to try and return to that place, even though the feeling is not usually experienced again as it was the first time.

Karl's Personal Experience with a Guiding Star

Karl's personal guiding star was touched upon in the introduction to this book, when he told the story of how he had experienced a moment of enlightenment on a beach and then spent the next 20 years trying to recreate it by constantly needing to travel and find himself on beaches. This guiding star was detrimental to his whole life until he realized it and worked on it.

Interestingly, Karl uncovered his guiding star while he was actually on the beach where he had originally had the experience, searching as usual for that perfect moment. While on the beach he was reading the section about guiding stars in Silvia Hartmann's *Advanced Patterns of EFT* and had the shocking realization that not only did he have a guiding star, but he was actually on that beach at that moment because of the guiding star! He was also listening to the same music (Kate Bush's *The Hounds of Love*), drinking cava, because that's what he had been drinking in that enlightenment moment, even though it wasn't his usual drink, and sitting on a deckchair that was positioned at exactly the same angle as the one on which he'd had the experience. Until he'd recognized that he was running a guiding star, he had not been conscious of recreating the same scene. It was his subconscious that had been driving him to do it.

While the scene itself was not detrimental, Karl didn't have any peace because he was trying to get back to the earlier experience. So it wasn't the beach itself that was the problem, but the effort he was going to subconsciously to try and recreate that scene.

Realizing this was a tremendously significant turning point for Karl, as he stopped seeking the experience of enlightenment outside himself and was able to start fully engaging with living in the present.

Sasha's Personal Experience with a Guiding Star

Sasha's personal guiding star was based around the moment that she got her GCSE results and found she had done really well. With a poor school attendance record due to ill-health and emotional problems, she had below average predicted grades for her GCSEs. Despite being off sick and having lots of emotional disruption in her life, however, she had still studied hard at home and got the joint highest grades out of all the girls in her school year. This was a massive achievement and she received lots of praise and encouragement. This became her guiding star. When she learned about guiding stars at 34, she realized that she had spent the previous 18 years trying to recreate that moment.

She had stayed behind to repeat her A-levels when her friends went to university, as she had not been happy with the grades that she had got, and had worked extremely hard to get exceptional grades. She had refused to finish university the year she was going to graduate, as she did not feel that she had put enough work in to get the grade she desired, so she stayed on another year to ensure she got a higher grade. She then took courses continually up until she was 34, repeatedly having to get excellent grades and be top of the class. She even studied whilst she was disabled with ME and could hardly walk, read or concentrate! She had countless qualifications and certificates and was always studying. The consequence was that she pushed herself very hard and had frequently put achieving over joy and fun.

When she realized what her guiding star was, she was utterly shocked and dismayed, and had to tap for some time on the consequences. That was several years ago and she has not felt the need to gain a certificate since!

How to Treat Guiding Stars with Matrix Reimprinting

Just as you cannot change negative subconscious beliefs by willpower alone, it is very challenging to go against guiding stars. The way to work with them is not to treat the actual memory where they were created. It can be really devastating for people if you suggest that you are going to take away the emotional intensity of the perfect moment. So instead of treating the moment, transform the moment. Show the younger self in the memory that they can still have that experience, but in other situations. For example, the young girl could experience love from her father without him being drunk or Karl could have the spiritual connection in other places, rather than just on the beach. This will stop your recipient from trying to recreate that single perfect moment.

CHAPTER 17

Matrix Reimprinting in Action

The following are two live sessions of Matrix Reimprinting, which will give you a sense of the techniques in action. In the first session Karl uses Matrix Scene Reimprinting and demonstrates working ECHO to ECHO. In the second session Sasha uses Matrix Memory Reimprinting on a single memory.

SARAH AND THE LIFT

Karl worked with Sarah on an issue of claustrophobia.

Karl: *Sarah, what's the problem you are facing?*

Sarah: *I have claustrophobia. I've had it for years.*

Karl: *What triggers it?*

Sarah: *The most recent thing is probably the en-suite shower in my flat. It's really small, and sometimes when it's really hot and steamy in there I start to get a little bit…*

Karl: *Just close your eyes and get into that feeling of being in that closed space when it's hot and steamy.*

Sarah: *I already have it.*

Karl: *What do you feel and where do you feel it? Am I OK to tap on you?*

Sarah: *Yes, you're OK. It's all in my chest.*

Karl: *How intense is it right now?*

Sarah: *It's about a five.*

Karl: *Does it get higher than this?*

Sarah: *Yes. But right now it just feels as though I've a weight in my chest.*

Karl: *OK. What colour is that weight in your chest?*

Sarah: *It's a smoky grey.*

Karl: *What size is that smoky grey colour in your chest?*

Sarah: *It's quite big. It's quite dense.*

Karl: *What would it be made of? Metal, wood, air, water?*

Sarah: *Something like really thick smoke.*

Karl: *What would the emotion be in that thick, dense, heavy, smoky feeling in your chest?*

Sarah: *Panic.*

Karl: *Is it still a five? Is it getting worse now as we're tapping? Does it bring up more information?*

Sarah: *It's about a six.*

Karl: *That grey dense smoke in your chest, what's the earliest time you can remember feeling that? Just whatever comes to mind. Don't try to force anything.*

Sarah: *The first memory that pops up is when I was staying at my aunt's house years ago. I was probably in my late twenties. I'm in the bedroom. She has a four-storey house and I'm on the top floor. I'm sharing a room with my friend Louise. She's in bed and I'm sleeping on a mattress on the floor.*

Karl: *You can see yourself in that picture, can you?*

Sarah: *Yes. I've just woken up and the room is pitch black. There is no light coming in.*

Karl: *What do you feel now, when you look at that picture and it's pitch black?*

Sarah: *My chest is getting tighter. The smoke is getting denser in my chest.*

Karl: *OK. What I want you to do is imagine stepping into that picture and explaining who you are to yourself in your late twenties. Does she know who you are?*

Sarah: *No. Basically, she's woken up and she can't see any light and she can't breathe, so she's running up and down the walls, slapping the walls, trying to find the light switch.*

Karl: *So maybe the first thing you need to do is turn the light on for her?*

Sarah: *OK. The light's on now.*

Karl: *Just tell her to be calm. Tell her you've come to help her because you're sick of feeling claustrophobic and you've found a way to sort this out once and for all.*

Sarah: *OK.*

Karl: *She's alright with you being there, I take it?*

Sarah: *Oh, yes. She's really happy.*

Karl: *So start tapping on her to calm her down and ask her what she's feeling.*

Sarah: *She's really panicky. She was feeling completely swamped by the darkness and now she's stunned because the light has gone on really brightly.*

Karl: *Just tap on her and talk to her. Tap on her until she calms right down.*

Sarah communicates with her ECHO.

Sarah: *She's alright. She's laughing a bit. She doesn't want the light off again because it's so dark, but she doesn't want it on all night because Louise won't be able to sleep then.*

Karl: *OK. Just ask her what she's feeling right now. I want to leave her in a good place before we go any further.*

Sarah: *She feels better now. It's just been a bit of a shock. She was so disoriented when she woke up, it really freaked her out.*

Karl: *Does a time come to mind when she felt this feeling before?*

Sarah: *Yes. She says the first time was on the boat.*

Karl: *Can you see the picture of being on the boat?*

Sarah: *Yes. I'm on an RAF sailing boat. I'm on an expedition. I think I'm 19.*

Karl: *What's happening in that picture?*

Sarah: *I'm asleep at the front of the boat, the bow. There are only two girls in the crew and we're both at the front.*

Karl: *OK. What's happening in that picture?*

Sarah: *It's night-time. I wake up and it feels as though the ceiling of the boat is practically touching my face. I have to get off.*

Karl: *Again I want you to imagine stepping into that picture. Make it light if you need to.*

Sarah: *I think I need to make that space bigger. I'm going to put a door in above her and I'm going to open that now.*

Karl: *I want you to tap on her. Is she OK? Does she know who you are? Explain why you're here.*

Sarah: *I need to take her up on deck.*

Karl: *So take her up on deck.*

Sarah: *OK, we're walking through the door and standing on the top deck. We're in a marina somewhere.*

Karl: *Tap on her until she calms down.*

Sarah: *OK.*

Karl: *How is she feeling? Is it the grey feeling or is it a different feeling? Ask her where she feels the panicky feeling.*

Sarah: *She's saying it felt as though the ceiling was moving down and going to squash her.*

Karl: *How is she feeling now, though?*

Sarah: *She's finding it really hard to get her breath, so she's just sucking the air in.*

Karl: *Just tap on her karate chop point and say 'Even though you're finding it hard to breathe, you're OK.'*

Several rounds of tapping are carried out on Sarah's ECHO.

Karl: *How is she doing now?*

Sarah: *She's alright. She's calmed down.*

Karl: *Good. I want you to ask her where to go now. If she has an early memory of feeling like this, when is that? How old was she?*

Sarah: *Thirteen just popped into my head.*

Karl: *OK. Do you have a picture of when you were 13 when you had this pressure in your head, this tightness in your chest and this inability to breathe?*

Sarah: *Not yet.*

Karl: *It's alright. Don't try too hard, just focus on the pressure, the pain in your chest and the inability to breathe.*

Sarah: *I still can't remember a specific time, but I know when I was 13 I felt suffocated. I wasn't getting on with Mum and my stepdad. We were living in Norwich and I absolutely hated it. So I felt suffocated then.*

Karl: *Do you have a picture of around that time? What picture comes to mind of when you're 13 and feel suffocated and trapped by life?*

Sarah: *I'm sitting up in my room, looking out of the window, wishing I was somewhere else. I just feel really sad.*

Karl: *Where's all that sadness? Where do you feel that?*

Sarah: *Around my eyes.*

Karl: *I'm just going to tap on you and see what comes up: 'Even though I feel all this sadness I love and accept myself anyway.'*

A round of EFT is carried out on the sadness.

Karl: *How is it now?*

Sarah: *It's about a seven.*

Karl: *What do you think the sadness is connected to?*

Sarah: *She's stuck in a house and she thinks nobody cares about her. She feels completely isolated and alone.*

Karl: *Imagine stepping into this picture where she feels isolated and alone and start to talk to her. Tell her you're there to help her, you love her and you know how lonely she's feeling right now. Ask her where she feels all that loneliness.*

Sarah: *It's in her chest.*

Karl: *Go over to her and imagine picking up her hand and saying that even though she feels really lonely and really sad, she's still a good girl.*

Sarah: *I don't think the words 'good girl' are right for her. She's looking at me as if to say 'What?' I'll say 'still OK' instead.*

Karl: *Start to tap on her and tell her that things will work out great, but you know how sad she's feeling right now, how alone she's feeling and how suffocated she's feeling. Take as long as you need and bring in any resources you need.*

Sarah communicates with her ECHO.

Karl: *What's happening now?*

Sarah: *It's quite a stark bedroom, so what I've done is moved the bunk beds and put a big squashy sofa there. I'm sitting on it next to her, I've got my arm round her and I've told her all the positive things that are going to happen to her in the future.*

Karl: *How is she with that?*

Sarah: *She's starting to relax and she's laughing. She's amazed by what's going to happen. I'm saying, 'I always hated this house and it's really funny being back here.'*

Karl: *Ask her what else she'd like to do to the room to make it really special.*

Sarah: *She'd like to move her bedroom downstairs and make it an extension off the kitchen. She wants her space. It was claustrophobic upstairs in that house because there was only a tiny little square patch of landing so she was right next door to her mum and stepdad and baby sister and she could hear everything. She heard her mum and stepdad having sex one night and it completely freaked her out. She screamed, 'Shut up!'*

Karl: *Ask her about this feeling of suffocation. Is it just this house or does she often feel suffocated?*

Sarah: *She often feels suffocated.*

Karl: *Ask her if she has any memories of where this came from. Can she show you a picture of it?*

Sarah: *She's saying, 'Nana's bedroom. Go back to when we used to have to sleep in that bedroom.'*

Karl: *How old are you in the picture in your nana's bedroom? Can you see yourself there?*

Sarah: *Yes. I'm around ten.*

Karl: *Do you have a picture of being ten years old and in your nana's bedroom and feeling this grey smoky feeling in your chest?*

Sarah: *I'm not sure if she has that feeling in her chest right now... She's in bed and it's night-time and there's a cupboard on the other side of the room with a door which is always a little bit ajar and she's really scared of what's inside the cupboard.*

Karl: *Again, step into that picture and do whatever you need to do. Turn on the light, reassure her she's OK and you're there to help her. How is she?*

Sarah: *She's looking pretty amazed. She's standing behind me now and I'm going to open the cupboard and have a look inside and show her it's just a tiny little cupboard with some bits and bobs inside.*

Karl: *She's seen it's safe now?*

Sarah: *Yes.*

Karl: *Ask her what she would like to do to make this room warmer and lighter and happier and safer.*

Sarah: *She wants her mum to sleep in there with her.*

Karl: *Do you want to bring Mum into the room?*

Sarah: *Yes. There are two single beds in there, so Mum is going to sleep in there with her.*

Karl: *I want you to go and speak to Mum and little Sarah and just say you have this problem with feeling claustrophobic and you want to see where it comes from. Ask Mum if she knows.*

Sarah: *She's saying she used to get stuck in the lift a lot when they lived in a tower block in Singapore.*

Karl: *Does she have a memory of one of the times when she got stuck in Singapore?*

Sarah: *Yes.*

Karl: *You have that picture now, have you?*

Sarah: *Yes. I'm standing behind her in the lift when the door jams.*

Karl: *Are you going to get the doors to open or step out of the lift? Do whatever you need to do.*

Sarah: *I think we'll step out of the lift.*

Karl: *Just get down on your knees and talk to young Sarah and ask her what she's feeling. How old is she?*

Sarah: *I think she's four.*

Karl: *What is she feeling right now?*

Sarah: *She's scared.*

Karl: *What of? Is it of being trapped in the lift?*

Sarah: *Yes. She's saying that the lifts are so scary here.*

Karl: *So do a set-up with her and tap through the points with her. What does she feel and where does she feel it?*

Sarah: *I think she's a little bit angry with the lift.*

Karl: *OK. Tap on that anger. What would she like to have happen? Say it's a lift that does exactly what she wants all the time. What would it do? What would it be like?*

Sarah: *I think it would be a glass lift.*

Karl: *What can she see from the glass lift? Can she see things that she really wants to see, like the sea?*

Sarah: *Yes, that's a good idea, we'll make it that way. And really big. I'll put some big cushions on the floor so it's comfy in there as well.*

Karl: *Tell her it's her picture. She can make it whatever she wants. It can be a happy place now.*

Sarah: *She has fairies flying around. I never thought I would say that! It's just a real little magical land that a four-year-old would love.*

Karl: *When you look at that magical lift now, what are the colours and emotions around the picture?*

Sarah: *Purple and raspberry colours.*

Karl: *Wonderful. Make that picture bigger and brighter. Bring that through your mind. Feel all the feelings washing through your body. Bring it up into your heart and send that picture back out into the Matrix.*

There is a pause while Sarah does this.

Karl: *Now ask her if there are any other times when she would like to go and change a scary lift into a magical lift. Does she have another picture of that?*

Sarah: *No. I think that one sums up a lot of similar times.*

Karl: *So the lift is OK now?*

Sarah: *Yes. Every time the door opens it just seems like something out of Disney!*

Karl: *OK, let's test what we've done. Go back to the first picture, the one of being at your aunt's house, and speak to the you that's in that house. How is she feeling now?*

Sarah: *She's OK. She's quite calm actually.*

Karl: *Ask her, 'Could you turn off the light now?' If she were to think about turning off the light, how would she feel?*

Sarah: *She would be just fine.*

Karl: *Try it and see. You can stand there and turn it back on if it bothers her. (Pause.) How is she?*

Sarah: *Fine. There's no reaction.*

Karl: *Can she go back to sleep now?*

Sarah: *Yes.*

Karl: *Imagine going to the picture on the boat with the two girls. Are you up on the deck there with the 19-year-old Sarah?*

Sarah: *Yes.*

Karl: *Ask her if she feels OK to go back below deck now and go to sleep. If she wants, she can leave that porthole there.*

Sarah: *She says she would rather be sleeping in the bigger part of the boat.*

Karl: *Create that. Make that part of the boat the bigger part. Make it so that she can see there's a really starry night and a full moon and maybe leave the porthole open.*

Sarah: *That's better. There's a big porthole above her now that she can open and close.*

Karl: *What about the picture of the ten-year-old in Nan's bedroom?*

Sarah: *That one is fine. She's cuddling Mum.*

Karl: *The four-year-old in the lift, how is she?*

Sarah: *She's really happy.*

Karl: *How do you feel now? How's the smoke in your chest right now?*

Sarah: *My chest feels clearer. I feel a bit disorientated because I've had my eyes closed for so long.*

Karl: *OK, I want to test the original thought that caused the feeling of claustrophobia. Imagine being in the hot steamy shower – how does that feel now?*

Sarah: *There's none of the grey smoky feeling in my chest.*

Following the session Sarah was able to use the shower without any of the feelings of claustrophobia.

MILLIE AND THE EYEDROPS

In this session Sasha worked with Millie, who had a traumatic memory of a hospital visit as a small child.

Sasha: *So you've got a memory from when you were five or six years old that's still traumatic for you?*

Millie: *Yes.*

Sasha: *Start telling me about it before there is any emotional intensity and I'll stop you, or you stop yourself, if the intensity gets above a two or three.*

Millie: *Basically, my mum's getting together a little pot of sweets and a load of colouring books because we're on our way to hospital.*

Sasha: *Can I tap on you?*

Millie: *Yes, sure.*

Sasha: *Close your eyes. Can you see that little girl on the way to hospital?*

Millie: *Yes.*

Sasha: *What does she look like?*

Millie: *Tiny. She has brown hair, big glasses.*

Sasha: *What does she look like in terms of emotion? What's going on for her?*

Millie: *She's apprehensive – she knows something is going on.*

Sasha: *Just pause that scene for me a moment. Stand in front of her, step into the scene and let her know that you've come to help her let go of some of the feelings she's having. Check she's OK with that.*

Millie: *She's fine with that.*

Sasha: *Silently in your mind ask her what her fears and worries are.*

Millie communicates with ECHO.

Millie: *She's scared of being held down, scared of going blind.*

Sasha: *Take her hand in your hand and start tapping on her as I tap on you. Is she OK with being tapped on?*

Millie: *Yes.*

Sasha: *Keep tapping on her. Ask her where she feels that fear.*

Millie: *It's in her mid-section.*

Sasha: *Repeat after me as you tap on the side of her hand: 'Even though you've got this fear in your mid-section that you're going to go blind, you're still a great little girl.'*

This is repeated by Millie. They then repeat the reminder phrases 'fear of going blind' and 'fear in the mid-section' while tapping on the ECHO's points.

Sasha: *How's she feeling now?*

Millie: *She isn't feeling safe.*

Sasha: *Is there anyone or anything she would bring in to help her feel safe?*

Millie: *Actually, she just wants to go outside on the swings for a while.*

Sasha: *Let her do that.*

Millie: *OK.*

Sasha: *How has that changed things?*

Millie: *She feels a lot calmer. She's ready to face what's going to happen now.*

Sasha: *Tap on her again. With all the knowledge and the wisdom you have now, speaking as your higher self, what would you say to that younger self about what she's about to go through?*

Millie: *That it's really not that bad. That the fear is worse than actually going through it.*

Sasha: *How is she responding to that?*

Millie: *She doesn't believe me.*

Sasha: *Ask her what she needs in order to believe you.*

Millie: *I think for me to be there with her throughout.*

Sasha: *Does she need anything else – a teddy bear, a friend?*

Millie: *No, she's alright with me.*

Sasha: *OK. Facing her now, take her hand and let her know she's completely safe. Ask her if it's OK to go through that memory now, knowing that you're there and you're going to help her to release the fears or the feelings she's having. How is she with that?*

Millie: *She's a bit nervous.*

Sasha: *Where is she feeling the nerves?*

Millie: *In her shoulders. It's as if she wants to be held back.*

Sasha: *Take her hands again very gently. 'Even though you have this nervousness in your shoulders, you are still a great little girl.'*

This is repeated by Millie as she taps on her ECHO.

Sasha: *What colour is the nervousness?*

Millie: *Purple.*

Sasha: OK. *'Even though you have this purple nervousness in your shoulders you're still a great little girl.'*

Repeated whilst Millie taps on her ECHO and followed by a round of tapping with a reminder phrase.

Millie: *It's better.*

Sasha: *Ask her if there's something she would like inside her body to help her feel courage, to help her feel strong.*

Millie: *Pink and white clouds.*

Sasha: *Where are those pink and white clouds going to come from?*

Millie: *A Care Bear that I used to have.*

Sasha: *Perfect. She's got it there with her now?*

Millie: *Yes.*

Sasha: *Brilliant. Are those pink and white clouds going in?*

Millie: *Yes.*

Sasha: *That's perfect. Let her know she can keep the Care Bear with her the whole time and he can keep giving her those pink and white clouds if that makes her feel good. Ask her if there's anything else she needs in order to be able to go forward now.*

Millie: *She wants Mum there with her.*

Sasha: *Bring Mum in.*

Millie: *Mum's there. She's ready now, to go through it.*

Sasha: *Continue to talk me through the memory. Where do we go next?*

Millie: *To when he was trying to hold me down on the table and…*

Sasha: *Do you have an image of that?*

Millie: *Yes. She's being pinned down. She's screaming.*

Sasha: *OK. Just pause the scene there. Take hold of her hand. Tap on her as you did before.*

Millie taps on her ECHO.

Sasha: *I want you to ask her what she needs in order to feel differently about the situation.*

Millie: *It needs to be done differently.*

Sasha: *We'll make sure it is. Check in with her – I want to know what she's feeling right now. What are her life messages in this situation? What has she learned about being pinned down like this?*

Millie: *I don't know.*

Sasha: *OK, we'll come back to that in a bit. For now, where's the intensity for her?*

Millie: *In her head. He's got her pinned down by her head.*

Sasha: *Ask her what she wants to do.*

Millie: *She doesn't want him to put his hand on her head and hold her. And my mum's crying.*

Sasha: *We need to sort this out, don't we? If it were to play out differently, would you need your mum to assert herself?*

Millie: *Yes. I would be sitting on her lap, I think.*

Sasha: *OK. Just reassure your younger self. Take her hand. The doctor has let go now, has he?*

Millie: *Yes.*

Sasha: *Just tap on her and reassure her that she's going to be really safe and the best way for this to happen is for her to sit on Mum's lap. Does that feel OK?*

Millie: *Yes. But she's still afraid of what's going to happen.*

Sasha: *OK. Do we need to do something about that doctor?*

Millie: *Yes. Actually, she's a nurse.*

Sasha: *A nurse. What do we need to do about her?*

Millie: *Make her hands not so big.*

Sasha: *OK. How should we do it? Does she need to take one of those 'Shrink me' Alice in Wonderland pills?*

Millie: *Yes. That pill would work very well!*

Sasha: *Has that shifted it?*

Millie: *Yes.*

Sasha: *Is she more in proportion now?*

Millie: *Yes.*

Sasha: *So what happens next?*

Millie: *She wants to see if the eyedrops are going to be OK.*

Sasha: *So before she has the drops put in her eyes, take her hand and start tapping on the side of it. Just let her know you're there for her and she has those clouds swirling round from the Care Bear. Let her peacefully and calmly have that experience. Let me know when that feels complete or if you need any help or support to get to the next stage.*

Millie: *No, she's fine.*

Sasha: *She's had the eyedrops?*

Millie: *Yes.*

Sasha: *It was quite painless?*

Millie: *Yes.*

Sasha: *That's brilliant. Is there anything else that happens after that?*

Millie: *No.*

Sasha: *That's great. Where would she like to go now?*

Millie: *Just home. Back to the swings.*

Sasha: *Great. Take her there. Does she want anybody else with her?*

Millie: *My mum and dad.*

Sasha: *Bring them in. What is she doing now? Is she laughing, playing?*

Millie: *She's just swinging on her swings.*

Sasha: *OK. A smile on her face?*

Millie: *Yes.*

Sasha: *Take that image of her on the swings and make it really strong, so you have a very strong sense of her enjoyment and happiness. Take that image into your mind and send a signal throughout your whole body, letting it know that this is released now, that this is a positive memory. Let that travel through every cell in your body, reprogramming and rewiring them on every level, and then take that image into your heart. Make it really bold and bright. What colours are associated with that image?*

Millie: *Pink and white.*

Sasha: *Ah, the colours of the Care Bear! Make those pink and white colours really bright around that picture. Get a really strong sense of that in your heart. Let all the freedom, all the joy, all the happiness, all the positivity of that moment soak into the image. When they feel really strong, take that image from your heart and send it back out into the universe. Let me know when that feels complete.*

There is a pause whilst Millie carries out the work.

Millie: *OK.*

Sasha: *Brilliant. Just come back now for a second. Open your eyes. When we go back what I want you to do is close your eyes and silently play the original memory. I just want you to see, first of all, if anything has changed and if there's any intensity remaining at any point. Just play it through gently.*

There is a pause whilst Millie tests the work.

Millie: *There's still a little bit of intensity. It's when I was trying to escape and I got out of the door and got under some seats. They got hold of my waist and pulled me back out.*

Sasha: *OK, so we've missed a bit. Go back into the picture. Where's the intensity?*

Millie: *It's all over. It's panic because they've got hold of me.*

The scene is paused and several rounds of tapping are carried out on the panic.

Sasha: *Now talk to her. With all the knowledge and wisdom that you have, and speaking as your higher self, let her know it's going to be alright.*

Millie: *She's fine now.*

Sasha: *Take that part of yourself to the swings.*

Millie: *She's there. She's happy.*

Sasha: *OK, test that part again. Can you see them pulling you by the waist?*

Millie: *No. It's fine. She's on the swings.*

Sasha: *Now I want to test the whole thing again. Run the memory through, really intensely now. Make it a big vivid picture on a big screen. Make the sounds really loud. Make the eyedrops and the nurse's hands really vivid.*

Millie: *I don't really see it like that any more.*

Sasha: *What do you see? You can open your eyes.*

Millie: *It doesn't seem like anything at all now. It seems a bit silly that I got myself in that much of a state!*

Sasha: *But understandable, because you were tiny.*

Millie: *Yes.*

Sasha: *Great work. Well done!*

After the session Sasha and Millie discussed the theme of powerlessness that had arisen in the session, and Millie revealed that it had been a theme for her throughout her life.

CHAPTER 18

Further Case Studies

The following are case studies from other Matrix Reimprinting practitioners which highlight the power and simplicity of this technique. The contact details of the practitioners who carried out the following sessions can be found at the back of the book. The names of the clients have been changed to protect their privacy.

Josh and the Peanuts

Rebekah Roberts

I worked with an eight-year-old boy called Josh on a fear that had been having an increasing negative effect on his day-to-day life. He had a nut allergy, meaning that his mum had to carry an antihistamine injector with her at all times and they had both got into the habit of checking the labelling on all food to see whether it might contain traces of nuts. This had been manageable until an incident which turned Josh's caution when eating food into outright fear.

Josh loved pumpkin seeds and on this particular day had eaten a few mouthfuls of his favourite brand when his mum picked up the packet and declared, 'It says, "May contain traces of nuts!"' in an alarmed voice. Actually, the contents of the packet hadn't changed; the company had just taken a more cautious approach to labelling. However, in that split-second, hearing the alarm in his mum's voice and being aware that he'd now ingested the seeds, Josh went into shock and so a new fear was created.

Over the next few months Josh began refusing more and more foods until his diet was reducing down to bagels and Marmite and little else, and he was losing weight as a result. He had also started to have panic attacks at night and he told his mum that it felt as though his throat was closing up when he lay down to sleep, which was very distressing for both of them.

Josh knew about EFT as his mum was an EFT practitioner and he'd used it in the past on other issues, but with this he refused to let his mum tap on him and wouldn't accept help from anyone else, including other professionals. He was a bright boy and very independent, and it was very challenging for his mum, as she had all the tools literally at her fingertips.

I knew I had to approach this from a different angle and so while we were having lunch one day I started telling Josh about Matrix Reimprinting and how we can effectively time-travel to overcome fears that developed in our past. He was intrigued, so I asked him to picture the day when he first became scared of eating food in case it had nuts in it. Like most children, he is incredibly visual and creative and so he had a vivid picture of his younger self immediately in his mind. I told him that in a moment we were going to step into that picture and help him. Before we did, I asked him if he would like to gain any superpowers or bring anyone with him, like his hero, Spiderman, or someone similar. He said, 'No, just me.' He felt he had everything he needed already.

Munching away on his bagel, he closed his eyes and imagined walking up to his ECHO. He didn't want me to tap on him, so I tapped on myself as a surrogate for him. I told him to ask his ECHO how he was feeling, which he did, but said he didn't want to tell me anything about it. I said, 'That's absolutely fine, I don't need to know anything. Just be a best friend to that younger you and teach him how to tap.' This was all he needed to become enthusiastic about it.

For two minutes we sat there, him with his eyes closed munching away and me tapping silently on myself on his behalf. Once he had finished he opened his eyes and said, 'That looks a little bit happier now,' in a matter-of-fact kind of way. I asked him what the picture looked like now and he told me that at first it had been like one of those old-fashioned picture books where when you flick through the pages quickly it looks like an animation. Once he'd tapped on his ECHO it had turned into a 'frozen picture'. There was more work to do and he was very happy to make this his new project and go in bit by bit to help his younger self more and more. He decided that each time he did that he'd give himself a smiley face sticker to congratulate himself.

Then his mum came into the room and he proceeded to do a Matrix Reimprinting session on her, remembering that she had a fear of heights from when they had been hillwalking a couple of years before. It was such a beautiful moment, seeing that he truly understood this work and was empowered to help his mum too.

Two months later I rang and spoke to Josh and his mum to find out how things were with his eating. He was very chatty on the phone and what I noticed was that he was also comfortable with talking about his issues. He'd been very private before and his new openness made it obvious that changes had taken place. He told me that he'd been 'time-travelling' quite a lot and now the food phobia was completely gone and he'd been eating chocolate, biscuits, cake, ice cream and custard! He was also happy to eat a wider variety of food, including vegetables, chicken and rice. All in all, he was brighter, more alert, happier and free of the fear that had curtailed his eating habits so drastically before.

Baby Peggy and the Pram

Caroline Rolling

Now in her early seventies, Margaret had been claustrophobic for as long as she could remember. She felt unable to travel in the back seat of a car, or by train, bus, plane or boat, and often felt uncomfortable in unfamiliar places where she was unsure of how to open windows or get out easily. Even parking in multi-storey car parks was a problem. Things had become worse for her when her husband had accidently locked her in their car. She had only been trapped for a minute or two, but that was more than enough for her to feel panic. She told me she had sought help for this phobia a few years before but had been told that as it had been with her for such a long time, she would always have it. Thankfully, she had recently heard about EFT and decided to see if it would help.

As the memory of being trapped in her car had left Margaret feeling uncomfortable in the only means of transport she used, we started the session there. Margaret rated her level of intensity at the mention of being trapped as 'higher than ten'. Her face was flushed and heart pounding, so we tapped on the physical symptoms she was experiencing. After one round she rated the SUDS level as seven and her face had lost some of the redness; the second round saw a drop to a SUDS level of five. Halfway through the third round Margaret stopped tapping and described a memory of herself at 15 months old.

Her mother was picking up baby Peggy (as she was called then), saying, 'I don't have time to deal with you now, you'll have to go to sleep,' and putting her in a pram, securing the cover in place. Margaret said Peggy didn't want to be in the pram, didn't like the smell (like oilcloth) and wanted to play with her brother. She told me that Peggy couldn't see over the pram cover and was trying to pull it down with her fingers but couldn't do it. She was crying.

I asked Margaret to explain to baby Peggy who she was and that she was there to help her. Margaret said that Peggy understood. As I tapped on Margaret, she tapped on baby Peggy. We began by focusing on Peggy feeling upset and crying, and when she had calmed down a little, we tapped on her anger with her mother for putting her in the pram. Importantly, Margaret herself was not distressed throughout this process.

Once Margaret said baby Peggy was alright now and understood that her mother had been doing the best she could, I asked her if there was anything Peggy needed to make things better. She told me she wanted her to ask her mother to take off the pram cover. She did so, the cover was removed and Margaret's face and posture visibly calmed and relaxed. When asked how Peggy was, she replied, 'Happy. She's asleep now.' Before ending the session, I checked to see how Margaret felt on thinking about being trapped in her car. She could see the comedy in it and actually laughed.

I saw Margaret a few days later and gave her a lift in my car. Without any thought, she offered to make room for another passenger and sat in the back seat, where she stayed calmly and happily until reaching her destination. She now regularly uses a lift (in a multi-storey car park!) and says she feels comfortable in unfamiliar buildings. The intense fear that had been there for over 70 years had gone in about 25 minutes with only a minimal amount of distress.

Jo's Allergies

Jo Trewartha writes her own remarkable case study…

Being a delegate on Karl's EFT Level 3 course and having had chronic autoimmune disease, including food intolerances, for most of my life, I was very much looking forward to finding out about how EFT could benefit allergy sufferers. Karl invited me to be his demo for the session in which he blended Matrix Reimprinting with traditional EFT. The end result was amazing.

In order to fully appreciate exactly how staggering the changes have been, it is first necessary to explain a little of the background to my condition. Shortly after having my wonderful little son in the summer of 2003 my health plummeted to an all-time low. I had virtually no strength or energy, was covered in psoriasis, had intense arthritic joint pain and could barely lift myself out of a chair or walk. Having a baby to care for, it was necessary that my own health was optimal. As soon as the aforementioned problems began to manifest, I put myself on a strict dairy-free and anti-candida diet and started taking probiotics. This treatment had been recommended to me two years previously by a kinaesiologist and had kept my joints pain-free until this severe flare-up.

During pregnancy I reintroduced wheat, dairy and sugar because I craved such foods, and happily I appeared not to be reacting to them. Unfortunately, though, despite being extremely strict about my diet once again when my child was born, I could not alleviate the joint pain with a restricted diet.

By January 2004 my condition had become life-threatening; in addition to the pain and mobility problems I was hospitalized with pustular psoriasis and acute cellulitis. Antibiotics and immune-suppressing medications eventually brought relief from the skin symptoms, but I was still plagued with joint stiffness, pain and exhaustion each day. Out of sheer desperation, in August 2005 I privately paid a small fortune for consultation, testing and low-dose immunotherapy from a doctor specializing in the treatment of allergy and environmental illness. Over six days of testing I selected a combination of 48 different foods and chemicals to be tested for, and, alarmingly, I tested intolerant, in varying degrees, to all of them.

Reflecting back on the Matrix Reimprinting demonstration some months later, I certainly remember thinking, 'How can Matrix Reimprinting sort out food intolerances?' Karl began the demonstration by asking me which foods seemed to create health problems for me. We began by using conventional EFT and focusing merely on orange juice, a drink I enjoyed every day as a child. Karl then directed me back through when symptoms appeared and this led me into a memory of when I was 15 and having tests in hospital shortly before I was diagnosed with arthritis. I imagined tapping on the ECHO of myself in a hospital gown with huge swollen knees waiting for X-rays.

After this we went back to an earlier ECHO of me at my grandparents' farm as a young girl. The ECHO was of me feeling poorly with asthma and hay fever symptoms. The ECHO was also lonely, as her grandparents were too busy running the farm to give her attention. In the memory I sat down on the sofa with my ECHO and tapped on her and we left the ECHO happily playing Lego with my brother and my adult self.

The next ECHO we focused on was based on my feeling that my brother always ended up getting more exciting presents than me as a child. During this part of the session I remember, during the tapping, reframing myself with 'Oh well, I guess he was just more vocal in asking for what he wanted than me.'

This led into another memory of childhood: my young aunt dying as a result of a tragic road accident. The details had not been given to me fully as a six-year-old child and when I discovered the truth a few years later by finding a newspaper clipping about the accident, I was angry about being lied to. I'd been told that my aunt had slipped and banged her head. I tapped on my ECHO and had a conversation telling my father how sad she was that she'd not been told the truth. A reframe came that he thought that little Jo would never want to go in a car again if she had known the truth.

I didn't initially notice any major changes following the Matrix Reimprinting session, but five nights later uncharacteristically I woke up in the early hours unable to lift my left arm and so shivery my teeth were chattering. It was not a cold night, and although I tried to stay calm I did feel a bit scared. I also had a picture in my mind of my poorly legs covered in pustular psoriasis during the time of the cellulitis several years previously. When I thought about it, my arm had felt heavy back then too. The coldness persisted for quite some time and then I went to the other extreme and felt burning hot and sweaty. This feeling also persisted for quite a while. I assumed I had had a healing crisis and when I contacted Karl he confirmed that this was probably the case.

As I'd had such a challenging night I didn't go to work the following day. As I sat at home, another image came to mind – me as a young girl coming back from the farm late at night sharing the back seat of the car with a bagged-up pheasant. I thought this must be significant, so I reimprinted the image. A few hours later I was in the supermarket and I bizarrely felt the desire to eat meat, something I've not done for many years as I've found the idea repulsive.

A few weeks later, out of curiosity I had my food intolerances rechecked. Out of the original 48 substances, amazingly I was only reacting to wheat, sugar and strawberries.

I'm still trying to understand myself how focusing on these specific memories helped clear these longstanding issues for me. However, I am writing this case study five months after this short Matrix Reimprinting demonstration and the results have held. Understandably, I am delighted.

Jenny and the Coffee

Practitioner: James Robinson

Jenny had been suffering from an exceptionally rare coffee allergy for many years. It was so extreme that even the slight smell of coffee would send her into a state of paralysis. She would be rendered completely speechless and unable to move any part of her body, and would lose all control of her bowels and bladder.

Jenny's allergy caused her huge amounts of social unease, because it restricted the consumption of coffee of everyone around her. If she went to a restaurant with friends, they would not be able to order coffee and she would have to hope that no one nearby did either. At work no one was able to drink coffee near her or even speak to her after drinking it. Even walking down the high street and passing a cafe was potentially dangerous.

Jenny's life outside her home was very much a minefield and she had to carry an antidote with her everywhere she went in case of a reaction. The looming fear of a reaction had haunted her for a number of years and she had tried every form of conventional and alternative healing, with no success. When she came to me for a session it was for the experience of something she had never tried or even heard of before. She had given up hope of receiving any real help for her allergy, and was instead seeking something that might ease her distress a little.

I started off by tapping slowly on Jenny and asking her questions about when the allergy had started and what was happening around that time. Almost immediately a memory came to the forefront. Jenny had been in an extremely abusive relationship and a prominent memory that came to mind was when her partner had beaten her up and verbally abused her while she was naked, which had then created a huge fear of being naked in front of anyone since. I asked how she felt in response to this memory. She replied, 'I feel really ******* angry.' We tapped on the anger with conventional EFT and I encouraged her to vent her wrath whilst we did so, until some of it had dissipated.

I then guided Jenny into Matrix Scene Reimprinting at the point in the memory where she was naked and being beaten. I asked her to approach her ECHO to tell her who she was and then to give her a huge hug and tell her she loved her and had come to help her. I suggested that she asked her ECHO what she was feeling, and she replied, 'Anger,' so Jenny tapped on her for the anger. Jenny then asked her ECHO what she needed. She replied that she just wanted someone to beat her boyfriend up, so that he would know how it felt. Jenny chose to bring her brother in to help her retaliate, and I gave her time to do this.

Next I asked Jenny if there was anything her ECHO would like to communicate to the abusive partner, for instance how he had made her feel and the effects his behaviour had had on her. She was very keen to do this and her ECHO spent some time expressing her feelings with rage and anger.

When she had finished I got Jenny to check how her ECHO was feeling and she replied that she felt great now, the anger had all gone and there was a sense of peace. She took her ECHO to a new place and the image was sent through the mind, around the body and out into the Matrix in the usual way. I then asked her to revisit the original memory and let me know what was there. She told me that there was nothing there any more, apart from a sense of peace.

I felt that this wasn't the basis of the allergy but that it might have been a contributing factor, so I asked Jenny to question whether this was the root cause of the coffee allergy. I slowly tapped on her as she contemplated this. She then realized that the coffee allergy stemmed from her being sent to a safe house to protect her from the continuing violence of her partner. In the safe house lots of people had drunk coffee continuously and the smell was now subconsciously taking her back to the fear and trauma of that time.

I asked her to look for a prominent memory from the safe house, and when she had a good clear vision of herself, the surroundings and the other people involved, I guided her into a further Matrix Scene Reimprinting session. While tapping on her, I asked her to walk up to her younger self and tell her who she was and that she had come to help her. I then guided her to give her younger self a big hug and tell her that she loved her dearly, that she completely understood everything she'd been through and what she was going through now. I also told her to let her younger self know that she didn't have to suffer alone now because Jenny was there to help her and would do everything she possibly could to make her feel good.

Jenny asked her younger self how she was feeling as she tapped on her. She replied that she was feeling scared, so we tapped on the fear. Jenny then asked her younger self what we could do to make her feel safe and whether there was someone we could bring in to protect her. She wanted to bring in her father and brother, who both gave her a huge hug and let her know she was safe.

I suggested to Jenny that we grant some wishes for her younger self. She wished to leave the safe house and go for a walk in some beautiful meadows she used to play in. I told her to take her time and enjoy the beautiful walk with her younger self and when they had reached some kind of plateau to let me know so that we could take the next step. When this part of the process felt complete for Jenny, she gave her younger self a huge hug again and told her that she loved her. This new memory was taken in through the mind, around the body and out through the heart in the usual way.

When she was ready I asked Jenny to return to the original memory and tell me what she found. She replied that all that remained was the new memory of the meadow, which was happy and positive. To test the memory, I asked her how she felt about smelling coffee now. Amazingly, she told me she felt fine about it. I asked her to visualize herself smelling coffee and there was absolutely no reaction. This was very unusual, as normally just the thought of coffee would trigger a reaction.

Jenny was keen to test her progress. This contradicted the guidelines on my Matrix Reimprinting training, which clearly stated that such a severe allergy should not be tested. However, Jenny wanted to take responsibility for testing her reaction, as she pointed out that her allergy dominated her every moment anyway and she frequently encountered the smell of coffee. She got her antidote ready and instructed me on what to do if she went into paralysis. I then got a brand new jar of coffee and got her to hold it and look at it. I was ready to treat any reaction with conventional EFT. However, unusually, there was still no reaction.

Next Jenny wanted me to hold the jar, which was still closed, below her nose. I constantly monitored her for any signs of reaction, but there were none. I then took the jar back and removed the lid. Jenny was still feeling fine. I showed her that the foil was still on and explained that I had to test that there was no reaction before we opened it. She still felt fine.

When I was completely sure she was ready, I pierced the foil in front of her while sitting at some distance away. I then gradually moved the jar closer and closer while she inhaled through her nose. With every movement towards her I was constantly checking with her for signs of a reaction. I got slowly closer and closer, and then unexpectedly she grabbed the jar from me and held it right under her nose, inhaling deeply! She had a huge smile and couldn't believe that she could actually smell it and feel completely fine.

Jenny had no desire to drink the coffee, but her life had completely transformed now that she could smell it without going into paralysis. Afterwards she said she could now hold a jar of coffee with the lid off under her nose and breathe it in deeply with no physical or emotional effects. She felt totally at peace and also that she was now ready to be seen naked.

I also think that she was very brave to allow me to test the work that we did and I am profoundly grateful.

Please note that although the client insisted on testing her allergy, hers was an unusual circumstance and we do not usually recommend testing an allergy of this severity.

Adam and the Toolbox

Practitioner: Gina Schofield

Adam came to me with issues around lack of purpose; he was not really fulfilling his potential and was feeling very frustrated. He was a creative person and a trained ceramicist and carpenter, but had never made enough money out of his crafts and had often ended up doing DIY and decorating for people instead. Although he found this partially satisfying, he felt he wasn't being as freely creative as he would wish.

He also had issues around attracting money. He had always 'scraped by', but had rarely had the feeling of being very comfortable financially. I asked him to give a VOC level out of 100 per cent on how much he believed the following statements: 'It's not OK to have more money than others' was 70 per cent; 'I don't deserve love' was 70 per cent; 'It's not fair' was 80 per cent.

Through considering these core beliefs, he suddenly mentioned that he'd not completed a forestry course he'd started, because it involved teaching a group and he felt he couldn't do that. However, when a friend who employed him said that he could have used his existing group to do his teaching practice, Adam realized that he had sabotaged himself. He was disappointed with himself for not getting the qualifications and allowing himself to do something he really loved – being outdoors in the woods and being creative with children.

I asked him to think about this situation and to tune into the emotion. He said it was despair, and rated it at a SUDS level of eight. He described it as orange in colour and looking like shredded wheat. We did a round of tapping on 'this orange despair' in his tummy, also referring to it looking like shredded wheat, which produced a lot of laughter and shifted the emotion quickly. I then checked in with him and he said it had changed to disappointment and it was in his chest now. I asked, 'If it were an animal, what would it be?' He replied, 'A blue square antelope.' I asked what the animal wanted to say to Adam and it said, 'Why didn't you complete me? What stopped you? This is typical of you!'

We did a couple of rounds of conventional EFT on: 'This blue square antelope feeling disappointed.' I asked Adam whether he felt he deserved to be happy in life and he rated 'I don't deserve happiness' at 80 per cent. I asked how the antelope was feeling now and Adam told me it had stretched out and elongated along his shoulders and into his arms. I asked what it was feeling – the answer was 'Frustrated.' I asked him why it couldn't get out and he replied, 'I won't let it.' I asked him if that was because it wasn't safe, and he replied, 'Yes.' I asked if it wasn't safe to be creative or fulfil his potential. Again he replied, 'Yes!' Then the flash of a memory came of his father giving him a child's toolkit when he was five, and we were back there with the ECHO.

Adam went into the scene. He described being given a beautiful toolbox full of child-sized tools and feeling really excited about it. But his dad hadn't given him any wood or materials to work with. So, creative and eager little five-year-old Adam decided to bang a line of nails into the door threshold to stop the door opening so that burglars couldn't get in! I guided Adam to tap on his ECHO as he started to cry when his dad was furious with him for nailing the front door shut. His ECHO calmed down quickly. I asked what lesson little Adam had learned about life from this event and Adam said, 'To be fearful of trying something out and expressing myself.' Then adult Adam started to cry and said, 'This is a massive insight into why I've never been able to create and make a living out of it, and always sabotage myself. I learned it's not safe and I'll get punished if I'm creative and follow my own urges.' Adam tapped further on his ECHO. I asked him to ask his ECHO what he was feeling and he said, 'I can't play the way I want to.' We carried out a round of tapping on that.

Adam's ECHO was now much calmer. I suggested Adam ask him what he'd like to happen instead of his dad telling him off. He said he'd like his dad to show him how to use the tools and to give him some materials to work with. Adult Adam imagined tapping on his dad and his ECHO told his dad that he'd like him to show him how to use the tools. In this scene, his dad was eager to help and hadn't known it was his job to show his son, since he'd been waiting for little Adam to ask and he hadn't. So when Adam's ECHO asked his dad for help, he and his dad spontaneously built a miniature door and doorframe together and little Adam was ecstatic about this.

I then asked Adam to ask his ECHO if they would like to go somewhere to have some fun. Adult Adam, his ECHO and his dad went to build a tree-house. When they had all had a really good experience, I guided Adam into bringing a clear picture of the new scene into his mind, then heart, intensifying the colours and the good feelings, and then sending it out into the field.

When he had opened his eyes and returned to the present, I asked him to close his eyes briefly and go back to his dad giving him the toolkit to see if the image had changed. He said it was a very happy scene now, with little Adam asking his dad to show him how to use the toolkit and his dad responding by showing him how to use the tools and make things with him in his shed.

We rated the earlier despair and his feelings such as 'It's not fair', 'It's not OK to have more money than others', 'I don't deserve love' and 'I don't deserve happiness', and he said they were no longer a problem and found it hard to believe they ever had been.

As our session came to a close, Adam seemed much happier and more present. His cold symptoms, which had been very apparent at the beginning of the session, had lessened, and he now talked of being easily able to face sorting out getting his forestry qualifications and feeling no need to sabotage himself in his creativity. Also, the antelope had turned into two antelopes, one in each hand, both eager to work through him and create!

A couple of days later Adam told me that he was no longer obsessed with scouring second-hand shops for children's toolkits to give to his sons and he also felt much more able to connect and play with his boys and enjoy them fully.

From Allergy to Abundance

Practitioner: Sondra Rose

Amber was a life coach who had suffered from allergies and asthma all her life. She wanted to work on some of her early memories to help reduce and hopefully eliminate her symptoms. She had done previous work with another practitioner and was aware of the link between allergies and fear of the world. She had been a highly sensitive child who had grown up in a chaotic suburban household with lots of yelling and stress about lack of money. We decided to tackle a memory of her having an anaphylactic shock reaction to eating half a Brazil nut at Christmastime. This had happened when she was visiting her alcoholic uncle's family when she was eight years old. Amber had already cleared most of her distress around this memory in previous sessions using EFT and she was eager to try Matrix Reimprinting.

In the memory, she was in the Accident and Emergency ward at hospital, being treated for her allergic reaction. She stepped into the picture, approached her ECHO and found that she still had some fear of not being able to breathe and a slight constriction in her throat. We tapped on the bodily symptoms until the ECHO felt more relaxed and then asked her what else she needed. She disliked the cold environment of the hospital and wanted to leave. She didn't want to go home, because she didn't feel safe there, so I asked her where she wanted to go. What happened next was unexpected, though not completely surprising, considering Amber's fearful childhood.

Her ECHO decided she wanted a whole new childhood and created a new picture where she lived in an expensive townhouse in London. She had rich parents who looked like her real parents but were relaxed, happy, loving and very generous. The house was filled with red and gold Christmas decorations, lots of food and a huge sense of happiness and abundance.

Amber was enjoying this new picture so much she stayed with her ECHO for over 15 minutes, describing the evolving scene in detail. Practically every childhood Christmas wish that she had ever had was coming true in the new picture. Only family members that the ECHO liked were there. Amber had the most relaxed and beatific smile on her face while she was with her ECHO in this picture. I gave her all the time she needed and this was tremendously therapeutic.

We integrated her ECHO by breathing her into Amber's heart and out into the field, and I asked Amber to check out the original picture to see if any intensity remained. She felt clear and relaxed. Obviously it wasn't appropriate to test her Brazil nut allergy, but she felt fine about this, since it wasn't an issue in her daily life. She was more interested in spending time with her ECHO in the new picture and soaking up more of the energy there.

A week later, Amber checked in with me and was just astounded at the change in her life. She had doubled her client caseload and income just one week after our Matrix Reimprinting session. Three months on, her allergy symptoms have decreased in intensity and she rarely needs her asthma medication, though she sees there is more work to do here.

Amber has maintained her new level of financial abundance and is now ready to increase her fees. She has deepened her belief in her ability to attract what she wants and is feeling more relaxed and happy about money.

Charlie and his New School

Practitioner: Carol Crowther

Charlie is a very likeable, sensitive and intelligent 11-year-old boy. He adores playing football, is a devoted Manchester United fan and in my opinion is spiritual beyond his years.

Charlie's mum asked me to carry out a session with him in his final weeks at primary school. He had passed his 11-plus exams and was due to start grammar school in September. He was worried about an unpleasant incident that he had had with two older local boys who would be attending his new school. In the first session, I felt traditional EFT was more appropriate and we successfully used the Movie Technique to tap away the anxiety of the memory and also tapped on the anxiety he felt about the long bus journey he would be taking to his new school.

Charlie later attended a talk and demonstration I gave about EFT and displayed a poster he had drawn of the tapping points for the benefit of the members of the audience. He learned the whole process very quickly and seemed very confident in the application of EFT.

My second session with him was a few days before he was due to start his new school and he was worried about his first day. Because he had taken to using EFT so naturally I decided to try Matrix Reimprinting with him. I feel that what happened next was quite remarkable and is best expressed in his own words:

I was worried about starting my new grammar school. Carol showed me how to survive my fears and she asked me to think about a time when I had felt worried about going to school. While she tapped on me, I remembered my first day at my primary school. I didn't want to go. Carol asked me to step into the picture on the back seat of my dad's car behind seven-year-old Charlie and I tapped on his fears about going to school.

Carol helped me picture myself standing in the playground with my dad. I could see myself standing in my school aged seven. My dad was telling the teacher how frightened I was. I had my arms around my dad and my head buried in his stomach. I tapped on little me to get his attention. He turned around and saw me and I told him who I was. I gave him a tour of his new school while tapping on him. I took him back into the playground and showed him to his new friends. Then I told him I was going to look after him. He was very happy. I then took him back to the teacher and said goodbye. Dad had gone, but he was still very happy.

So now, because I was worried about starting my secondary school, I got my 18-year-old self to take me around my big new school, showing me where everything was and looking after me. Then I'll have my 21-year-old me when I start at university!

Josie's Need to be Taken Seriously

Psychotherapist and EFT practitioner: Rachel Kent

Sometimes in my psychotherapy practice I have invited clients to express their 'unfinished business' to a parent as if they were sitting in the room with us. They then may experience release and completion. On occasion, a client has struggled to do this as they had been used to emotionally supporting their parent by holding back from expressing their own negative feelings. In this situation, I have asked the client what would support the parent to be strong enough to hear their feelings and for them to imagine them having that. The following case study demonstrates how I have used Matrix Reimprinting with a client to achieve the same end, with very powerful results.

Josie came to see me for some EFT as she was feeling like 'a bit of a failure'. She had great plans for her life but somehow was stopping herself from carrying them out. She hadn't yet pinpointed where this was coming from. Through our initial discussion, it emerged that she held a belief that she was not being taken seriously by people in her professional life. She felt that this was holding her back from running personal development workshops on a self-employed basis.

I asked her to recall a specific memory of 'not being taken seriously'. She had a recent memory of enthusing to an old school friend about some powerful new techniques she was trying in her therapy practice. This friend had raised an eyebrow with an expression that Josie felt looked like 'Do me a favour.' Josie immediately felt some shame and wanted to hide, wishing she hadn't said anything. I invited her to notice what she was feeling in her body right now and we tapped on what she was feeling. This brought her shame down in intensity and anger emerged. We tapped on a series of emotions as they emerged.

As we tapped, it occurred to me that it might be useful to go back to an earlier memory related to the theme 'Not being taken seriously' and the subsequent impact on Josie. So I asked, 'Can you think of an earlier time, perhaps when you were a child, when you remember not being taken seriously and how that felt?' Josie paused thoughtfully, while looking down. I noticed a red colour flushing her face. 'What are you remembering?' I enquired. Josie's breathing became uneven and she struggled initially to get her words out. We kept tapping throughout.

Josie told me of being about seven years old and sitting in the kitchen of her family home with her parents and older brother and sister. They were all talking about something – she couldn't actually remember the content, as that wasn't the important bit. She had what for her felt like a really important contribution to the conversation and was waiting for a pause so she could speak. Everyone seemed to be talking at once and she felt that she was going to burst if she didn't get her bit in. Finally, there was a pause and she said her bit, but got muddled and forgot the important point, as she'd been waiting so long to speak. A number of things stood out that held an emotional intensity for her in that moment. The first was her dad not looking at her as she spoke. The second was his frown (which always made her feel in the wrong). The third was her sister's and brother's eyes meeting while they shared slight mocking smiles. Josie felt crushed and full of shame. She'd messed up and no one took her seriously.

I tapped on Josie and asked her to see her seven-year-old self in her mind and tell me what she was wearing and where she was in the room. Josie described a little girl with mousy brown hair wearing a green dress with pumps on her feet. She then explained to her seven-year-old ECHO who she was and what she was going to do. Her ECHO was fine with this. Josie started to tap on her and she felt her hurt feelings intensify then start to subside. I asked Josie to find out what her ECHO needed to happen. Did she need to talk with anyone about how she was feeling? Little Josie wanted to tell her father how hurt she was. She also wanted him to take her seriously when she had something to say. However, something was holding her back from speaking. I asked what needed to happen first. She felt protective towards her dad and said that he would *feel shame if she expressed her hurt and anger and she couldn't bear that. So what needed to happen?*

She suddenly had the idea that if her dad was tapped on too she might feel he was supported enough to hear her. So older Josie tapped on her dad and asked him to listen to what little Josie had to say and to take her seriously. Little Josie felt huge relief that Dad was supported, and so proceeded to express her hurt and anger towards him.

What she experienced then was profoundly healing as he said he was sorry that the family had treated her that way just because she was the youngest. She had a private conversation with him while I continued to tap on her.

When there was resolution for Josie, I asked what else needed to happen. She said that she was looking at her sister and brother to see if there was something to express to them. However, as they had witnessed what had happened with Dad, their expressions had changed and they were now looking on quite seriously. Josie now felt that she was finally being taken seriously. She cried with relief and felt it was important to forgive them for how they had treated her.

A beautiful new picture was created. Josie decided they would all go to a beach where in real life they had spent many holidays. The difference this time was that Josie felt just as important as the rest of the family and was left with a joyous new memory.

When the new picture was sent out into the field, I asked Josie to return to the original memory and see if there was any remaining hurt or shame. She said she struggled to bring the image back, as it seemed irrelevant. Now she had a beautiful memory that filled her with empowering feelings.

A few weeks later, I spoke with Josie and enquired as to how the training she was running had gone. She positively beamed at me. She had felt confident, had established good contact with the delegates and had definitely been taken seriously.

Izzy and the Unicorn

Practitioner: Emma Summers

We were on a camping holiday in France and our tent was pitched right next to an area of woodland. My nine-year-old daughter, Izzy, had heard that there were wild boar in the area and this began to really worry her at night-time. A few nights into our stay she was very frightened by a 'snuffling' noise that she heard in the middle of the night and had to climb into someone else's bed for reassurance.

The following evening, at bedtime, she was very anxious about what she called 'warthogs'. Despite lots of reassurance about 'warthogs' being very shy, the campsite being really safe and adults being close by, she refused to settle or to be left alone. I decided to try some Matrix Reimprinting, which Izzy prefers to conventional EFT, as it appeals to her vivid imagination.

I asked Izzy to close her eyes and began tapping on her. I asked her to imagine her future self asleep in the tent that night. I asked her how that future Izzy felt. She replied that she felt scared of warthogs getting into the tent. I asked her if she needed to bring anything into that picture to protect the sleeping Izzy, perhaps angels, light or a special animal (knowing that she has a special affinity with animals). She replied that she wanted to bring in a horse. I asked what colour it would be and she said it would be white. So I asked her to imagine a magical white horse standing next to the sleeping Izzy, guarding her and keeping her safe from any warthogs.

I asked her if the sleeping Izzy needed anything else to keep her safe. She said that the horse was giving off a white light that was surrounding her and had a horn. I asked if it was a unicorn and she replied that it was. I then asked if the unicorn had a name and she said it was Starlight (this is a character from a book that she likes). So I asked her to imagine the sleeping Izzy surrounded by a magical white light that was provided by Starlight who was staying right next to her all night to protect her from feeling scared of any warthogs. At this point Izzy seemed very peaceful and content with her visualization, so I asked her to bring that picture into her mind, send it down to her heart and then send it out into the universe.

After this session Izzy was happy for me to kiss her goodnight and leave the tent. The following morning I had pretty much forgotten about it until Izzy spontaneously told me that it had 'worked' and she hadn't been worried at all about the warthogs. She also took herself off for a little explore at the edge of the woods that morning for the first time. There were no more worries about warthogs for the rest of our stay.

Carol and her Mother's Love

Practitioner: Claire Hayes

Carol, an intelligent and aware middle-aged woman, was busy setting up her own coaching business. She was a therapist and had done a lot of work on herself, but came for EFT when she needed extra help. The occasions that led to her coming for the two sessions described here were different, yet, as often happens, the core memory that came up was the same. In the first session we used the Movie Technique and in the second session we also used Matrix Reimprinting. Both sessions led to huge relief and gains, yet there were substantial differences which are worth noting.

Carol's first session was an emergency EFT session. On the morning of the day when she was due to give a public talk in the evening where she was introducing her work locally for the first time, she realized she felt terrified. She was an experienced public speaker and workshop leader, so she knew this was something out of the ordinary. When I asked her what the feeling was when she imagined herself at the front of the group that evening, the answer came: 'I can't see myself. I'm not there.' She started crying. When I asked her for a memory where this was a familiar feeling, she went immediately to an incident in her childhood.

Carol was the eldest of several siblings and the memory was of her standing in her family's kitchen when she was perhaps five or six. Her mother had her back to her as she was going about her business and when Carol asked her something, she got no reply. She then blurted out to her mother that she never had time for her. Her mother replied that even though she was busy, she loved Carol and her daughter would always be special to her. One might assume that this was a positive memory, but not for adult Carol. 'I didn't believe her' was her response.

First we used the conventional EFT Movie Technique. We tapped on the feelings that came up, including 'I am invisible' and 'There isn't space for me in my family.' We then got down to the core belief: 'I don't deserve to breathe. I shouldn't exist.' Carol laughed as she realized that it was no wonder she couldn't see herself in front of the group that evening!

We tapped her beliefs around not deserving to breathe or exist and her SUDS levels fell from a ten to zero. She realized that her mother couldn't in fact have said anything better at the time and could now see herself glowing in front of her audience that evening, being seen, heard and appreciated. In fact, her presentation was brimming with confidence and brought her many new clients.

A few months later Carol came for a session with a general feeling of being overwhelmed by her business. She was again coming up to a key public moment when she would be launching a new product. She was quite distressed and put herself at a ten in terms of level of intensity. When she looked inside she found both a 'fear of success' and 'fear of failure'. The 'fear of success' was underpinned by a belief that 'I have to be successful' and the 'fear of failure' by 'I'm a fraud.' We tapped to relieve some of the prevailing emotion.

When I asked Carol for a memory, she again came up with the one in the kitchen. She was quite surprised, as she thought she had dealt with that. I explained that there was still an ECHO in that memory *that needed to be worked with and that we could revisit it with Matrix Reimprinting and see what happened. She was intrigued by this and eagerly re-entered the memory.*

I asked Carol to introduce herself to her ECHO and explain she was here to help her. The ECHO welcomed big Carol and together they went to the ECHO's safe place, her bedroom. The ECHO sat on big Carol's lap and learned how to tap on her 'magic points'. She loved being on big Carol's lap, but soon ran off to find her mother. She explained the 'magic points' to her and together they went back upstairs to the bedroom. This time the ECHO sat on her mother's lap and big Carol sat quietly to one side. The ECHO tapped on her mother and her mother was able to express her love in a way that the ECHO really heard. Her mother held her for a long time and together they looked out of the window, to the water, and felt connected in their love without pressure.

When Carol had been serene for some time and we had checked that there was no more that her ECHO wanted or needed, she brought her attention back to the present moment.

Carol was stunned by the beauty of this new relationship with her mother. It had healed the 'not believing' part of her. Before, she had understood with 100 per cent of her mind that her mother loved her and had done the best she could, but now she felt it in her heart too. Needless to say, the 'I have to be successful' and 'I am a fraud' thoughts had also collapsed. There was no fuel for these beliefs to feed on with her mother's love so fully experienced. Carol returned to her work with renewed optimism and energy.

Both sessions worked and both were useful. Carol felt, however, that the Matrix Reimprinting had truly healed a deep hurt in her. The benefits of this session continue to reverberate, not least with a more open relationship with her mother.

John and the Asthma Attacks

John Bullough uses Matrix Reimprinting on himself...

Last summer I departed from several decades of regular steroid- and antihistamine-based inhalers and oral drugs to work on my hay fever symptoms and asthma with EFT alone. I had good initial success, as the symptoms always subsided with the tapping, but they also tended to recur whenever I exposed myself to pollen again. I also found that my allergies to things like cats, house dust mites, smoke and perfumes seemed very resistant to EFT, perhaps even getting worse after six months without the drugs. Nevertheless, I decided to persist, since I was convinced that eventually I would find the core issues that supported my allergies.

I woke one day last week at 5 a.m. with a blocked nose and tight breathing after working in the garden the previous day. After tapping a few rounds on the symptoms themselves, I did a version of 'S-L-O-W EFT' (tapping continuously on one point at a time for a minute or two at a time, with my eyes closed) while allowing any old pictures/movies associated with the symptoms/feelings to come to the surface. What came up, to my surprise, was a rather fuzzy memory of my father and stepmother loudly arguing, with me standing impotently nearby, aged around five.

I tried to find a specific movie to work on so I could use the EFT Movie Technique, but without success. My memory is of countless such arguments sprinkled liberally throughout my childhood and teenage years, most of them a kaleidoscope of fierce looks, loud shouting, angry body language, sudden movements and banging of doors, and each one provoking in me a sense of unpredictability and a fear of physical violence. I now know that my main coping strategy as a young child was to dissociate, to disappear, to stop existing, and perhaps as a result, my memory of my childhood is very hazy. So in the absence of anything specific, I invented a short (two-minute) scenario that seemed typical and called it The Scary Mummy and Daddy Movie.

The child in the movie was about five years old, which was about the time I first went to live with my father and stepmother. I had lived with my grandmother up to this point because my mother had been taken into a nursing home with tuberculosis (from which she never recovered) when I was ten months old. This felt like a perfect opportunity to use Matrix Reimprinting, so I imagined my 61-year-old self physically tapping on the five-year-old child and asked him what he felt. He couldn't give me a level of intensity but he was clearly feeling very scared, so we then did several rounds of tapping on the movie title, with an assumption by my adult self that it was my stepmother's strong Italian temperament that had triggered me.

It was at this point that my 'tight breathing' suddenly developed into a full-blown asthma attack. I then fully felt the five-year-old's fear as I began to worry about whether I would survive this attack, which I seemed to be bringing on with the tapping. And the more we tapped on a fear of my stepmother's emotion, the worse it got! Looking back, it was one of the scariest asthma attacks I've ever had. Fortunately, from my experience as a therapist, I've found that a worsening of symptoms often means we're on the right track, and that above all persistence is vital, so I forced myself to keep going. And when the rather bossy adult me finally recovered enough presence of mind to ask the five-year-old ECHO what he was scared of, he replied straightaway, 'I'm scared of Daddy's shouting. I'm scared he'll hit me.' As soon as we tapped on this, the asthma immediately subsided almost to nothing! An attack such as this had never subsided so quickly, even with the strongest of drugs.

My adult self had absolutely no idea that my father shouting was the key underlying issue, although I have to admit that it does seem rather obvious now. Also, I found during the tapping that five-year-old me could not comfortably say 'I deeply and completely accept myself' or even 'I'm a good kid', but was very happy to say 'Granny loves me to bits.' And then later, with much emotion, 'Granny and John love me to bits.'

In the tapping that followed, it emerged that my ECHO felt huge love for my stepmother, experiencing her as a loving, warm, maternal and feminine presence, and also as vital physical protection from my father's anger. I can relate to all this now, having heard it directly from my ECHO, but at the time it came as a complete surprise, communicating itself to me as a remembered feeling rather than in words.

We tapped on how I felt about each of my parents, and five-year-old me was very happy to realize that my father's anger and frustration masked a deep love for all of us, and reflected in some way his pain at the loss of his wife, who had died of tuberculosis barely a year earlier. We ended the tapping bathing in a sea of love, with me (aged 61 and five) tightly hugging a stuffed toy dog which my wife and I keep on the bed, kissing it on the nose and feeling a powerful flow of love in both directions.

Although my clients have often experienced release of this magnitude, this is the first time it had happened to me, and I found it hugely liberating. Perhaps the most encouraging thing of all is that when I now go back in my mind to that time, aged five, it feels very different and deeply positive.

One year later John added:

I've continued to work on my asthma with EFT and have now been effectively free of asthma due to pollen and house dust mites for over ten months. Although some sensitivity to other allergens remains, I am very hopeful that over time a combination of Matrix Reimprinting and other EFT-related techniques will help me to put this condition behind me once and for all.

Please note that this next case study contains graphic descriptions of the 9/11 attack. Please do not read it if you are sensitive in nature or easily upset.

Claire and the Twin Towers

Practitioner: Susie Shelmerdine

Claire contacted me with regard to helping her with depression, which she had been diagnosed with after escaping the Twin Towers during the 9/11 terrorist attack. She had been referred to a psychologist for Cognitive Behavioural Therapy but was afraid to go for the appointment, as she didn't want to talk about what she saw or heard that day. Her friend suggested that she try Matrix Reimprinting first.

Claire informed me that she did not sleep, she did not go out and that her life seemed to be falling apart. She told me of a particular image that haunted her. It was there every time she closed her eyes. The image was of herself outside the Twin Towers. She had escaped from one of the towers and was outside when the shock hit her. At this point she didn't know what had happened. She asked if she had to step into the picture and I reassured her she only needed to do that when she was ready. She then asked if she could have a pair of red shoes like the ones Dorothy had in The Wizard of Oz and that if she clicked her heels she could come out of the picture. We decided to have a practice run stepping into the picture and stepping out of it, so that Claire could feel reassured that she could leave at any time. We did this successfully, placing the picture on freeze. The next time we stepped in, Claire could see her ECHO. I reminded her that she was there to help her ECHO with the conscious knowledge she had from the present day.

Claire introduced herself and immediately started tapping on her ECHO. Her ECHO was confused and distraught but, when it was suggested that they go somewhere safe, refused to leave. We explained to her that the whole world was on freeze while we helped her and she was fine with that, but wanted to remain there. She kept repeating, 'It's all wrong. It's all so wrong.' Claire continued to tap on her until she was calm. She then explained to her ECHO what happened that day so that she knew it was a terrorist attack and that the Twin Towers would collapse. The ECHO did not believe her and they tapped through her shock and fear. Claire then brought in a newspaper from the next day to prove the facts of the attack to her ECHO. She continued to tap on her the whole time.

At this point the image was still frozen. We discussed taking it off freeze and both Claire and her ECHO needed to tap on the fear of doing so. They held hands and reassured each other that they could get through. I reminded them both that they could freeze the image whenever they wanted. Claire allowed the scene to unfold and her ECHO became very emotional. She clicked her heels and came out of the scene. It was the sound that had traumatized her, the 'thuds' of people jumping from the towers. This sound had stayed with Claire. She went back into the picture with her ECHO and they tapped on the feelings that the sound had created. As they tapped, Claire mentioned how the people jumping had stopped help from getting into the building. Suddenly she said, 'Oh my God, they were angels. They stopped people from getting in. They may have saved someone's life, even though they couldn't save themselves.' She thanked them. She then clicked her heels to come out of the picture with her ECHO. She needed some time to reflect.

After a break, Claire and her ECHO returned to the picture. She said she could now see angels everywhere she looked. She said even though it was the worst day of her life she could see light in the picture that she had never seen before. She could now see the bravery of people from that day; she had heard people talk about this and yet never recognized it before. Her ECHO did not want to go to a new place of her choosing, she wanted to join Claire in this new image of the attack, the one that represented courage, bravery and light.

After the session, Claire was completely drained. We spoke a few days later and she mentioned that the first night she had dreamed heavily, but the following two nights she had slept right through. She said she felt that she had more energy now and felt more like herself every day.

Claire had a further session with me on her anger at certain events surrounding the attack. She is now off her antidepressants, with her doctor's consent. She has decided to take some time to enjoy her life and her family.

Joe's Fear of Winning

Practitioner: Susie Shelmerdine

Joe is a professional golfer who approached me about using EFT to improve his score. He had previously seen sports psychologists and cognitive therapists to aid his 'mental game', with some success, and he remained openly sceptical about EFT improving his performance.

During his initial consultation I noticed that he mentioned that he was in awe of his coach and felt pride in playing against others whom he admired. His language did not show he believed he could equal if not surpass these other players. I asked him how it would feel to win against them and he replied hesitantly that it would be fantastic. Through further investigation, it was established that he had always thought he was an average player – good, but nothing special.

Joe told me how one of his idols had given him praise about his game. He did not think it was genuine and thought that the other player was just being nice. He had a specific picture of this memory, so I asked him to freeze the picture and tap on himself in it.

In the picture, Joe looked quiet, withdrawn and completely lacking in confidence. He introduced himself to his younger self and explained who he was and why he was there. As he tapped on his younger self, he learned that there was a fear of not meeting his potential. He learned that there was a benefit to not winning – if he won he would have to make a speech.

From there we were led to three related memories: the time Joe froze during a winning speech, the time he stumbled on his words in an *award ceremony, and a school presentation which hadn't gone well. Joe replaced each memory with a happy and positive picture. I also gave him homework to do for the next session.*

Joe had two competitions in the two weeks following our session. He came third in the first one, and was pleased with this result, but he now wanted to win. He decided to write his winning speech and practise it, tapping on the fear. We used the Matrix Future-Self Reimprinting protocol, and he imagined crowds applauding and his idols congratulating him.

The second competition he won. It was the best he had ever played. His speech went well afterwards and he also went on to win a further game.

At the time of writing this case study, he is only a third of the way through his competitions for the year and has already surpassed his personal target.

Matrix Reimprinting and World Transformation

In this book we have introduced you to Matrix Reimprinting, a technique for rewriting your past and transforming your future. We have shown you how we are all connected by a unified energy field and how when we experience a trauma, part of our consciousness goes into that field or Matrix as an Energetic Consciousness Hologram (ECHO). We have also shown how these ECHOs affect our beliefs about ourselves and our lives, as well as our health and wellbeing on every level. Furthermore, we have introduced you to a unique set of techniques and protocols to transform your physical and emotional health.

We would like to suggest that by using these protocols you will do more than simply transform your own health and happiness. As we have already highlighted, the positive pictures in your field are far more powerful than the negative ones. By taking responsibility for transforming your own pictures, you will affect the whole, given that we are all connected by the Matrix. What is more, a number of Matrix Reimprinting practitioners have also started experimenting with using these techniques on behalf of others. The practice of using energy techniques to surrogate for others is not a new one, and the future of Matrix Reimprinting may well include being able to tap on the ECHOs of friends, family, animals or disaster victims to help them release the trauma that they are holding.

We would like to close with a poem by one of Karl's Matrix Reimprinting trainees, Hazel Trudeau, who shares her vision of Matrix Reimprinting far more eloquently in poetry than we could in words alone:

The Matrix

Wise Ones told me of 'The Field' – an inner place I could explore.
So I went beyond my thinking mind, to learn and find out more…

This storehouse for my memories of near and distant past,
A multi-coloured library, a vault deep, wide and vast.

A blaze of action movies, each playing out a scene,
Every possible scenario, drama, play and theme.

Some were pure and beautiful – they took my breath away,
Sacred holy places where I'll go, my dying day.

Others bruised my senses, tore in two my aching heart:
Little children trapped, ignored, alone and set apart.

Desperate, frightened ECHOs – little beings from the past,
Impregnated long ago, now locked in, iron cast.

Stored away through trauma, at times I could not cope,
A battlefield of drama, beyond a young mind's scope.

Those ECHOs in the shadows whispered poison to my life,
Which manifested trouble, fear, dis-ease and painful strife.

I knew I had to face them: I'd been distracted far too long,
Developed body troubles, felt my life had gone all wrong.

Inside I felt so frightened, yet dared to free myself,
For I sensed beyond the ECHOs lay an ocean of great health.

So painful step by painful step I worked to integrate
Each part of me: methodically, I changed the Matrix state.

With tools in mind, armed with light, I helped each little being
To find their way to happiness ... I felt my body freeing!

Pockets of stagnant energy, caught in my Auric field
Began to shift, let go, release, then into love they yield.

Breathing, freeing, working through every painful tale,
ECHO led to ECHO on a synergistic trail.

Link by link the pain was healed, my ECHOs gained new choices,
What a joy to sense and hear new hope within their voices.

It took some time to work it out. Divine I felt was guiding,
To show the way to another day without the need for hiding

Love the mighty healer had dissolved my worldly pains,
A perfect flow, and unto me many outstanding gains.

My spirit wove its magic, I attracted what I asked,
Animated by divinity, in peace all day I basked.

As nature flowed encompassing, my every cell now sings
My heart beats time, in unity, at oneness with all things.

Gratitude spills from my heart, I feel aligned and neat,
But most of all, worth more than gold, at last I feel complete!

And finally, a reminder that in order to change yourself you will need to practise the techniques that we present in this book. Just knowing about them will not transform the trauma that your ECHOs are holding. However, practising them regularly will transform you on many levels.

We wish you peace as your journey with Matrix Reimprinting unfolds.

References

Chapter 1

1. Braden, Gregg, *The Divine Matrix*, Hay House, 2007, p.26
2. Sheldrake, Rupert, *The Presence of the Past*, Inner Traditions, Bear and Company, 2000, p.198
3. Ibid., p.199
4. Ibid., p.132
5. Ibid., p.162
6. Ibid., p.167
7. Ibid., p.xvii
8, Ibid., p.160
9. Ibid., p.175
10. *Swarm: Nature's Incredible Invasion: One Million Heads, One Beautiful Mind*, BBC documentary, 2009
11. Hicks, Esther and Jerry, *Ask and It Is Given*, Hay House, 2005, p.84

Chapter 2

1. Hamilton, David, *It's the Thought that Counts*, Dr David R. Hamilton, 2005; reissued Hay House, 2007, p.20
2. Dossey, Larry, *Healing Breakthroughs*, Piatkus, 1993
3. Ibid., pp.76–7
4. Ibid.
5. Pert, Candace, *Everything You Need to Know to Feel Good*, Hay House, 2007, p.29

6. Ibid., p.30

7. Ibid., p.32

8. Ibid.

9. Hamilton, David, op. cit., p.43

10. Ibid., p.46

11. Ibid., p.107

12. Childre, Doc, and the Institute of HeartMath, *The Inside Story*, HeartMath, 2003, p.18

13. Ibid., p.5

14. Ibid., p.24

15. Childre, Doc, Martin, Howard, and Beech, Donna, *The HeartMath Solution*, HarperCollins, 1999, p.33

16. Ibid.

17. Ibid., pp.2-3

18. Childre, Martin and Beech, op. cit., p.36

19. Ibid., p.38

20. Pearsall, Paul, *The Heart's Code*, Thorsons, 1998, pp.7-8

21. Lipton, Bruce, *Biology of Belief*, Mountain of Love, 2005, p.50

22. Church, Dawson, *The Genie in Your Genes*, Elite Books, 2007, p.27

23. Lipton, op. cit., p.51

24. Ibid.

25. Church, op. cit., p.33

26. Lipton, op. cit., p.135

27. Church, op. cit., p.25

28. Lipton, op. cit., pp.167-8

29. Lipton, Bruce, 'The wisdom of the cells: Part 3', from *The Wisdom of Your Cells*, Sounds True, 2006-7

Chapter 3

1. Church, Dawson, *The Genie in Your Genes*, Elite Books, 2007, p.34

2. Lipton, Bruce, *Biology of Belief*, Mountain of Love, 2005, p.148

3. Church, op. cit., p.71

4. Childre, Doc, and the Institute of HeartMath, *The Inside Story*, HeartMath, 2003, p. 21

5. Scaer, Robert, *The Body Bears the Burden*, Haworth Medical Press, 2001; second edition, 2007, p.2

6. Ibid., p.5

7. Ibid., p.7

8. Ibid., pp.6–7

9. Ibid., pp.10–12

10. Ibid., p.17

11. Ibid., p.19

12. Ibid.

Chapter 5

1. Scaer, Robert, *Trauma, Transformation and Healing* [DVD], 2008

2. Ibid.

3. Hamilton, David, *How Your Mind Can Heal Your Body*, Hay House, 2008, p.48

4. Ibid., p.49

Chapter 6

1. Hamilton, David, *How Your Mind Can Heal Your Body*, Hay House, 2008, p.49

Chapter 11

1. Church, Dawson, *The Genie in Your Genes*, Elite Books, 2007, p.33

Chapter 14

1. Pearce, Joseph Chilton, *The Biology of Transcendence*, Park Street Press, 2004, p.27

Chapter 16

1. Hartmann, Silvia, *The Advanced Patterns of EFT*, DragonRising 2002, p. 134

Bibliography

Books

Gregg Braden, *The Divine Matrix: Bridging Time, Space, Miracles, and Beliefs*, Hay House, 2007

Doc Childre, *The Inside Story: Understanding the Power of Feelings*, HeartMath, 2003

Doc Childre, Howard Martin and Donna Beech, *The HeartMath Solution*, HarperCollins, 1999

Dawson Church, *The Genie in Your Genes: Epigenetic Medicine and the New Biology of Intention*, Elite Books, 2007

Larry Dossey, *Healing Breakthroughs: How Your Attitudes and Beliefs Can Affect Your Health*, Piatkus, 1993

Donna Eden, *Energy Medicine: How to Use Your Body's Energies for Optimum Health and Vitality*, Piatkus, 2008

Gill Edwards, *Living Magically*, Piatkus, 1992

—, *Pure Bliss: The Art of Living in Soft Time*, Piatkus, 1999

—, *Wild Love*, Piatkus, 2006

—, *Life is a Gift: A Practical Guide to Making Your Dreams Come True*, Piatkus, 2007

David Feinstein, Donna Eden and Gary Craig, *The Healing Power of EFT and Energy Psychology*, Piatkus, 2006

Richard Flook, *Why am I Sick? What's Wrong and How You Can Solve it Using META-Medicine®*, Booksurge, 2009

Peter H. Fraser, Harry Massey and Joan Parisi Wilcox, *Decoding the Human Body-Field*, Healing Arts Press, 2008

Donna Gates, *The Body Ecology Diet*, Batus, 1996

David Hamilton, *It's the Thought That Counts: The Astounding Evidence for the Power of Mind over Matter*, Dr David R. Hamilton, 2005

—, *How Your Mind Can Heal Your Body*, Hay House, 2008

—, *Why Kindness is Good for You*, Hay House, 2010

Silvia Hartmann, *The Advanced Patterns of EFT*, DragonRising, 2003

Louise Hay, *Heal Your Body*, Hay House, 1994

—, *You Can Heal Your Life*, Hay House, 1984

Esther and Jerry Hicks, *Ask and It Is Given*, Hay House, 2005

Byron Katie and Stephen Mitchell, *Loving What Is*, Rider, 2002

Bruce Lipton *The Biology of Belief,* Mountain of Love, 2005

Frank McNeil, *Learning with the Brain in Mind*, Sage, 2008

Lynne McTaggart, *The Field: The Quest for the Secret Force of the Universe*, HarperCollins, 2001

Dan Millman, *The Way of the Peaceful Warrior,* H. J. Kramer, 1991

—, *Sacred Journey of the Peaceful Warrior*, H. J. Kramer, 1991

—, *Wisdom of the Peaceful Warrior: A Companion to the Book That Changes Lives*, H. J. Kramer, 2007

Joseph Chilton Pearce, *The Biology of Transcendence: A Blueprint of the Human Spirit*, Park Street Press, 2004

Candace Pert, *Molecules of Emotion: Why You Feel the Way You Feel*, Pocket Books, 1999

—, *Everything You Need to Know to Feel Good*, Hay House, 2007

Stewart Robertson, *The Book of Reframes*, Lulu, 2008

Robert Scaer, *The Body Bears the Burden: Trauma, Dissociation and Disease*, Haworth Medical Press, 2001; second edition, 2007

Rupert Sheldrake, *The Presence of the Past: Morphic Resonance and the Fields of Nature. Inner Traditions*, Bear and Company, 2000

Eckhart Tolle, *The Power of Now: A Guide to Spiritual Enlightenment*, Mobius, 2001

Other Media

Greg Becker and Harry Massey, *The Living Matrix*, DVD, The Living Matrix and Becker, Massey, 2009

Rhonda Byrne *The Secret*, DVD, TS Productions, 2007

Betsy Chasse, Marc Vicente and William Arntz, *What the Bleep Do We Know?*, DVD, Revolver Entertainment, 2005

Donna Eden, *Energy Medicine Kit*, Sounds True, 2004

Bruce Lipton, *As Above, So Below: An Introduction to Fractal Evolution*, DVD, Spirit 2000, 2005

Robert Scaer, *Trauma, Transformation and Healing*, DVD#4, part of: Look, Carol, *A Vibrational Approach to Healing Pain and Illness*, DVD set, 2008

Swarm: Nature's Incredible Invasion: One Million Heads, One Beautiful Mind, BBC documentary, 2009

Debby Takikawa, *What Babies Want*, DVD, Hannah Peace Works, 2006

Articles

Bruce Lipton, 'The wisdom of the cells: Parts 1, 2 and 3', www.brucelipton.com, derived from *The Wisdom of Your Cells: How Your Beliefs Control Your Biology*, an audio listening course on eight CDs, Sounds True, www.soundstrue.com, 2006–7

Resources

Find a Matrix Reimprinting Practitioner

Practitioner listings can be found at www.matrixreimprinting.com.

Matrix Reimprinting Training

Train as a Matrix Reimprinting practitioner. Details of practitioner training courses can be found at: www.matrixreimprinting.com.

Join the Matrix Reimprinting Webinar Programme

You can learn more about Matrix Reimprinting through our online programme. Find out more at: www.matrixreimprintingtelecourses.com.

Essential Reading and Viewing

Top ten books and DVDs to reinforce your understanding of the topics presented in this book (in no particular order):

Gregg Braden, *The Divine Matrix: Bridging Time, Space, Miracles and Beliefs*, Hay House, 2007. A comprehensive and highly accessible explanation of the science behind the Matrix.

The Living Matrix, DVD, The Living Matrix and Becker, Massey, 2009. A cutting-edge documentary exploring the Matrix with interviews from Bruce Lipton, Rupert Sheldrake, Lynne McTaggart, Peter Fraser and many other scientists and leaders in this field.

Bruce Lipton, *The Biology of Belief*, Mountain of Love, 2005. This is a simple scientific explanation of how our thoughts affect our biology. It introduces us to epigenetics, showing that it is not the genes that are in charge. Also available as a DVD or audio book.

Dawson Church, *The Genie in Your Genes: Epigenetic Medicine and the New Biology of Intention*, Elite Books, 2007. A detailed scientific exploration of the field of epigenetics, with information on the science behind Energy Psychology.

Nicolas and Jessica Ortner, *Try It on Everything*, DVD, Try It Productions, 2008. This brilliant DVD features Jack Canfield, Joseph Mercola, Carol Look, Bruce Lipton, and many more. It is a great introduction to EFT.

Richard Flook, *Why am I Sick? What's Wrong and How You Can Solve It Using META-Medicine*®, Booksurge, 2009. A thorough exploration of META-Medicine® and the emotional causes behind physical disease.

Karl Dawson, *META-Medicine*® *and EFT/Matrix Reimprinting*, DVD set, Karl Dawson, 2008. Learn the basic principles of META-Medicine® and discover how it goes hand in hand with Matrix Reimprinting.

David Hamilton, *How Your Mind Can Heal Your Body*, Hay House, 2008. This book contains a plethora of scientific experiments which prove the astonishing power of the mind over the body.

Robert Scaer, *The Body Bears the Burden: Trauma, Dissociation and Disease*, Haworth Medical Press, 2001; second edition, 2007. In this book you can learn more about trauma and the freeze response. Ensure you buy the second edition, as the first edition is not written with laypeople in mind.

Rupert Sheldrake, *The Presence of the Past: Morphic Resonance and the Fields of Nature*, Inner Traditions, Bear and Company, 2000. A detailed exploration of the science behind morphic fields and morphic resonance. This is an excellent read if you are scientifically minded.

Further Reading and Viewing

EFT

Sasha Allenby, *Joyful Recovery from Chronic Fatigue Syndrome/ ME: Accelerated Healing with Emotional Freedom Techniques (EFT)*, Strategic Book Publishing, 2008. Read Sasha's remarkable healing story from CFS/ME using EFT. This book is also a simple self-help manual for those in recovery from the condition.

Pamela Bruner and John Bullough (eds), *EFT and Beyond*, 2009.

Advanced EFT book containing contributions from many of the EFT Masters, including a chapter on Matrix Reimprinting.

Karl Dawson, *EFT Practitioner Course, Levels 1 and 2*, DVD set, 2008. Karl's EFT training course is recommended if you want to learn EFT for your personal use or if you are an EFT practitioner and want to enhance your skills.

—, *EFT for Serious Diseases*, DVD set, 2008. Featuring Matrix Reimprinting. Recommended if you want to learn about Karl's Serious Disease work.

Stewart Robertson, *The Book of Reframes*, Lulu, 2008. This is an excellent resource for practitioners who want to help their clients reframe or change the meaning of situations, memories or events.

Robert Scaer, *Trauma, Transformation and Healing*, DVD, 2008. Part of a four-DVD set, *A Vibrational Approach to Healing Pain and Illness*, by Carol Look. This DVD shows a lecture from Dr Scaer on healing trauma.

Science and the Matrix

Peter H. Fraser, Harry Massey, Joan Parisi Wilcox, *Decoding the Human Body-Field*, Healing Arts Press, 2008. This book expands in detail our understanding of the human body-field.

Bruce Lipton, *As Above, So Below: An Introduction to Fractal Evolution*, Spirit 2000, 2005. This DVD explains how we tune into ourselves in the Matrix.

Lynne McTaggart, *The Field*, HarperCollins, 2001. A fascinating exploration of some of the scientific evidence behind the Matrix.

The Secret, DVD, TS Productions, 2007. A life-changing movie that will help you understand more about the Law of Attraction.

What the Bleep Do We Know?, DVD, Revolver Entertainment, 2005. An exploration of quantum physics, showing the convergence of science and spirituality. Also available as a book.

Nutrition

Donna Gates, *The Body Ecology Diet*, Batus, 1996. Helps you to rebuild your gut flora and immunity.

Practitioners

Practitioners who contributed case studies to this book:

John Bullough, http://www.intuitive-connections.co.uk, john@energypublications.co.uk

Carol Crowther, http://www.eft-reiki.co.uk, carollcrowther@yahoo.co.uk

Claire Hayes, http://www.eft4change.co.uk, claire@eft4change.co.uk

Rachel Kent, http://www.eftbirmingham.co.uk, rachjkent@talktalk.net

Sharon King, http://www.magicalnewbeginnings.com, Sharon@magicalnewbeginnings.com

Brett Moran, http://www.matrixmind.co.uk, brett@matrixmind.co.uk

James Robinson, http://www.matrix-illumination.com, james@matrix-illumination.com

Sondra Rose, http://www.sondrarose.com, Sondra@sondrarose.com

Gina Schofield, gina.schofield@btinternet.com

Susie Shelmerdine, http://www.eftmidlands.co.uk, info@eftmidlands.co.uk

Emma Summers, http://www.stopsmokingeft.co.uk, emmalsummers@hotmail.com

About the Authors

Karl Dawson

Karl Dawson is the creator of Matrix Reimprinting, a cutting-edge Energy Psychology technique which combines EFT with all the latest developments in quantum physics and the New Sciences.

As one of only 29 EFT Masters worldwide, Karl has been at the leading edge of the personal development industry since 2003. He previously created the 'EFT for Serious Disease' training which has been attended by doctors, health professionals and laypeople alike. He has also trained over 1,000 EFT practitioners worldwide.

Karl has presented at large conferences all over the world. He has also created a number of DVD sets, including *Matrix Reimprinting, EFT for the Prevention and Treatment of Serious Disease, EFT with META-Medicine®* (featuring Richard Flook) and *EFT Practitioner Training.*

Karl currently resides in Warwickshire with his partner, Rebekah Roberts.

Sasha Allenby

Sasha Allenby has contributed much to the development of Matrix Reimprinting. She has helped to shape the techniques and protocols and, in addition, has created her own. Sasha has presented at various events in the UK, including the 2009 EFT Masterclass. She has also made contributions to *EFT World Magazine.*

Sasha is a Matrix Reimprinting and EFT AAMET trainer and over the years has worked extensively with clients who are overcoming long-term illness, serious disease and severe trauma. She now focuses almost exclusively on training and writing.

Sasha has overcome two 'incurable' health conditions using Matrix Reimprinting and EFT, and her first book, *Joyful Recovery from*

Chronic Fatigue Syndrome/ME: Accelerated Healing with Emotional Freedom Techniques, was released worldwide in 2008.

She currently resides in Bournemouth with her partner, Rupert Wood.

Visit www.matrixreimprinting.com for more information on Karl and Sasha's Matrix Reimprinting training courses.

NOTES

NOTES

Notes

NOTES

NOTES

NOTES

Matrix Reimprinting Workshops and Training Courses

Train as a Matrix Reimprinting Practitioner

You can train as a Matrix Reimprinting Practitioner and learn this technique for your professional or personal use:

Brand New to EFT and Matrix Reimprinting?

This two-day introductory course will give you a basic grounding in EFT. You will learn the basics of EFT and the EFT Movie Technique. In this experiential learning course, you'll get to practise the tools on other group members, and also experience whole group sessions on phobias, cravings and physical pain. This course will enable you to go on to the Practitioner Training.

Already Experienced or Qualified in EFT?

The two-day Practitioner Training will give you a basic grounding in Matrix Reimprinting. You will learn the two Foundation Techniques (Matrix Scene Reimprinting and Matrix Memory Reimprinting). You will also learn a whole host of protocols for working with addictions, phobias, relationship issues, birth issues, past-lives, future-selves, and so on. This is an experiential learning course meaning you will have opportunities to practise these skills on others during the course. Following the course, you can qualify by completing case studies and a short exam, and participating in 12 weeks of the Matrix Reimprinting Webinar Programme.

Matrix Reimprinting Webinar Programme

The Matrix Reimprinting Webinar Programme is for everyone interested in Matrix Reimprinting – from beginners to experienced practitioners. This rolling programme takes place weekly throughout the year, and brings Matrix Reimprinting to the comfort of your own home. The webinar is presented live by Sasha and a host of experts in the field of Matrix Reimprinting, and is accompanied by a PowerPoint presentation to your computer. This is an interactive programme where you can ask Sasha questions live on the calls, or through the members only forum.

Visit **www.matrixreimprinting.com** for information on these and other speciality Matrix Reimprinting workshops and courses.

Hay House Titles of Related Interest

Tapping for Life,
by Janet Thomson

ThetaHealing,
by Vianna Stibal

Why Kindness Is Good for You,
by David R. Hamilton, PhD

Waking from Sleep,
by Steve Taylor

The Good Retreat Guide,
by Stafford Whiteaker

Dowsing,
by Elizabeth Brown

Energy Secrets,
by Alla Svirinskaya

Feel Happy Now!,
by Michael Neill

Take Your Soul on a Vacation

Visit www.HealYourLife.com® to regroup, recharge,
and reconnect with your own magnificence.

Featuring blogs, mind-body-spirit news,
and life-changing wisdom from Louise Hay and friends.

Visit www.HealYourLife.com today!